Regionalism in Trade Policy

Essays on Preferential Trading

Regionalism in Trade Policy

Essays on Preferential Trading

Arvind Panagariya
University of Maryland, College Park

World Scientific
Singapore • New Jersey • London • Hong Kong

Published by

World Scientific Publishing Co. Pte. Ltd.

P O Box 128, Farrer Road, Singapore 912805

USA office: Suite 1B, 1060 Main Street, River Edge, NJ 07661

UK office: 57 Shelton Street, Covent Garden, London WC2H 9HE

Library of Congress Cataloging-in-Publication Data
Panagariya, Arvind.
   Regionalism in trade policy essays on preferential trading / Arvind Panagariya.
      p.   cm.
   Includes bibliographical references and index.
   ISBN 981023841X -- ISBN 9810238428 (pbk)
      1. International economic integration.   2. Commercial policy.   3. Regionalism.   I. Title.
HF1418.5.P32   1999
382'.3 21--dc21   99-045509

British Library Cataloguing-in-Publication Data
A catalogue record for this book is available from the British Library.

Cover Design: Ananth Panagariya

Printed in Singapore.

To: Amita

Contents

Preface

This volume contains six of my essays on preferential trading, written over a period of as many years (1993-98). In the public debate that ensued following the launching of the current wave of regionalism, I have take a critical view of preferential trade arrangements (PTAs). These essays represent that view.

The volume is divided into three parts, each consisting of two essays. Part I offers an overview and discusses various aspects of preferential trading from a conceptual standpoint. Part II focuses on the implications of the proliferation of regional arrangements for East Asia, a region that has itself kept generally clear of these discriminatory arrangements. Part III covers Latin America that has, on the other hand, enthusiastically embraced PTAs. The essays argue why Asia has been right in sticking to a nondiscriminatory approach while Latin America is compromising its own interest by taking the preferential route to trade liberalization.

The first essay was written recently and presented at a conference, co-hosted by the University of Warwick and WTO, to celebrate the 50th anniversary of the signing of the General Agreement on Tariffs and Trade (GATT). This essay is forthcoming in the *World Economy* as a part of a mini symposium based on the papers presented at the conference. It brings the reader up to date on the current debate on regionalism versus multilateralism as viewed by a multilateralist. It begins with a discussion of the WTO provisions that permit PTAs and the events that led to their current proliferation. The essay then offers a number of criticisms of PTAs, based on both static welfare effects and their harmful implications for the multilateral trading system. The essay also explains the pitfalls of the so-called "open regionalism" and "deep" integration. It concludes by offering a number of suggestions on what can be done to minimize the damage from PTAs and ensure that nondiscrimination in trade policy, enshrined in the Most Favored Nation (MFN) principle of the GATT and WTO, guides future policy.

The second essay, reproduced as Chapter 2 here, was written jointly with Professor Jagdish Bhagwati of Columbia University. Along with Bhagwati's earlier essay, published in the World Bank volume that I co-edited with Jaime de Melo, this essay played an important role in making economists and policy analysts rethink their unqualified support of PTAs.[1] At the time this essay was written, policy analysts and many prominent economists carried a religious faith in the "natural trading partners hypothesis," introduced by Paul Wonnacott and Mark Lutz and popularized by Paul Krugman and Lawrence Summers. This is the idea that if potential PTA members already import a large proportion of their total imports from each other, trade creation will outweigh trade diversion and the PTA will necessarily improve the member countries' welfare. Chapter 2 systematically demolishes this idea, with the result that, within a short period of its original publication, the defense of PTAs on the basis of "natural trading partners" hypothesis has virtually disappeared.

More broadly, chapter 2 draws a sharp distinction between Viner's trade creation versus trade diversion terminology as it relates to "static" welfare effects of PTAs and Bhagwati's "building blocks" versus "stumbling blocks" terminology as it relates to the "dynamic" time-path issue.[2] It then uses these concepts to unify the theoretical literature on static as well as dynamic aspects of PTAs. The chapter concludes with a number of policy judgements.

Chapter 3, in Part II, asks the critical question facing Asia today: should the region join the race to form regional arrangements? Though the article on which this chapter is based was originally written in 1993, the question it raises and the analysis it offers remain valid today. The chapter begins by examining the only serious attempt at preferential trading in the region—the Association of South East Asian Nations (ASEAN) —, which aims to form the ASEAN Free Trade Area (AFTA) by the year 2003. My analysis leads to the conclusion that the costs of this arrangement far outweigh their expected benefits. I also evaluate the case for a formal East Asian trading bloc along the lines of NAFTA or European Union and conclude that though the *threat* of such a bloc may serve some purpose, its actual execution is fraught with problems. The diverse levels of protection across different countries in the region and the possibility of retaliation from the United States through in-

---

[1] Bhagwati, Jagdish, 1993, "Regionalism and Multilateralism: An Overview," in Melo and Panagariya, eds., *New Dimensions in Regional Integration*, Cambridge, Great Britain: Cambridge University Press.

[2] Viner, Jacob, 1950, *The Customs Union Issue*, New York: Carnegie Endowment for International Peace.

creased protection against East Asian goods pose insurmountable barriers to such a bloc. Finally, the chapter looks at the case for a *simultaneous*, MFN style, nondiscriminatory liberalization on a *region-wide* basis. I argue that though such a *regional* approach may be feasible, the case for it is far from airtight. On the one hand, this approach will face less resistance from the United States and is likely to promote an open world trading system in the long run. But on the other, in the short run, it is likely to be resisted due to adverse terms of trade effects on the participating countries.

Chapter 4 goes on to examine the role of the Asia-Pacific Economic Co-operation (APEC) forum in promoting trade liberalization and its relationship with the United States. I argue that, in recent years, the U.S. conversion to preferential trading creates a fundamental conflict within APEC: while the Asian members want to liberalize trade on an MFN basis, the United States demands reciprocity. In particular, the United States is unwilling to give trade concessions within the APEC framework on an MFN basis lest they become available to the European Union without any reciprocal concessions. Thus, effectively, the United States will be an active participant in the APEC-liberalization process only if it takes the form of a PTA. I argue against turning APEC into an FTA, however, and advocate transforming the goal of *APEC-wide* free trade in all member countries by the year 2020, set out in the Bogor Declaration, into the WTO goal of *worldwide* free trade by that date.

In Part III, I examine the case for preferential trading in Latin America. My focus is principally on the arrangements between countries in Latin America and the United States. These, in turn, include NAFTA and its extensions and the proposed Free Trade Area of the Americas (FTAA). The essay in Chapter 5, published originally in the *World Economy,* attracted much attention of the policy community and press. It introduced the idea that the formation of a Free Trade Area between a high-tariff country (Mexico) and a low-tariff country (United States) results in a net transfer by the former to the latter. The essential point is that a tariff preference results in the transfer of tariff revenue, previously collected on the imports from the partner, to the latter's exporters. For the first time, the essay also questioned systematically the assertion, made by PTA proponents, that NAFTA was an effective instrument of making Mexico's economic reforms more credible and that other developing countries could achieve the same objective by forging PTAs with developed countries. Finally, Chapter 6 contains an as yet unpublished note. It makes a simple calculation of the tariff revenue transferred by Mexico to

U.S. exporters as a result of the preferential access it has given them to its markets. I estimate that NAFTA has resulted in an annual transfer of income from the Mexican treasury to U.S. exporters that could be as large as three and a quarter billion dollars. Since this figure was reported in the leading newspapers such as the *Financial Times* and the *Economist*, I thought the readers might find the original note itself of some interest.

The papers in this volume can be read independently of one another. The concepts necessary to follow a particular essay are fully developed in that essay itself. This naturally means that some key ideas such as trade creation and trade diversion are explained and developed more than once. I could have economized on space by eliminating this repetition but that would have interfered with the continuity of the essay.

I will be remiss if, in addition to the acknowledgements in the specific essays, I did not repeat my intellectual debt to Jagdish Bhagwati. I have not only drawn freely on his ideas—with and without attribution—but also benefited greatly from his generosity in reading, discussing and commenting on my papers.

I would also like to thank my children, Hirsh and Ajay, who have helped me in various ways in the preparation of the manuscript. Ajay's "technical" expertise in handling the intricacies of Microsoft Word was especially critical to the completion of the project.

Above all, I want to express my deep appreciation of the highest priority that Amita, my wife, has given to my academic pursuits. Without her all-round support, this book would not have seen the light of day.

Arvind Panagariya
May 1999

List of Figures

List of Tables

PART I   OVERVIEW

1. The Regionalism Debate: An Overview

1.1 Introduction

This chapter offers an overview of the debate on the merits of regional arrangements as an instrument of trade liberalization. While the advocates of these arrangements view them as moving the member countries and the world towards freer trade, multilateralists argue that they detract from true liberalization and fragment the global trading system. Because I count myself among multilateralists, the chapter has a strong bias in favor of the latter view.[3]

In this introductory section, I spell out some key definitions, describe the WTO provisions permitting regional arrangements, and recount the main historical events that led to the current wave of regionalism. A review of the economic effects of PTAs on union members (Section 1.2) and the global trading system (Section 1.3) follows this introduction.[4] Two terms, "Open Regionalism" and "Deep Integration" have received much attention in recent years from the advocates of PTAs. Given the importance these terms have acquired in policy discussions, it is appropriate to subject them to a close examination. Thus, open regionalism is dissected in Section 1.4 and deep integration in Section 1.5. I conclude the chapter in Section 1.6 with suggestions for reforming the WTO rules on PTAs.

Originally published in the *World Economy* 22, 1999. Thanks go to Jagdish Bhagwati for innumerable conversations over the years and to Douglas Irwin for comments.

[3] For a pro-regionalism view, see Frankel (1997). Winters (1996) is a more neutral survey.

[4] The two sets of effects are not entirely separable so that the division should not be viewed as watertight. An alternative classification, employed in Bhagwati (1993), Bhagwati and Panagariya (1996a) (1996b) and Bhagwati, Greenaway and Panagariya (1998), divides the implications of PTAs into static welfare effects and the "dynamic" time-path issue. The key feature distinguishing the classification in the present paper is that it places all systemic effects, including those relating to the time-path question, into a single category.

1.1.1 Definitions

Three key concepts, all relating to arrangements confined to trade in goods, appear frequently in the academic as well as policy literature: Preferential Trade Area, Free Trade Area and Customs Union. A Preferential Trade Area or PTA is a union between two or more countries in which goods produced within the union are subject to lower trade barriers than the goods produced outside the union. A Free Trade Area or FTA is a PTA in which member countries do not impose *any* trade barriers on goods produced within the union but do so on those produced outside the union. A customs Union or CU is an FTA in which member countries apply a common external tariff (CET) on a good imported from outside countries. The CET can, of course, differ across goods but not across union partners.

In policy documents and debates, the acronym FTA is often used to refer to a Free Trade *Agreement* or Free Trade *Arrangement* rather than Free Trade *Area*. This usage of the term gives the misleading impression that an FTA is equivalent to nondiscriminatory free trade. The term PTA—whether used to stand for Preferential Trade Area, Preferential Trade Agreement or Preferential Trade Arrangement—avoids this confusion by making explicit the discriminatory nature of the arrangement. For this reason, at the urging of Bhagwati (1995), economists have increasingly adopted the term PTA to refer to Free Trade Areas. The term has the additional advantage of being wider in that it can be used to describe FTAs, CUs and arrangements involving partial trade preferences.

In practice, PTAs rarely do away with all trade barriers among member countries. For instance, in the North American Free Trade Agreement (NAFTA), member countries can use anti-dumping measures against one another. Similarly, in the European Union (EU), competition policy can be invoked to restrict the flow of imports from partner countries. In addition, PTAs may exclude entirely certain goods or sectors from liberalization. A prime example of such exclusion is agriculture in the EU.

PTAs are sometimes accompanied by agreements in areas other than trade in goods. For example, the EU has gone some ways towards introducing harmonization of product standards, competition policies and tax laws and is poised for a complete monetary union among at least a subset of member countries. NAFTA has provisions relating to investment liberalization, intellectual property rights, dispute settlement and, through side agreements, environmental and labor standards.

The term "Regional Arrangement" (RA) is sometimes used either as substitutes for PTA or to describe an arrangement which is not a PTA[5] I will use this term only for arrangements that cannot be justifiably called PTAs. For instance, the Asia Pacific Economic Cooperation (APEC) forum is not a PTA and is, as such, better described as a regional arrangement. As mentioned in the previous paragraph, arrangements such as the EU and NAFTA go beyond a PTA but I will continue to call them PTAs rather than risk creating confusion by introducing a new term distinguishing them from pure PTAs.

1.1.2 WTO Provisions for PTAs

The Most Favored Nation (MFN) clause in Article I of the General Agreement on Tariffs and Trade (GATT) forbids Member countries from pursuing discriminatory trade policies against one another. Indeed, the language in the 1947 Agreement subsumed within the 1994 Marrakesh Agreement establishing the World Trade Organization (WTO) is quite unequivocal.

"With respect to customs duties and charges of any kind...any advantage, favour, privilege or immunity granted by any contracting party to any product originating in or destined for any other country shall be accorded immediately and unconditionally to the like product originating in or destined for the territories of all other contracting parties" (GATT 1994, p. 486).

PTAs have, nevertheless, been accommodated into GATT through Article XXIV, which allows Members to form such arrangements provided they eliminate, rather than just lower, within-union trade barriers on "substantially all trade."[6] The arrangements must also not raise trade barriers on goods produced outside the union. These provisions together legalize FTAs in which member countries do not raise their tariffs on outside countries and CUs in which the CET is chosen so as to leave the average external tariff unchanged. The provisions rule out partial PTAs, however. Article V in the General Agreement on Trade in Services (GATS) introduces

---

[5] Two other terms, "Regional Trade Arrangement" and "Regional Integration Arrangements" also appear in the literature sometimes. But these are poor substitutes for either PTA or RA and I will not use them in this paper. Qualifier "regional" in terms such as RA, RTA and RIA should be interpreted to mean that the membership falls short of all countries on the globe without any implication that it is concentrated in a specific geographical region of the world.

[6] Trade barriers such as anti-dumping, which are permitted by other provisions of GATT, can be maintained within the union.

provisions for PTAs in services that parallel those in Article XXIV of GATT for goods.

In the original GATT, signed in 1947, Article XXIV offered the only provisions for new PTAs.[7] Subsequently, however, with the addition of Part IV in 1965 and the Enabling Clause in 1979, GATT permitted partial PTAs under two circumstances. First, developed countries were allowed to grant one-way *partial* tariff preferences to developing countries (through Article I exemption). And second, two or more developing countries were given the right to exchange two-way *partial* trade preferences. Under the former provision, developing countries have benefited from tariff preferences granted by developed countries under the rubric of the Generalized System of Preferences (GSP). Under the latter provision, developing countries have exchanged partial tariff preferences within arrangements such as the ASEAN Preferential Trading Area (APTA) and South Asian Preferential Trading Area (SAPTA).[8] Not being full-fledged FTAs or CUs, these arrangements would not have been permitted under Article XXIV.

It is important to emphasize that the presence of even a single developed country in a PTA imposes an important constraint on the nature of the arrangement: to be GATT consistent, it must satisfy the requirements of Article XXIV, which are far more demanding than those of the Enabling Clause. This has made, for example, the exchange of partial tariff preferences among members of the Asia Pacific Economic Cooperation (APEC) forum a difficult task. On the other hand, the bulk of PTAs consisting exclusively of developing countries, have been concluded under the Enabling Clause provisions and can stop well short of a genuine FTA or CU if the members so desire. Even the prominent developing-country PTAs such as the Southern Cone Common Market (MERCOSUR) and ASEAN Free Trade Area (AFTA) fall in this category. Admittedly, in the past, developed-country PTAs have also violated the spirit of Article XXIV provisions; on balance, however, the Enabling Clause offers a much greater scope for the exchange arbitrary preferences than Article XXIV.

---

[7] The existing arrangements involving partial preferences, principally those between former colonies and their colonial powers, were granted exemption from the MFN provision within Article I.

[8] ASEAN stands for the Association of South East Asian Nations.

1.1.3 Historical Evolution

Prior to early 1980s, PTAs were limited to arrangements within Western Europe, among developing countries, and trade preferences by developed to developing countries. Because the developing-country arrangements, undertaken principally in Latin America and Africa, were largely ineffective and trade preferences by developed to developing countries limited, effective PTAs were confined to the two arrangements in Western Europe: the European Community (EC) and European Free Trade Area (EFTA). The limited role for PTAs meant that the architects of the global trading system did not have to fear that regional arrangements might undermine the multilateral process of trade liberalization. Indeed, with the EC negotiating its common external tariffs as a single unit, the United States, who was strongly committed to the multilateral process, was successful in leading the world into as many as seven rounds of multilateral trade negotiations (MTNs).

Throughout this earlier period, while the European Community widened and deepened its integration, the United States remained singularly committed to the multilateral approach. Having witnessed the pernicious effects of discriminatory trade and payments regimes during the Great Depression, at the end of the Second World War she had emerged as the champion of a nondiscriminatory global trade regime, grounded firmly in the MFN principle. Speaking for the U.S. policy makers, Howard Ellis (1945) denounced bilateral arrangements in the strongest terms:

> There are good reasons for believing that no device portends more restrictions of international trade in the postwar setting than bilateral arrangements.

Proposals were made during 1960s for a North Atlantic Free Trade Area but received no attention from the United States. All this changed, however, when, at the GATT Ministerial in November 1982, the United States began efforts to start the eighth round of multilateral trade negotiations. Unable to persuade the EC to go along, she felt obliged to abandon her long-standing opposition to regional arrangements. Recognizing that PTAs were the only means left for keeping the process of trade liberalization afloat, the United States went on to conclude an FTA with Israel in 1985 and Canada in 1989. Though the Uruguay Round was launched in the meantime, because the EC remained a reluctant player at the negotiating table, the United States moved ahead with yet another PTA, this time jointly with Mexico and Canada. Side by side, the European Community continued its expansion, adding Greece in 1981, Portugal and Spain in 1986 and Austria, Finland and Sweden in 1995.

Today, with the Uruguay Round having been successfully concluded and the multilateral process working well, the original rationale for the U.S. pursuit of PTAs has disappeared. But what was originally viewed as a temporary diversion to force the European Community to the negotiating table has turned into a race for securing preferentially the neighbors' markets for one's exports. The European Community, renamed the European Union following the Maastricht Treaty, has moved aggressively to conclude FTAs with its neighbors in Eastern and Central Europe and with Baltic Republics while the United States has gone on to promote the idea of a Free Trade Area of the Americas. This race between two giants has, in turn, led to a renewal of efforts for PTAs by and among smaller countries in Africa, Latin America, South and Central Asia, Central and Eastern Europe and Baltic Republics. The only region, which has so far remained firmly committed to the MFN approach to liberalization, is East Asia.

Because PTAs are inherently discriminatory, their proliferation has led to fears that they may undermine the multilateral process of trade liberalization. The issue became a key subject of discussions at several WTO working parties, which had been looking at the regional arrangements notified to WTO in recent years. In February 1996, recognizing the importance of the issue, WTO appointed a Committee on Regional Trade Agreements (CRTA) to give coherence to these discussions. A key charge of CRTA is to examine in detail whether regional arrangements are compatible with multilateralism.

Though the Committee's work is still in progress, the Singapore Ministerial Declaration provides a preliminary impression of the Member countries' view on the subject. The paragraph dealing with regional arrangements states,

> We note that trade relations of WTO Members are being increasingly influenced by regional trade agreements, which have expanded vastly in number, scope and coverage. Such initiatives can promote further liberalization and may assist least-developed, developing and transition economies in integrating into the international trading system. In this context, we note the importance of existing regional arrangements involving developing and least-developed countries. The expansion and extent of regional trade agreements make it important to analyse whether the system of WTO rights and obligations as it relates to regional trade agreements needs to be further clarified. We reaffirm the primacy of the multilateral trading system, which includes a framework for the development of regional trade agree-

ments, and we renew our commitment to ensure that regional trade agreements are complementary to it and consistent with its rules. In this regard, we welcome the establishment and endorse the work of the new Committee on Regional Trade Agreements. We shall continue to work through progressive liberalization in the WTO as we are committed in the WTO Agreement and Decisions adopted at Marrakesh, and in so doing facilitate mutually supportive processes of global and regional trade liberalization.

Thus, the view taken by the Conference and, indeed, by the participating Ministers in their individual statements, is that regional arrangements are compatible with multilateralism. As we will see, this view is not shared by free-trade purists who see PTAs as a source of fragmentation of the global trading system rather than a unifying force.

1.2 Effects on Union Members

The effects on union members can be studied under four headings: (i) Vinerian analysis which focuses on the welfare effects of a PTA, holding the tariffs on outside countries unchanged, (ii) the implications of differences in transport costs across potential union members, (iii) the implications of the rules of origin, and (iv) nontraditional gains including guaranteed market access, shelter from contingent protection, locking-in the reforms and dispute settlement. We take each of these effects in turn.

1.2.1 Vinerian Analysis: Welfare Effects of a Tariff Preference

Advocates of regional arrangements sometimes claim that the conventional static welfare analysis is too narrow a criterion to judge overall desirability of the arrangements. But this is not a defensible position since PTAs are the principal, often only, component of regional arrangements with serious economic effects of which the static welfare effect is a key and best understood component. It is no accident that economists evaluating regional arrangements, be it various EC extensions or NAFTA, have almost always focused on their static welfare effects.

In static analysis, Viner's (1950) seminal concepts of trade creation and trade diversion remain central today. Viner noted that since PTAs liberalize trade preferentially, on one hand, they "create" new trade between union members while, on the other, they "divert" trade from low-cost outside suppliers to high-cost within-union suppliers. The former effect arises from a union partner undermining another union member's less efficient industry and is beneficial. The latter effect arises from a union member displacing a more efficient outside supplier by taking advantage of the tariff preference it enjoys in a partner country. This effect is harmful. Unions, which are primarily trade creating, are beneficial and those that are primarily trade diverting are harmful to member countries taken together and to the world as a whole. As we will see shortly, however, an individual member of the union can reap large benefits even from a primarily trade diverting union through a shift in intra-union terms of trade in its favor.

It is easy to see that when trade is multilateral, that is, countries import from and export to union members as well as outside countries, trade diversion is inevitable. Moreover, if potential union members are small in relation to the outside world as is likely, little trade creation will be forthcoming. This rather surprising point has not been fully appreciated but can be made easily with the help of a simple partial-equilibrium example.

Suppose Indonesia and Singapore form an FTA under which Indonesia removes its tariff on imports of video-cassette recorders (VCRs) from Singapore but retains it on outside countries (which include such competitive suppliers as China, Republic of Korea and Taiwan). The outcome of such an FTA is shown in Figure 1.1. In this figure, subscript I distinguishes Indonesia, S Singapore and W the rest of the world. Curve $M_I M_I$ represents Indonesia's import demand for VCRs (assumed to be homogeneous), $E_S E_S$ represents Singapore's supply of exports of VCRs, and $P_W P_W$ gives the supply of VCRs from the world market. It is assumed that Indonesia and Singapore are small in relation to the world and take the world VCR price as given.

Initially, Indonesia levies a nondiscriminatory tariff on imports equaling $P_W P^t_W$ per VCR. Export supply curves of Singapore and the rest of the world, as viewed by Indonesian consumers and producers, are given by $E^t_S E^t_S$ and $P^t_W P^t_W$, respectively. The price of VCRs in Indonesia is P^t_W. The country imports OQ_1 from Indonesia and $Q_1 Q_3$ from the rest of the world, collecting GSNH in tariff revenue. The consumers' surplus is given by triangle KSG.

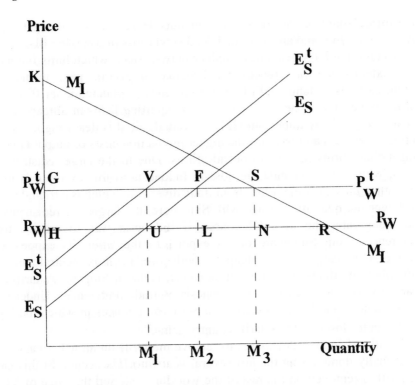

Figure 1.1: The Welfare Effects of a Preferential Removal of Tariff by Indonesia.

An FTA with Singapore results in the elimination of the tariff on Singapore but its retention on the rest of the world. This change shifts the supply curve from Singapore down to $E_S E_S$. As long as any VCRs continue to comefrom the rest of the world, the price in Indonesia remains unchanged at P^t_W. Imports from Singapore rise to OQ_2 and those from the rest of the world fall to $Q_2 Q_3$.

Several conclusions can now be drawn. First, as noted above, the FTA turns out to be wholly trade diverting. With no change in the external tariff, as long as VCR imports continue to come from the rest of the world, the domestic price of VCRs in Indonesia cannot change and domestic producers are unaffected by increased competition from Singapore. The margin on which they must compete is defined by the rest of the world before as well as after the formation of the FTA. There is no trade creation. On the other hand, taking advantage of the preference, Singaporean suppliers of VCRs are able to displace some of the more efficient outside suppliers, leading to trade diversion of Q_1Q_2 and an associated deadweight loss of triangle FLU.

Second, the FTA generates a redistributive effect, which hurts Indonesia who extends the preference and benefits Singapore who receives it. Indonesia loses rectangle GFLH that it previously collected in tariff revenue but no longer does. The rectangle goes to exporting firms in Singapore who boost their profit by trapezium GFUH. Triangle FLU is deadweight loss due to trade diversion and pays for the higher production costs of output Q_1Q_2 by Singaporean firms relative to outside firms. Due to the large redistribution effect, which is a rectangle, the loss to Indonesia in this example is much larger than the deadweight loss from trade diversion, which is a triangle. And the larger the quantity of trade with Singapore, the larger the redistribution and the greater the loss. Of course, if Indonesia was to receive trade preferences from Singapore on its exports to the latter, its exports will receive a rectangle and Singapore will lose it, thus neutralizing the redistribution effects. The problem, however, is that if Singapore's tariffs are near zero, as is true, it can offer Indonesia no trade preferences. Under such circumstances, the FTA amounts to one-way preferences in which the high-tariff country loses and low-tariff country gains.[9]

Finally, if Indonesia chooses to remove the tariff on an MFN basis as it has actually done during the last several years, no loss occurs. In this case, the tariff is removed on the rest of the world as well and the price of VCRs in Indonesia falls to the world level. The lost tariff revenue, which was transferred to Singaporean exporters under the FTA, is now transferred to Indonesian consumers. In addition, the country makes a net gain of triangle SNR from improved efficiency. Thus, for small countries, unilateral liberalization on an MFN basis remains a vastly superior option to a PTA.

It has been argued by many, most prominently Summers (1991), that while considering PTAs, we should not worry about trade diversion. To quote him,

> I find it surprising that this issue is taken so seriously—in most other situations, economists laugh off second best considerations and focus on direct impacts.

---

[9] Using a simulation model, a recent paper by Spilimbergo and Stein (1996) shows that the "rectangle effect" continues to dominate in models of product differentiation of the Krugman (1980) variety. They find that a high-tariff country is better off forming an FTA with a high-tariff rather than a low-tariff country.

The analysis just presented shows that trade diversion is not something that can be laughed off. Especially when unions are between a high-tariff country such as Mexico and a low-tariff country such as the United States, losses from the PTA to the former can be considerable. In Panagariya (1997a), I have estimated that the redistributive effect shown in Figure 1.1 may be costing Mexico as much as $3.25 billion per year.

Summers rests his conclusion on the claim that when union members are "Natural Trading Partners," that is, they already trade a lot with each other and are geographically proximate, the risk of trade diversion is minimal. In his own words,[10]

> Are trading blocs likely to divert large amounts of trade? In answering this question, the issue of natural trading blocs is crucial because to the extent that blocs are created between countries that already trade disproportionately, the risk of large amounts of trade diversion is reduced.

Bhagwati (1995), Panagariya (1996) and Bhagwati and Panagariya (1996a) have offered detailed critiques of this view. Bhagwati and Panagariya (1996a), in particular, show systematically that the natural trading partners hypothesis has no analytic basis. To give some flavor of their critique, note that this criterion is neither symmetric not transitive. According to Summers' definition, the United States may be the natural trading partner of Mexico but the reverse is not true. Similarly, the United States is a natural trading partner of both Mexico and Canada but these two are not natural trading partners of each other. More directly, it should be obvious from Figure 1.1 that trade diversion is a marginal concept and, therefore, has nothing to do with the initial *level* of trade. While the *scope* for trade diversion may depend on the extent of intra-union trade, the actual trade diversion depends entirely on the response of partner country's exports to the tariff preference at the *margin*. Yet another point, made forcefully by Panagariya (1995, 1996) and illustrated in Figure 1.1, is that if a country forms a PTA with another country with substantially lower tariffs than its own, its losses are larger the more it imports from the partner!

---

[10] The natural trading partners idea was originally proposed by Wonnacott and Lutz (1989) and was also discussed by Jacquemin and Sapir (1991). Krugman (1991a) endorses the idea as follows: "To reemphasize why this matters: if a disproportionate share of world trade would take place within trading blocs even in the absence of any preferential trading arrangement, then the gains from trade creation within blocs are likely to outweigh any possible losses from external trade diversion."

Because weaker, uncompetitive industries are usually the ones that succeed in lobbying against foreign competition, PTAs get voted in precisely when trade diversion is the dominant force. This is a point made formally in the recent political-economy-theoretic analyses of Grossman and Helpman (1995) and Krishna (1996). The careful empirical work by Kowalczyk and Davis (1996) on the tariff phase out in NAFTA shows that the sectors which were allowed the longest phase out periods in the United States were the ones in which import-competing lobbies were the strongest.

More direct empirical evidence supporting trade diversion is also beginning to accumulate. A recent, widely publicized, World Bank study by Yeats (1996) provides systematic evidence of wholesale trade diversion in MERCOSUR.[11] Similarly, Wei and Frankel (1996) find that various extensions of the European Community were accompanied by a considerable trade diversion. Referring to the EC expansion during 1980s, Wei and Frankel note, "Overall, the evidence suggests massive trade diversion resulted from the membership expansion." According to the key finding on which this conclusion is based, "Imports from non-member countries in 1990 were 30% lower than in 1980, after controlling for economic growth."[12] Thus, the possibility of trade diversion cannot be taken lightly.

1.2.2 Transport Costs and PTAs

Following an initial suggestion by Krugman (1991a), Frankel (1996) and his associates [Frankel, Stein and Wei (1995), Frankel and Wei (1997)] have strongly pushed the idea that the presence of transport costs make PTAs among proximate countries an attractive option. This is a surprising development since none of the original pioneers including Viner (1950), Meade (1955) and Lipsey (1958) had mentioned transport costs or proximity as a factor in determining the desirability of PTAs. Building on the earlier critique in Bhagwati (1993) and Bhagwati and Panagariya (1996a), I have recently subjected this view to a thorough examination [Panagariya (1997b)].

---

[11] Richard Eckaus of M.I.T. and Robert Scott of the University of Maryland have found that even in the case of NAFTA, there has been a substantial trade diversion in the textile and clothing industry.

[12] It is important to note that establishing trade creation and trade diversion empirically is a difficult task. As such these studies are not without flaws. In the case of Yeats (1996), despite pitfalls of specific measures used, the overall evidence is compelling. Wei and Frankel (1996) employ the gravity equation that, despite many modifications by different authors, is likely to remain misspecified and, thus, open to criticism (e.g., see Polak 1996).

My unequivocal conclusion is that transport costs are no different than any other costs and as such deserve no special attention in considering PTAs. Here I discuss some key points.

There is nothing in economic theory that says that countries located far apart must gain less from trade than those located close to each other. This should be clear enough from the analysis associated with Figure 1.1, which does not depend on the source of cost differences between Singapore and the rest of the world. As long as the delivery price of Singapore is given by the height of the curve $E_S E_S$, regardless of whether transport costs contribute a large, small or no part of it, the analysis remains unchanged.

Alternatively, consider an example, given in Panagariya (1997b), in which trade blocs between proximate countries confer no gains while those between distant countries do. Suppose the world consists of two continents, two countries per continent, and two goods produced at constant but different labor costs a la Ricardo. Suppose further that the countries located on the same continent are identical in all respects but differ across continents. Despite positive transport costs across continents but none within a continent, there are no gains from forming continental blocs whereas, with sufficiently large comparative cost differences across continents, gains are available to blocs between countries across continents.

Bhagwati and Panagariya (1996a) show that in general even a limited proposition, which makes a PTA between proximate partners *ceteris paribus* superior to that between distant partners, is false. These authors provide an example in which a country facing a proximate and a distant partner who are otherwise identical is better off giving a tariff preference to the latter.

1.2.3 Rules of Origin in FTAs

In FTAs as distinct from CUs, member countries retain their own outside tariffs. Ignoring internal transport costs, this feature opens the possibility that a product destined to a high-tariff member country will be first imported into the lowest-tariff member country and then re-exported to the former. Or, more subtly, if inputs imported from outside countries constitute a large part of the value added of a product, producers in the member country with lowest tariffs on inputs can undercut producers in other member countries. To guard against these possibilities, FTAs are usually supplemented by rules of origin, which can take various forms. For example, the agreement may specify that a product will qualify for duty-free movement within the union only if a pre-specified proportion of its value added has originated within the union. Alternatively, it may require that a product undergo a substantial transformation in a country before being permitted to cross the border of a partner country free of duty.

Analytic literature on the rules of origin in the context of PTAs is still in its infancy.[13] But from a policy perspective, some simple points can be made. First, at least in the absence of traded intermediate inputs, rules of origin have an unambiguously harmful effect. If there are no rules of origin, each product will be imported through the member country that has the lowest external tariff. This will minimize the trade diversion effect of internal preference in higher-tariff member countries by lowering the effective external tariff down to the level of the member with the lowest tariff on the product. Effectively, the FTA will be turned into a CU with the lowest tariff among union members serving as the common external tariff. Rules of origin, by contrast, allow more trade diversion in a member country with higher tariff by requiring that goods destined to a high-tariff country be imported through the border of that country.

Second, if traded inputs are used in production, rules of origin can paradoxically reduce trade diversion. Thus, recall that tariff preferences can give rise to harmful trade diversion by giving within-union producers an extra advantage over outside suppliers. Rules of origin may be beneficial to the extent that rules of origin may counteract this advantage. For example, taking advantage of a tariff preference in a partner country, the producer of a final good in a member country may be able to outcompete his outside competitor provided he can import the input from outside sources. But if the rules of origin require that he purchase the input from more expensive internal sources to qualify for the tariff preference on the final good, and such a purchase raises the cost of production above the tariff inclusive price of outside suppliers, harmful trade diversion in the final good will be avoided.

Third, for the same reason that rules of origin may counteract trade diversion, they may also counteract trade creation. The ability of a partner country to undermine an inefficient domestic industry is reduced by rules of origin, which require it to purchase inputs from less efficient internal sources.

---

[13] See Krueger (1993) and Krishna and Krueger (1995) for a preliminary analysis of some policy issues. Theoretical literature on the subject is so far sparse. Thus, see Falvey and Reed (1997a, 1997b) and the references therein

Fourth, in intermediate goods production itself, the rules of origin are likely to be harmful. To take advantage of the tariff preference in the final good, union members will shift their purchases towards intra-union sources of inputs even though these sources may be more expensive. It is this harmful role of rules of origin that is emphasized by Krueger (1993) in her critique of FTAs.

Fifth, the rules of origin can multiply distortions as overlapping FTAs begin to form. For example, if Chile, who already has an FTA with MERCOSUR, joins NAFTA, a Chilean firm will have to buy components in Brazil if it wants to take advantage of the preferential tariff in MERCOSUR and in the United States if it wants to exploit the preference in NAFTA. This may happen even though the most efficient supplier of the components may be in Asia.

Finally, in a political-economy context, rules of origin can turn into yet another instrument available to lobbies for adding to trade diversion or frustrating trade creation. That this may indeed have happened in NAFTA is illustrated by the fact that the stringent rules of origin were sought by the United States even though U.S. tariffs were generally lower than those in Mexico. In the absence of rules of origin, the possibility of final goods imports coming into the United States through Mexico was minimal. Nor would it have made sense for a producer in the United States to import inputs through Mexico. The intent of the rules of origin had to be protectionist: a stringent rule of origin would undermine Mexico's ability to outcompete an inefficient U.S. firm producing final goods and also make internal market in inputs more profitable. In one area, textiles and clothing, where U.S. tariffs were high and the scope for trade creation substantial, the triple transformation rule of origin was adopted to maintain a high level of protection for U.S. producers.

1.2.4 Non-traditional Gains: Guaranteed Market Access, Shelter from Contingent Protection, Locking-in the Reforms and Dispute Settlement

The debate on regionalism initiated by NAFTA brought several new elements into the analysis of PTAs. Many economists and policy analysts expressed the view, though without supporting evidence or analysis, that the gains to a small developing country from a PTA with a large developed economy go well beyond the traditional static welfare effects. In addition it has been argued that since the dispute settlement mechanism in a PTA such as NAFTA or the EU gives direct access to private parties, it works more effectively than the dispute settlement mechanism of WTO which is available exclusively to member-country governments.

Three non-traditional benefits to a developing country from entering into a PTA agreement with a large developed country were identified during NAFTA debate. First, such arrangements guarantee access to a large market. The agreement ensures the small developing country that if the rich partner turns protectionist in the future, its access to the latter's market will be preserved. The cost in terms of opening one's own market preferentially to the large country can, thus, be seen as the cost of insurance against possible loss of access to the partner's market.

Second, the PTA can shield the developing-country member from administered protection in the rich country. For instance, the country may escape anti-dumping and safeguards actions by the rich partner to which other trading partners can be subject.

Finally, a regional arrangement with a large, rich trading partner can be an effective instrument of imparting credibility to reforms. An international treaty with a large and rich country can "lock" the reforms, making it difficult for more protection-minded future governments to reverse the actions of their predecessors. An important element of this "lock," emphasized recently, is the more effective dispute settlement process of PTAs that in the case of NAFTA is available to private parties including labor unions, business groups and activists. The WTO dispute settlement process, by contrast, is available to the governments of member countries only.

Panagariya (1995, 1996) offers a systematic critique of these arguments. Since the benefits were identified originally as accruing to Mexico from NAFTA, let us examine them in that context. Consider first the market access argument. Under normal circumstances, access to the U.S. market is guaranteed by WTO agreements. In order for market access to be curtailed in the absence of NAFTA, the united States will have to go back on its WTO obligations including the possibility of a complete withdrawal from that institution. Under such circumstances, it is not clear that the United States will adhere to its NAFTA obligations. The bottom line is the following: Is the U.S. commitment to NAFTA more credible than to WTO? If not, the insurance argument is quite weak.

Next, take the argument that NAFTA shelters Mexico from administered protection. At least in principle, this is a misleading claim since NAFTA agreement contains nothing that says that member-country firms are to be treated differently from firms in outside countries for purposes of administered protection. Indeed, the special agreements on sugar and orange juice explicitly allow for the play of administered protection in the event of import surges from Mexico in these sectors. Furthermore, side agreements on labor standards and environment give the United States *new* powers to subject Mexico to dispute settlement procedures which can lead to fines of up to $20 million.

Turning to "lock-in" effects, it is unlikely that NAFTA can "lock in" all reforms. For instance, it surely does not guarantee macroeconomic stability as was demonstrated by the peso crisis. It also does not advance the cause of privatization in any meaningful way. The main area where the lock-in argument may apply is trade policy. But here there are two problems. First, the lock applies only to trade preferences granted to NAFTA members. If these preferences were harmful to Mexico in the first place, the lock is not a benefit but cost. Second, Mexico could have as easily locked in its trade reforms on a multilateral basis by binding tariffs with WTO at the applied rates. Instead, it chose to bind tariffs at levels much higher than applied rates. Paradoxically, NAFTA may have contributed to the water in the bindings. Recognizing that it will not be possible to raise tariffs on the bulk of imports coming from the United states, Mexican authorities may have decided to leave themselves considerable room in the choice of external tariffs in case pressures from domestic industry necessitate a rolling back of trade liberalization. As it turned out, this flexibility was used after the peso crisis with tariffs on 503 items rising from less than 20% to 35%.

Finally, consider the benefits of the alternative dispute settlement process in the EU and NAFTA. The argument here is that it is more effective since it is available directly to private parties whereas WTO process is available to member-country governments only. But as Levy and Srinivasan (1996) show, this is not a compelling argument. They show that the access of private parties can lead governments not to sign agreements that are otherwise beneficial.

1.3 Implications for the Global Trading System

There are several questions one may ask about the relationship between PTAs and multilateral liberalization. Can a PTA expand continuously to yield worldwide free trade? Can it make an otherwise feasible multilateral liberalization infeasible? Does it offer an incentive to increase or reduce trade barriers against outside countries? What kind of transition trade regimes are we likely to have with the formation of criss-crossing PTAs? Let us take these and related questions in turn.

1.3.1 Can PTA Expansion Lead to Global Free Trade?

Assuming the PTA and multilateral processes to be independent, can the expansion of a PTA continue until we achieve worldwide free trade? This is what Bhagwati and Panagariya (1996a) labeled Question I relating to the time path issue, introduced originally by Bhagwati (1993). As noted by them, this question is not about the existence of a PTA path along which world welfare increases monotonically as analyzed by Kemp and Wan (1976) and Panagariya and Krishna (1997).[14] Nor is it about the relationship between the number of trade blocs and welfare as analyzed by Krugman (1991b). Instead, it concerns the monotonicity of incentive to seek entry on the part of outsiders and to offer entry on the part of insiders until global free trade is achieved.

Baldwin (1995) deals with this issue focusing on the incentives of outsiders to seek entry. Using a variant of what have come to be known as models of economic geography, he identifies a "domino" effect. Accordingly, idiosyncratic events such as the European Single Market initiative create economic incentives for outside countries to seek entry into an existing PTA. Unless there are sufficiently strong non-economic factors that counter these incentives, as the PTA expands, eventually all countries want to enter the PTA. Then, as long as entry into the PTA is free, as indeed assumed by Baldwin, this process can lead to global free trade.[15]

There are two key limitations of Baldwin's otherwise elegant analysis. First, working in the tradition of economic-geography models, he formalizes

---

[14] Kemp and Wan (1976) demonstrated that two or more countries can always form a customs union which makes member countries better off without making outside countries worse off. A analogous result for FTAs was not available until the recent contribution of Panagariya and Krishna (1997).

[15] Yi (1996) obtains a similar result in a somewhat different model than that of Baldwin.

trade barriers as transport costs. As such, accession to the PTA becomes equivalent to a reduction in transport costs. This means that the tariff revenue aspect of trade barriers is completely absent in his analysis. It is not clear whether his result will remain valid once transport costs are replaced by tariffs with tariff-revenue effect of the entry into the PTA taken into account. Second, even if we ignore this problem, Baldwin (1995) assumes that "insiders" have no incentive to block the entry. It may be hypothesized that after the PTA reaches a certain size, insiders will have an incentive to block further entry.

This is indeed the message of a recent elegant paper of Andriamananjara (1998) that explicitly models the incentives facing outsiders to seek entry and willingness of outsiders to give entry. He uses a Cournot oligopoly model of identical countries in which the outside tariff is assumed to be fixed and decisions to seek and offer entry are driven by profits. He shows that in this model as the PTA expands, profits of insiders first rise, reach a maximum and then decline. Moreover, the maximum-profit point reaches before the PTA comes to encompass all countries. Profits of outsiders, on the other hand, decline monotonically as the PTA expands. Thus, while outsiders have an increasing incentive seek entry, insiders stop short of taking all of them into the club. The PTA fails to expand into a global bloc.

Using the symmetric Krugman (1991b) model, modified to allow for comparative advantage, Bond and Syropoulos (1996) ask the following related question. Suppose countries and blocs behave as Nash players and choose tariffs to maximize welfare. The world is initially divided into two or more identical blocs. If one of these blocs now begins to expand by drawing one country from each of the remaining blocs at a time, with Nash-optimum tariffs chosen at all times by all blocs, will the expanding bloc eventually turn into a global bloc or stop short of it. Using simulations, they show that as this bloc expands, the welfare of its members peaks before it absorbs the other blocs in their entirety. The process stops short of yielding global free trade.

1.3.2 Do PTAs Make Multilateral Liberalization Less Likely?

Assuming the PTA process interacts with multilateral process, does it serve as a building block or stumbling block to global free trade? This is the alternative time-path Question II identified in Bhagwati and Panagariya (1996a). There are both formal models and informal arguments focusing on this issue. Let us take them in order.

Formal Models

Using the median voter model, Levy (1997) asks the question whether presenting the option to form an FTA can make a previously infeasible multilateral liberalization feasible and whether it can render a previously feasible multilateral liberalization infeasible. The question is addressed in a multi-country world in which voters in two countries are given the option to vote on an FTA and multilateral liberalization in that order. The FTA is modeled as complete free trade between union members with a prohibitive tariff on nonmembers. Levy shows that in the Heckscher-Ohlin set up, a previously feasible multilateral liberalization cannot be rendered infeasible by the FTA option. Essentially, when multilateral liberalization is feasible, the FTA offers a lower utility than global free trade to the median voter in at least one country so that the FTA is necessarily rejected by at least one country. Levy also shows that the FTA cannot make a previously infeasible multilateral liberalization feasible. This is simply because the FTA is voted favorably only if it raises the median voter's utility over the autarky equilibrium. But that change only raises his reservation utility.

If the problem is considered in a Krugman (1980) type of model with product differentiation, Levy shows that the FTA can turn into a stumbling block to global free trade. With the gains from trade deriving from differences in factor endowments as well as increased variety, it now becomes possible for median voters in both countries forming the FTA to achieve a higher level of utility under this alternative than available under the multilateral option.

Krishna (1998) offers another example of FTAs turning into stumbling blocks to global liberalization. He uses a three-country, partial-equilibrium, oligopoly model in which trade policy is chosen to maximize national firms' profits. He shows that more trade diverting the FTA between two countries in this set up, the greater the backing it receives and more it reduces the incentive to eventually liberalize with the third country. With sufficiently large trade diversion, an initially feasible multilateral liberalization can be rendered infeasible by the FTA option.

Informal Arguments

In addition to these formal analyses, several informal arguments have been made to support the building blocks or stumbling blocks hypothesis.

First, it has been suggested by Summers (1991) and others that multilateral negotiations will move more rapidly if the number of negotiators is reduced to approximately three via bloc formation. This argument gained some popularity at the time the Uruguay Round negotiations were stalled but has lost force since the successful completion of the round. The argument is that due to a large number of members involved at the WTO and the associated free rider problem, negotiations there are slow and difficult. If the world is first divided into a handful of blocs, multilateral negotiations will become easier.

There are at least two problems with this argument, however. First, theoretically speaking, if blocs take the form of FTAs, they have no effect on the number of participants. For FTA members retain their own external tariffs and must negotiate these tariffs individually. So far, the only PTA, which participates as a single unit in multilateral negotiations, is the EU. Second, as a practical matter, it is not clear that the existence of the European Community, now the EU, has been an unmixed blessing for multilateral negotiations. Preoccupied with its internal problems and agenda, it was the EC, which first delayed the launching, and then the conclusion of the Uruguay Round. It is possible that if EC members were participating individually in negotiations, they would see greater merit in multilateral liberalization and be more eager to negotiate.

According to the second informal argument, PTAs may serve as a threat to force unwilling parties to negotiate in earnest at the multilateral level. Bergsten (1994) argues that the upgrading of the November 1993 APEC ministers meeting in Seattle by President Clinton to high-profile Leaders' Meeting signaled to the European Community that if they dragged their feet at the Uruguay Round, the United states would go ahead with an FTA with Asian countries. This threat led the European Community to conclude negotiations. Bhagwati (1996) disagrees with this interpretation of events. He argues that the Uruguay Round was completed essentially because the United States wisely decided to close the deal, taking the offer on the table rather than seeking more concessions. Given how distant and remote was, and still is, the possibility of an APEC FTA, it is difficult to imagine that the European Community would have taken the threat seriously, suggesting that Bhagwati's interpretation is correct.

Third, on the stumbling blocks side, it is argued that due to their high visibility, PTAs can energize and unify protectionist lobbies, turning them into effective obstacles against multilateral liberalization. This is especially true since the PTAs likely to be negotiated by developed countries are with developing countries. Such PTAs are associated in public mind (in developed countries) with large inflows of labor-intensive goods and reduced wages for the unskilled. Multilateral negotiations, by contrast, involve both developed and developing countries and draw less attention of protectionist lobbies. Thus, the NAFTA debate in the United States was fiercer than the debate for any multilateral trade negotiation including the Uruguay Round. More recently, President Clinton's efforts to obtain the fast track authority, aimed principally at bringing Chile into NAFTA, met with failure. It is possible that if the President had sought this authority to negotiate a multilateral round, instead, he would have faced less opposition.

Finally, there is the related issue of attention diversion and scarce negotiating resource. If the President of the United States and his Trade Representative are preoccupied with cutting deals in Latin America, they will have less time and motivation for multilateral negotiations. Furthermore, even if they had the time and motivation, it may become difficult to persuade the U.S. Congress to go along with a multilateral round with negotiating capital having been used up for regional deals.

1.3.3 Do PTAs Lead to a Rise in Trade Barriers
against Nonmembers?

Closely related to the issue, whether PTAs make multilateral liberalization less likely, is the question whether they lead to a rise in trade barriers against nonmembers.[16] Like the former question, this one is also a political-economy theoretic question and the answer depends on the political process at work in a given situation. The theoretical literature, summarized below, offers arguments on both sides. Although the analysis is generally couched in terms of tariffs, it should be interpreted to apply to trade barriers in general, which include WTO-sanctioned instruments such as anti-dumping and safeguard measures.

---

[16] In the case of developing countries, applied tariffs are generally below GATT bindings so that barriers can be raised by raising tariffs. In developed countries where actual tariffs are constrained by GATT bindings, this objective can be achieved through safeguard measures including anti-dumping actions.

An FTA Leading to a Reduction in Tariffs on Inputs

Suppose that in the pre-PTA equilibrium, relative to its potential partner, a union member faces lower tariffs on final goods and higher tariffs on intermediate inputs in some sectors. The PTA then places the country's final goods producers at a disadvantage vis-a-vis its union partner in these sectors. If the final goods producers are politically powerful, they will succeed in getting the external tariff on the input reduced to the partner country's level. A similar process will operate in the partner country in sectors with lower tariff on final goods and higher tariffs on intermediate inputs. Thus, the PTA will lead to further liberalization. It has been suggested that this factor has played some role in the MFN liberalization of certain inputs in Canada.

This seemingly neat argument favoring PTAs has three important limitations. First, the liberalization envisaged by it is in all likelihood a welfare-reducing proposition. As is well known, a reduction in the tariff on an input increases effective protection to the final good and can turn out to be a move away from rather than towards free trade. In trying to explain why so many free traders of his time supported PTAs, Viner (1950) had warned against precisely this type of liberalization. To quote him,

> The major explanation [of why so many free traders support PTAs] seems to lie in an unreflecting association on their part of any removal or reduction of trade barriers with movement in the direction of free trade. Businessmen, however, and governments which had to try simultaneously to satisfy both special interests seeking increased protection and voters hostile to protection, have long known ways of making increased protection look like movement in a free-trade direction.... Let us suppose that there are import duties both on wool and on woolen cloth, but that no wool is produced at home despite the duty. Removing the duty on wool while leaving the duty unchanged on woolen cloth results in increased protection for the cloth industry while having no significance for wool-raising. (Viner 1950, p. 48)

Second, the argument assumes that the option of raising the external tariff on the final product is not available. In virtually all developing countries, external tariffs are bound at levels above their applied levels. As a result, lobbying by producers of final goods can very well result in increased tariff on the final good rather than a reduction in the tariff on the input.

Finally, the argument relies on an essentially flawed political-economy model. It assumes that the producers of intermediate inputs do not lobby against the reduction in tariff and, thus, relies on an ad hoc asymmetry between the availability of protection to final goods and intermediate inputs. The asymmetry could be justified if intermediate inputs were not produced at home. But in that case, there will be no reason for a tariff on them in the first place.

Reducing the External Tariff to Reverse Trade Diversion

Richardson (1993) has provided an interesting case in which, following the formation of PTA, a reduction in the external tariff can result from the government's desire to maximize a political support function. This case, illustrated in Figure 1.2, occurs when a union member faces a constant supply price of a product from its partner as well as the rest of the world and the partner's price is higher. It is well known that the FTA between Singapore and Indonesia in Figure 1.2 is trade diverting. Letting $P_W P_W^t$ be pre-FTA per-unit tariff, all imports come from the rest of the world initially and the price in Indonesia is P_W^t. The FTA brings the internal price down to P_S with all imports diverted to the union partner, Singapore. In Indonesia, pre-FTA tariff revenue, represented by area a+b, disappears. The expansion of imports due to the price decline increases joint gains of consumers and producers by area a+c. Thus, the net gain to Indonesia from the FTA is b−c which is likely to be negative though not necessarily.

Richardson's argument is that once the FTA is in place, by reducing the tariff on the outside world by $P_S P_W^t + \varepsilon$, where ε is an arbitrarily small number, Indonesia can switch imports back to the rest of the world and, thus, reverse the initial trade diversion. The switch allows the country to recover the lost area b in tariff revenue. Richardson shows that such a tariff reduction necessarily obtains in an incentive-theoretic model in which the government maximizes a political support function, which gives a positive weight to consumers' surplus and tariff revenue, no matter how small in relation to the producers' surplus.

There are three key limitations of this argument, which considerably limit its practical relevance. First, if we take Richardson's political support function seriously, it is not clear why the FTA will be approved in the first place. The domestic price declines due to FTA from P_W^t to P_S so that producers will most surely resist it. Moreover, area b−c is likely to be negative implying that the sum of tariff revenue, consumers' surplus and

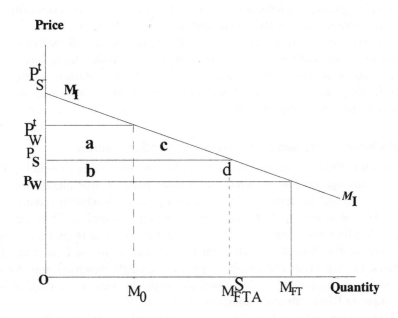

Figure 1.2. The Richardson Case: PTA Leading to a Reduction in the External Tariff

producers' surplus declines. The FTA will be resisted. Alternatively, a political support function compatible with FTA will also be compatible with an MFN tariff reduction by $P_W^t P_S$ which is precisely what Richardson obtains through the FTA plus external tariff reduction of $P_W^t + \varepsilon$.

Second, for a moment, let us make the unrealistic assumption that despite their equivalence, the FTA and MFN liberalization up to $P_W^t P_S$ are subject to different political processes so that the former is feasible but not the latter. Even then, Richardson's argument has very unrealistic setting in that it *requires* a model in which, at any time, the good in question is imported from a single source. Note that in Figure 1.2, all imports come from the outside country under an MFN tariff and from the partner under an FTA. If we were to assume, as in Figure 1.1, that the partner's supply is upward sloped permitting imports from both sources, Richardson's argument no longer holds.

Finally, it is not clear why Singapore will enter into a PTA with Indonesia in the setting shown in Figure 1.2. Singapore has nothing to gain from the FTA so that it will not be willing to pay the political costs of the

FTA. If Singapore did have to gain, as in Figure 1.1, it will necessarily resist outside liberalization by Indonesia after the FTA is formed.

Empirically, so far, no evidence has been provided by advocates of PTAs supporting the point that Richardson type of considerations have led to liberalization of tariffs on outside countries. On the contrary, as discussed later in this section, much of the evidence suggests increases in tariffs following the formation of PTAs.

Lobbying and Increased Barriers against Outside Countries

Bhagwati (1993) argues that in a political-economy setting in which producers play the central role in determining trade policies, liberalization through FTA is likely to be replaced by increased protection against outside countries. To the extent that the country's applied external tariff is below its GATT binding, the country can accomplish this increase in protection by increasing tariffs. And if the actual tariff corresponds to the bound tariff, the increase in protection can be accomplished through increased anti-dumping actions. This argument is demonstrated with the help of a diagrammatic technique in Bhagwati and Panagariya (1996a).

Panagariya and Findlay (1996) offer a formal general-equilibrium model in which tariffs in importable sectors are determined by firms' lobbying activity that uses labor. There are two importables of which one comes from the potential partner and the other from the outside country. The FTA leads to an institutional change which renders lobbying for protection against imports of the partner's good ineffective. This releases labor, lowers the wage and makes lobbying in the other import-competing sector more profitable. The tariff on that good, imported from the outside country, rises. This rise in the tariff can make an otherwise welfare-improving FTA a welfare-reducing proposition and makes the world trading system less liberal.

Cadot, Melo and Olarreaga (1996) also consider the issue of the external tariff in a model in which trade policy is determined by the Grossman-Helpman (1996) political support function. Their analysis turns out to be more complicated and the answer ambiguous. If rules of origin are present, the FTA may result in one or both partners raising the outside tariff though such an outcome is not necessary.

A Tariff-Revenue Objective and the Outside Tariff

If a country is dependent on tariffs for revenue purposes as is true of the countries in Africa, South Asia and even Central and Eastern Europe, an FTA that requires a removal of tariff on the partner country may force it to raise the external tariff. The more the country imports from the FTA partner (i.e., more natural is the FTA partner according to Summers), the larger the loss of revenue, the greater the increase in the external tariff required to maintain fiscal balance and greater the trade diversion. In the same vein, after the formation of an FTA, suppose a country is faced with a fiscal crisis and has to resort to tariffs. Because the bulk of imports coming from the union partner are no longer in the tax base, the necessary increase in the tariff rate is likely to be much larger than in the absence of the FTA.

Empirical Evidence

Theoretical arguments aside, what is the empirical evidence on the impact of PTAs on outside tariffs? There is certainly a considerable evidence of increases in outside tariffs following the implementation of PTAs. After Israel concluded FTAs with both the United States and EU, tariffs on outside sources of imports—principally located in Asia—went up (Halevi and Kleiman, 1994). In the aftermath of the Peso crisis in Mexico, tariffs on outside countries on 503 items went up from 20% or less to 35% [Bhagwati and Panagariya (1996a)]. The same phenomenon has also been observed recently in the Central African Customs and Economic Union (UDEAC) which introduced an across-the-board increase in tariffs on nonmembers to support trade preferences among member countries. In the wake of the recent fiscal crisis in Brazil, MERCOSUR had to raise its common external tariff by 3 percentage points. In the EC, it has been found that internal liberalization there was accompanied by more vigorous anti-dumping against outside countries (Hindley and Masserlin 1993). Finally, now that Eastern and Central European countries must start implementing tariff preferences under the Association Agreements with the EU, they too are having to raise tariffs on outside imports to make up for the revenue shortfall (Masserlin 1997).

Many advocates of PTAs argue that tariff increases in Mexico in the aftermath of the recent peso crisis were minuscule in comparison to the increases in the wake of the macroeconomic crisis there in mid 1980s. They, thus, conclude that the effect of NAFTA was to actually contain tariff increases on outside countries, which could have been much more widespread in its absence. There are three problems with this argument.

First, since early 1980s, there has been a complete reversal in the conventional wisdom on how countries should respond to balance-of-payments crises. In the past, the uniform advice, including that given by the International Monetary Fund, to countries facing balance-of-payments crises was to raise trade barriers. Today, the advice is to take the opportunity to carry out trade reforms that are difficult in times of stability. As a result, even in India, a bastion of protectionism until 1990, the balance-of-payments crisis of 1991 led to an unprecedented and unthinkable wave of trade liberalization which has not been reversed so far and, with some pressure from the WTO, is likely to continue. India, of course, has no PTA with a powerful entity such as the United States or EU. Second, Mexico was given a massive $40 billion debt-relief package to deal with the recent peso crisis which was not available at the time of the previous crisis. If Mexico had shown a lack of commitment on its reforms, the fate of the package would have been in grave doubt. Finally, though the reversal of trade reforms in Mexico was deeper in mid 1980s than that following the crisis of 1994, trade liberalization resumed soon and achieved sufficient success to impress the United States into calling for NAFTA negotiations. By contrast, since the NAFTA and the crisis of 1994, Mexico has shown no significant progress towards cutting its outside tariffs.

1.3.4 The Spaghetti-Bowl Phenomenon

As discussed in Section 1.2.3, in FTAs as opposed to CUs, member countries fear that imports from outside countries destined to a high-tariff member may enter through a low-tariff member. Or more subtly, entrepreneurs in the low-tariff country may import a product in almost finished form, add a small value to it and export it to the high tariff country free of duty. To avoid this trade deflection, FTA agreements usually include the rules of origin according to which products receive the duty-free status only if a pre-specified proportion of value added in the product originates within the union.

Even in the absence of any increase in trade barriers against nonmembers, the proliferation of crisscrossing FTAs leads to a replacement of the nondiscriminatory MFN tariff by a spaghetti bowl whereby tariffs vary according to the ostensible origin of the product. This process is indeed at work as Figure 1.3, adapted from Snape (1996), illustrates. Complicated as it looks, the figure actually understates the complexity of the trade regime, which has come to prevail in Europe as a result of FTAs among different countries there and in neighboring countries in North Africa. For each FTA has its own rules of origin which vary across products and transition phase. As a result, for a given product, there are several different tariff rates depending on what origin is assigned to it. A similar picture can be drawn for Latin America.

1.3.5 WTO-Illegal Policies in PTAs

Yet another way in which PTAs can undermine the global trading system by introducing into such arrangements measures which are otherwise WTO inconsistent. One such example is the trade-balancing requirement within MERCOSUR. The WTO has just outlawed this Trade-Related Investment Measure or TRIM. Yet, the members of MERCOSUR have introduced the provision on the firms operating within the union. Thus, an Argentine company operating in Brazil must export as much Brazilian goods to Argentina as it imports from the latter. Yet another example of this kind is appearance of a voluntary export restraint or VER on tomatoes in NAFTA. Recall that the Agreement on Safeguards in the Uruguay Round Agreement had outlawed VERs. At the moment, we do not have evidence of such WTO-inconsistent measures being widespread, nor are we clear on its legality within the WTO, but it is a problem that deserves attention.

1.4 Open Regionalism

In the policy debate, advocates of the current wave of PTAs also defend it on the ground that it represents "open regionalism" in contrast to closed, import-substituting regionalism of 1950s and 1960s. While references to open regionalism are repeatedly made, few attempts have been made to define the term systematically. In a recent paper even Bergsten (1997a), a staunch advocate of open regionalism, acknowledges, "Yet neither APEC nor any other official body has defined 'open regionalism.'...There is thus considerable confusion about the implications, and even the relevance, of the basic idea." As for critics, they find the term inherently contradictory: arrangements that are open cannot be regionally confined and those that are regionally confined cannot be open. Srinivasan (1995), the most vocal critic of the idea, goes so far as to call open regionalism an oxymoron.

An early attempt at defining open regionalism was made by the Eminent Persons' Group (EPG), appointed by APEC and headed by Fred Bergsten, in

Figure 1.3: The European Spaghetti Bowl

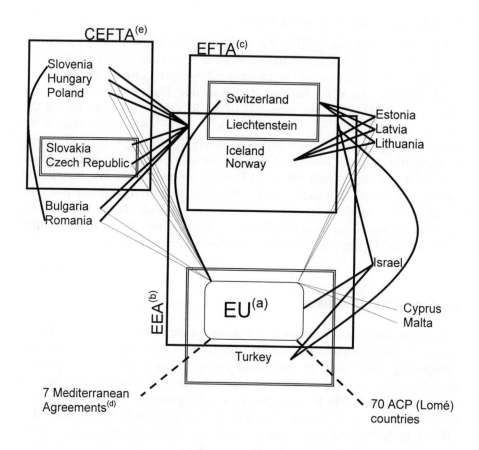

Figure 1.3 (continued): Key to the Spaghetti Bowl

NB: Does not include countries of the former Soviet Union other than Baltic countries.

(a)   European Union comprises: Austria, Belgium, Denmark, Finland, France, Germany, Greece, Ireland, Italy, Luxembourg, Netherlands, Portugal, Spain, Sweden, and United Kingdom.

(b)   European Economic Area

(c)   European Free Trade Association

(d)   Algeria, Egypt, Jordan, Lebanon, Morocco, Syria, Tunisia

(e)   Czech Republic, Hungary, Poland, Slovakia, Slovenia

☐ EU Single Market

═══ Customs Union

▬▬ Free Trade Area

········· EU Association Agreements

▬▬ Non-reciprocal agreements

Source: Adopted from Snape (1996)

its second report [APEC (1994)]. The Council of Economic Advisors to the President of the United States, from which I quote below, subsequently defined the idea in very similar terms:

"Open regionalism refers to plurilateral agreements that are nonexclusive and open to new members to join. It requires first that plurilateral initiatives be fully consistent with Article XXIV of the GATT, which prohibits an increase in average external barriers. Beyond that, it requires that plurilateral agreements not constrain members from pursuing additional liberalization either with non-members on a reciprocal basis or unilaterally. Because member countries are able to choose their external tariffs unilaterally, open agreements are less likely to develop into competing bargaining blocs. Finally, open regionalism implies that plurilateral agreements both allow and encourage non-members to join." [CEA (1995, p. 220)]

This definition offers three criteria for open regionalism: (i) open membership with positive encouragement to nonmembers to join, (ii) consistency with GATT Article XXIV, and (iii) freedom to member countries liberalize further unilaterally or with non-members on a reciprocal basis. Though the report is not entirely explicit about it, the requirement seems to be that all three criteria be applied rather than just any one of them. Let us examine the criteria carefully, taking them in the reverse order.

The requirement that members be free to pursue unilateral or bilateral liberalization rules out customs unions as being compatible with open regionalism even though they are perfectly compatible with GATT Article XXIV. Recall that in a customs union, individual members are not free to lower their tariffs; the common external tariff cannot be lowered unless all members are willing to do it. Nor are members permitted to conclude PTAs with outside countries on their own. Entry of new members into the customs union or a bilateral FTA has to be a joint decision. The criterion rules out the EU as pursuing open regionalism while it accepts NAFTA to be doing so despite the fact that *ex post* the former has signed more new PTAs than the latter. It must be abandoned as either necessary or sufficient for defining a PTA as open.

The second criterion, compatibility with Article XXIV, can serve as a necessary but not sufficient condition for an arrangement to be open. If two countries start with prohibitive tariffs and then form an FTA, keeping their prohibitive tariffs on outside countries, they will satisfy the requirements of Article XXIV. Yet, such arrangements can hardly be characterized as open regionalism. In more practical terms, this criterion says nothing about why the regionalism of 1950s and 1960s was closed while that being pursued today is open. The criterion can be regarded as necessary but far from sufficient.

The remaining criterion, open membership, is perhaps the most important one and is, indeed, what gives the term "open regionalism" substance. It opens the possibility that if outsiders find it attractive to seek membership, a PTA can eventually encompass the entire world and thus lead to multilateral free trade. Despite this possibility, the open-membership criterion has three important limitations, which give critics reason to be skeptical of open regionalism. First, discrimination against nonmembers at any point in time remains in place by definition as long as the regionalism is of Article XXIV variety. Therefore, "open" club is still likely to harm nonmembers. Second, openness is not as innocuous as it sounds; as Bhagwati (1995, 1997) notes, the admission price can include several unpleasant "side payments" that are essentially unrelated to trade. These include acceptance of a stronger intellectual-property-rights regime, investment rules, and higher labor and environmental standards. Finally, open membership does not necessarily translate into speedy membership. It has taken the EU more than 40 years to grow from 6 members to 15. The Canada-U.S. Free Trade Agreement was concluded almost a decade ago and, taking into account NAFTA, its membership has grown to only three so far. Attempts by even a tiny country such as Chile have faced serious resistance. And it will be a long time, if ever, before countries in South Asia and Africa are admitted to either the EU or NAFTA. Until that happens, the world trading system can become fragmented with complex rules of origin and tariff phase-outs contributing to the spaghetti bowl phenomenon.

It is this fear of fragmentation, which prompted Mr. Renato Ruggeiro, the Director-General of the WTO to go a step beyond the CEA (1995) in defining open regionalism. In WTO (1996), he contrasted two interpretations of open regionalism. The first interpretation stops at consistency with Article XXIV of GATT 1994 and the understanding on its interpretation incorporated in the Uruguay Round agreements on Trade in Goods. In the second interpretation,

> "... (T)he gradual elimination of internal barriers to trade within a re-
> gional grouping will be implemented at more or less the same rate
> and on the same timetable as the lowering of barriers towards non-
> members. This would mean that regional liberalization would in

practice as well as in law be generally consistent with the m.f.n. principle." [WTO (1996 p. 11)]

Interestingly, this was the option considered in detail and preferred by the author in the context of regionalism in East Asia [Panagariya (1993) (1994)]. The Director General expressed a clear preference for this option when he concluded

"The choice between these alternatives is a critical one; they point to very different outcomes. In the first case, the point at which we would arrive in no more than 20 to 25 years would be a division of the trading world into two or three intercontinental preferential areas, each with its own rules and with free trade inside the area, but with external barriers still existing among the blocs." [Ibid, p. 11]

In my judgement, if regionalism is to be truly open, it cannot escape being nondiscriminatory. As we have seen, Article-XXIV consistency is a necessary but far from sufficient criterion for ensuring the openness of the world trading system. Open membership can, in principle, lead to global free trade but will lead to fragmentation during transition which will be long and, in practice, may even dead-end at two or three large blocs. Adherence to the MFN principle, by contrast, will eliminate the need for any rules of origin and prevent the growth of the spaghetti-bowl phenomenon.

Some critics find the idea of adherence to the MFN principle to be incompatible with regionalism, however. Thus, Srinivasan (1997) retorts, "if regional liberalization is to be extended *on the same time table* 'in practice and in law' to non-member countries on an MFN basis, it would be multilateral and not regional. If that is the case, why would any group initiate it on a regional basis in the first place?"

There is one other definition of open regionalism, which deserves consideration. Some observers have noted that a distinguishing feature of current regional arrangements is that they are taking place in an environment in which trade barriers have been brought down to low levels through eight rounds of multilateral trade negotiations. Therefore, open regionalism can be defined as FTAs and customs unions with low trade barriers on outside countries. While this definition distinguishes recent regionalism from earlier ones, it does not overcome the fundamental contradiction between openness and discrimination: outsiders may face low barriers but they are nonetheless subject to discrimination relative to insiders.

But suppose for a moment we accept the view that it is possible to discriminate, albeit with low barriers, and still be open. But what is the level of discrimination at which closed regionalism turns into open regionalism? This is not idle discourse. When Mexico maintains a large number of external tariffs in the 15-20% range, keeps open the option of raising them up to 35%, and also has the instrument of anti-dumping at its disposal, can we say that it is pursuing open regionalism under NAFTA? Or should we adopt external trade barriers in the United States as the critical level that distinguishes open from closed regionalism? But this latter definition is also problematic: even after the Uruguay Round liberalization, more than half of textiles and clothing products will remain subject to 15-35% tariffs in the United States and anti-dumping will remain a major trade barrier. To put the matter differently, despite lower (though by no means low) external trade barriers today, the motivating force behind regional arrangements is no different than in the 1950s and 1960s. Now as then, discrimination is the name of the game as member countries continue to be driven by a desire to secure a *preferential* access to the partner country's market. This is clearly the impression conveyed, for example, in the recent report by the United States Trade Representative, "Operation and Effect of NAFTA."[17]

Since the term open regionalism has been used most frequently to describe the developments in Asia, our discussion will be incomplete without brief comments on regionalism in that region. Asian regionalism has been truly "open" in that liberalization undertaken by members of Asian regional groups has been largely non-discriminatory. APEC has created no trade preferences and the members of ASEAN, despite having signed the ASEAN Free Trade Area (AFTA) agreement, which is a PTA in principle, have undertaken much of their liberalization on a nondiscriminatory basis. Thus, if one was looking for an example of Director-General Ruggeiro's preferred form of regionalism, Asia provides it. Regional arrangements in North America, Latin America or Europe do not meet the standards of openness laid out in the Director-General's definition.

---

[17] As discussed in Panagariya (1997), the United States certainly sees APEC as an instrument for seeking increased access for the US goods and has refused to give tariff or other trade concessions under the APEC auspices except on a discriminatory basis.

1.5 "Deep" Integration

Lawrence (1996) has advocated regional arrangements by arguing that, unlike multilateral trade liberalization, they promote "deeper" integration. Rather than being confined to "shallow" integration in terms of liberalization of trade among members, they involve "deep" integration through coordination, if not complete harmonization, of other policies including competition policies, product standards, regulatory regimes, investment codes, environmental policies, labor standards and so on. He argues that such deep integration may confer gains on member countries by lowering the costs of production and improving efficiency in general.

The phrase "deep integration" conveys the impression that whatever it stands for must be a good thing—both deep and integration are "good" words. But there are reasons to be skeptical of such a conclusion. First, a substantial part of the deep integration agenda is itself undesirable from the viewpoint of efficiency and welfare. The careful analysis in Bhagwati (1996) and Wilson (1996) shows that there are good reasons for diversity in domestic polices across nations and that harmonization is, in general, not a welfare-enhancing proposition. Optimal pollution and labor standards depend on income levels. Developed countries may be more concerned about air pollution while developing countries may be worried about water pollution. Likewise, optimal standards with respect to minimum wage, worker-safety, and child labor depend on income levels.

Second, in regional arrangements between countries with uneven bargaining power, smaller, developing countries fear that deep integration can become an instrument for extracting concessions of all kinds not just in trade but in other "non-trade" matters by their larger, more powerful counterparts.[18] The agenda for deep integration is likely to be determined by rich, developed countries. And it is the smaller, developing countries who will have to adjust their standards to those of developed countries, regardless of whether these are appropriate to their conditions. As it happens, the non-trade agenda for future regional arrangements has been dominated in the

---

[18] This sentiment was expressed in slightly different form by Whalley (1993) when he wrote, "The current danger for Mexico in NAFTA is that the price will be paid in the form of adverse exclusionary arrangements which are against Mexican national interest, particularly autos, with potential impediments to third-country inward capital flows and arrangements which effectively reserve the Mexican import market for US suppliers."

United States by demands for higher labor and environmental standards in potential partners. Whatever their social merit, deep integration along these dimensions is unlikely to be a welfare-enhancing move for countries integrating with the United States.

According to the available evidence, when deep integration is attempted among entities with uneven bargaining power, penetration may end up being one way.[19] Lawrence (1996) offers NAFTA as an example of deep integration. Yet, all said and done, it offers increased scope for the penetration of Mexican markets by the United States but not the other way around. Fred Bergsten, who championed the cause of NAFTA, has himself gone on the record stating that under NAFTA the U.S. made no concessions to Mexico while she got every concession she sought.[20] The rules of origin including triple transformation rules in textiles and clothing, side agreements on orange juice and sugar, and subsequent restrictions on Mexican tomatoes bear testimony to the fact that NAFTA generally resisted deep penetration of the U.S. markets by Mexico.

Finally, even if we are able to identify dimensions along which deep integration is desirable, it does not follow that a PTA is necessary complement to it. In principle, much of deep integration agenda can be pursued independently of a PTA. To justify PTA, one must identify extra gains resulting from a simultaneous pursuit of PTA and other deep integration agenda. Short of that, the two policies must be justified on their own merit. This, proponents of deep integration have failed to do.

1.6 Conclusions: Minimizing the Adverse Effects of PTAs

Rather than try to summarize, I conclude the chapter with suggestions that have been made to minimize the adverse effects of PTAs. Because the en-

---

[19] Bhagwati (1994) makes the further argument that a hegemonic power is likely to gain a greater payoff by bargaining *sequentially* with a group of non-hegemonic powers than *simultaneously*. He cites provisions with respect to intellectual property protection and environmental and labor standards as extra benefits secured by the United States through the uneven bargain. Mexico was unable to obtain similar benefits in return.

[20] To quote him, [Bergsten (1997b, p. 26)], "NAFTA amounted to a 4% expansion of the American economy, to include a country that accepted virtually every demand placed upon it in the negotiations and which made virtually all the concessions."

thusiasm for PTAs remains strong, this is a useful exercise. Many proposals have been made of which I list the more important ones here.[21]

First and foremost, we can consider placing a moratorium on the expansion of PTAs beyond those already in an advanced stage of negotiation, particularly the big FTAs such as Transatlantic Free Trade Area and APEC. At the same time, we should move speedily to bring the unfinished agenda of multilateral trade liberalization to its logical conclusion. Such liberalization will not only promote the cause of multilateral liberalization directly, it will also do so indirectly by neutralizing the impact of trade preferences within PTAs. In the limit, if all external barriers drop to zero, PTAs will be effectively eliminated.

Second, for future FTAs, we should modify the GATT Article XXIV so as to require each FTA member to bind its tariffs to the actual levels prevailing at the time of negotiations for the FTA. This will ensure that tariff protection against nonmembers is not raised in the future. For example, if this provision had been present, Israel and Mexico would not have been able to raise their external tariffs following FTAs with the United States. In the case of customs unions, as Bhagwati (1991) suggested, it may be required that the common external tariff be set at the minimum of the pre-union import tariffs of the member countries.[22]

Third, since anti-dumping and safeguard measures can be substituted for higher tariffs on outside countries by enforcing these measures more aggressively against the latter, we also need to introduce changes in Article XXIV which will prevent such a shift in policy.

Fourth, to minimize trade diversion, we should require that within a specified time period, say, five to ten years, following the grant of a tariff

---

[21] Serra et al. (1997) and Panagariya and Srinivasan (1998) provide more details in this context.

[22] In an early contribution to the debate on how GATT rules should be modified to minimize trade diversion, McMillan (1993) had suggested that member countries of PTAs be required to ensure through appropriate policies that their trade with outside countries does not decline. According to the current rules, FTA members are not be permitted to raise their external tariffs and a customs union must adopt a common external tariff no higher than the average of the member countries' tariffs. These rules leave considerable room for a reduction in the union's trade with outside countries. McMillan's proposal is aimed at overcoming this weakness. A difficulty with the proposal, however, is that in a world of growing incomes, trade diversion is consistent with growing trade with outside countries. Moreover, it substitutes an *outcome* variable for an *instrument* variable which is harder to predict *ex ante*.

preference to an FTA member, the external tariff should be reduced to the level of the preferential tariff as well. This means that countries forming a full FTA will have to go to free trade with the rest of the world as well within the specified time limit.[23]

Finally, to contain the spaghetti-bowl phenomenon, we could require that there be no rule of origin on a product in a member country with the lowest tariff in the union. Such a requirement would have eliminated the need for the rules of origin in the United States in a large majority of products. We could also require that whenever the difference between the highest and lowest external tariff rates in the union is less than a pre-specified limit, say, 5%, no rules of origin are permitted.[24] With multilateral liberalization moving ahead, this requirement could help kill the rules of origin on many products in many FTAs faster than otherwise.

An advantage of the proposals on binding the external tariff and then bringing it down to the levels of the preferential tariff is that it will help arrest the proliferation of trade-diverting PTAs. For in that case only the countries truly interested in eventual multilateral free trade will muster the courage to enter into FTAs.

---

[23] See Srinivasan (1996) for this suggestion. The suggestion is a modification of the proposal by Panagariya (1994) that in pursuing regional trade liberalization, the countries in East Asia should proceed in a nondiscriminatory manner. He suggested that the countries could negotiate reductions in trade barriers regionally and implement them on a nondiscriminatory basis.

[24] See Wonnacott (1996) for proposals along these lines.

References

Andriamananjara, Soamiley, 1998, "On the Size and Number of Regional Integration Arrangements: A Political Economy Model," University of Maryland, mimeo.

Asia-pacific Economic Cooperation (APEC), 1994, "Achieving the APEC Vision." Second report of the Eminent Persons Group, Singapore: APEC.

Baldwin, Richard, 1995, "A Domino Theory of Regionalism." In Baldwin, Richard, Haaparnata, P. and Kiander, J., eds., *Expanding Membership of the European Union*, Cambridge, U.K.: Cambridge University Press.

Bergsten, Fred, 1994, "Sunrise in Seattle," *International Economic Insights* 5(1), January/February.

Bergsten, Fred, 1997a, "Open Regionalism," Institute for International Economics, mimeo.

Bergsten, Fred, 1997b, "American Politics, Global Trade," *Economist*, September 27, 23-26.

Bhagwati, Jagdish, 1991, *The World Trading System at Risk*, Princeton, N.J.: Princeton University Press.

Bhagwati, Jagdish, 1993, "Regionalism and Multilateralism: An Overview," in Melo and Panagariya, ed., *New Dimensions in Regional Integration*, Cambridge, Great Britain: Cambridge University Press.

Bhagwati, Jagdish, 1994, "Threats to the World trading System: Income Distribution and the Selfish Hegemon," *Journal of International Affairs*, Spring.

Bhagwati, Jagdish, 1995, "U.S. Trade Policy: The Infatuation with Free Trade Areas," in Bhagwati, Jagdish and Anne O. Krueger, eds., *The Dangerous Drift to Preferential Trade Agreements*, Washington, D.C.: American Enterprise Institute for Public Policy Research.

Bhagwati, Jagdish, 1996a, "Dissent at APEC Meeting cannot be Ignored," Letters to the Editor, *Financial Times*, December 6.

Bhagwati, Jagdish, 1996b, "The Demand to Reduce Domestic Diversity among Nations," in Jagdish Bhagwati and Robert Hudec, eds., *Fair Trade and Harmonization*, Cambridge, MA: MIT Press.

Bhagwati, Jagdish, 1997, "Fast Track to Nowhere," *Economist*, October 18, pp. 21-23.

Bhagwati, Jagdish, David Greenaway and Arvind Panagariya, 1998, "Trading Preferentially: Theory and Policy," *Economic Journal*, forthcoming.

Bhagwati, Jagdish and Panagariya, Arvind, 1996a, "Preferential Trading Areas and Multilateralism: Strangers, Friends or Foes?" in Jagdish Bhagwati and Arvind

Panagariya, eds., *The Economics of Preferential Trade Agreements*, AEI Press, Washington, D.C. (Chapter 2, this volume)

Bhagwati, Jagdish and Panagariya, Arvind, 1996b, "The Theory of Preferential Trade Agreements: Historical Evolution and Current Trends." *American Economic Review* 86, May, 82-87.

Bond, Eric W. and Syropulos, Constantinos, 1996, "The Size of Trading Blocs, Market Power and World Welfare Effects," *Journal of International Economics* 40, 411-437.

Cadot, O, Melo, Jaime de and Olarreaga, J., 1996, "Regional Integration and Lobbying for Tariffs Against Non-Members," mimeo, University of Geneva.

Council of Economic Advisors, 1995, *Economic Report of the President*. Council of Economic Advisors: Washington, D.C.

Ellis, Howard, 1945, "Bilateralism and the Future of International Trade," *Essays in International Finance* No. 5, Summer.

Falvey, Rod and Geoff Reed, 1997a, "Economic Effects of Rules of Origin," mimeo, University of Nottingham.

Falvey, Rod and Geoff Reed, 1997b, "Rules of Origin as Commercial Policy Instruments," mimeo, University of Nottingham.

Frankel, J., 1997, *Regional Trading Blocs in the World Economic System*, Washington, D.C.: Institute for International Economics.

Frankel, J., Stein, E. and Wei, S., 1995, "Trading Blocs and the Americas: The Natural, the Unnatural and the Supernatural," *Journal of Development Economics* 47, 61-96.

Frankel, J. and Shang-Jin Wei, 1997, "The New Regionalism and Asia: Impact and Options," in A. Panagariya, M.G. Quibria and N. Rao, eds., *The Global trading System and Developing Asia*, Hong Kong: Oxford University Press, forthcoming.

GATT (1994), *The Results of the Uruguay Found of Multilateral Trade Negotiations—The Legal Texts*, Geneva: GATT Secretariat.

Grossman, Gene and Helpman, Elhanan, 1995, "The Politics of Free Trade Agreements," *American Economic Review*, September, 667-690.

Halevi, N. and E. Kleiman, 1994, "Israel's Trade and Payments Regime," paper prepared for the Regional Trade Group, Institute for Social and Economic Policy in the Middle East, Kennedy School of Government, Cambridge, MA.

Hindley, B. and P. Messerlin, 1993, "Guarantees of market Access and Regionalism," in K. Anderson and R. Blackhurst, eds., *Regional Integration and the Global Trading System* (London: Harvester Wheatsheaf).

Jacquemin, Alexis and Andre Sapir, 1991, "Europe Post-1992: Internal and External Liberalization," *American Economic Review: Papers and Proceedings* 81, no. 2, May, 166-170.

Kemp, M. and Wan, Henry Jr., 1976, "An Elementary Proposition Concerning the Formation of Customs Unions", *Journal of International Economics* 6 (February), 95-8.

Kowalczyk, Carsten and Donald Davis, 1996, "Tariff Phase Outs: Theory and Evidence from GATT and NAFTA," in Jeffrey Frankel, *Regionalization of the World Economy*, Chicago: University of Chicago Press, forthcoming.

Krishna, K. and A. O. Krueger, 1995, "Implementing Free Trade Areas: Rules of Origin and Hidden Protection," in Deardorff, A, Levinsohn, J. and Stern, R., eds., *New Directions in Trade Theory*, Ann Arbor: University of Michigan Press, 149-187.

Krishna, Pravin, 1998, "Regionalism and Multilateralism: A Political Economy Approach," *Quarterly Journal of Economics*, forthcoming.

Krueger, Anne O., 1993, "Free Trade Agreements as Protectionist devices: Rules of Origin," NBER Working Paper No. 4352.

Krugman, P., 1991a, "The Move to Free Trade Zones," Symposium Sponsored by the Federal Reserve Bank of Kansas City, *Policy Implications of Trade and Currency Zones*.

Krugman, P., 1991b, "Is Bilateralism Bad?" in E. Helpman and A. Razin (eds.), *International Trade and Trade Policy*, Cambridge, Mass.: MIT Press.

Krugman, P., 1993, "Regionalism versus Multilateralism: Analytical Notes," in Melo and Panagariya (eds.)

Lawrence, Robert, 1997, *Regionalism, Multilateralism and Deeper Integration*, Washington: Brookings Institution.

Levy, Philip. 1997, "A Political-Economic Analysis of Free-Trade Agreements," *American Economic Review* 87(4), September.

McMillan, John, 1993, "Does Regional Integration Foster Open Trade? Economic Theory and GATT's Article XXIV," in Kym Anderson and Richard Blackhurst, eds., *Regional Integration and the Global Trading System*, London: Harvester Wheatsheaf.

Panagariya, Arvind, 1993, "Should East Asia Go Regional? No, No and Maybe," WPS 1209, World Bank, October. (Chapter 3, this volume)

Panagariya, Arvind (1994) 'East Asia and the New Regionalism,' *World Economy* 17, No. 6, November, 817-39.

Panagariya, Arvind, 1995, "Rethinking the New Regionalism," presented at the World Bank Conference on Trade Expansion Program, January 23-24, 1995. Forthcoming in John Nash and Wendy Takacs, eds., *Lessons in Trade Policy Reform*, Washington, D.C.: World Bank.

Panagariya, Arvind, 1996, 'The Free Trade Area of the Americas: Good for Latin America?' *World Economy* 19, no. 5, September, 485-515. (Chapter 5, this volume)

Panagariya, Arvind, 1997a, "An Empirical Estimate of Static Welfare Losses to Mexico from NAFTA," mimeo, Center for International economics, University of Maryland, mimeo. (Chapter 6, this volume)

Panagariya, Arvind, 1997b, "Do Transport Costs Justify *Regional* Preferential Trade Arrangements? No." Paper presented at International Economic Study Group Conference on "Regulation of International trade and Investment," October 1997.

Panagariya, Arvind and Ronald Findlay, 1996, "A Political Economy Analysis of Free Trade Areas and Customs Unions," Robert Feenstra, Douglas Irwin and Gene Grossman, eds., *The Political Economy of Trade Reform*, Essays in Honor of jagdish Bhagwati, MIT Press.

Panagariya, Arvind and Pravin Krishna, 1997, "On the Existence of Necessarily Welfare-Enhancing Free Trade Areas," Center for International Economics, Department of Economics, University of Maryland, mimeo.

Panagariya, Arvind and T. N. Srinivasan, "The New Regionalism: A Benign or Malign Growth?" in Jagdish Bhagwati and Mathias Hirsch, Essays in Honor of Arthur Dunkel, Ann Arbor: University of Michigan Press, forthcoming.

Polak, J.J., "Is APEC a Natural Regional trading Bloc?", *World Economy* 19, No. 3, September.

Richardson, Martin, 1993, "Endogenous Protection and Trade Diversion, " *Journal of International Economics* 34(3-4), 309-24.

Serra, Jaime, G. Aguilar, J. Cordoba, G. Grossman, C. Hills, J. Jackson, J. Katz, P. Noyola, and M. Wilson, 1997, *Reflections on Regionalism: Report of the Study Group on International Trade*, Washington, D.C.: Carnegie Endowment for International Peace.

Snape, Richard, 1996, "Trade Discrimination—Yesterday's Problem?" *Economic Record* 72(219), 381-396, December.

Spilimbergo, A. and E. Stein, 1996, "The Welfare Implications of Trading Blocs Among Countries with Different Endowments, " NBER Working Paper #5472 (March). Forthcoming in Frankel, Jeffrey, ed., *The Regionalization of the World Economy*, Chicago: University of Chicago Press.

Srinivasan, T.N., 1995, "APEC and Open Regionalism," Yale University, processed.

Srinivasan, T.N., 1997, "Regionalism and the World Trade Organization: Is Non-Discrimination Passe?", in Anne O. Krueger, ed., *The World Trade Organization as an International Institution*, The University of Chicago Press.

Summers, L., 1991, "Regionalism and the World Trading System," Symposium Sponsored by the Federal Reserve Bank of Kansas City, *Policy Implications of Trade and Currency Zones*.

Wei, Shang-Jin and Jeffrey Frankel, 1996, "Open Regionalism in a World of Continental Trade Blocs," May, presented at the American Economic Association meetings, January 3-6, 1997 at a joint AEA-Korea-American Economic Association session.

Whalley, John, 1993, Regional Trade Arrangements in North America: CUSTA and NAFTA," in Melo and Panagariya, ed., *New Dimensions in Regional Integration*, Cambridge, Great Britain: Cambridge University Press.

Wilson, John D., 1996, "Capital Mobility and Environmental Standards: Is There a Theoretical Basis for a Race to the Bottom?" in Jagdish Bhagwati and Robert Hudec, eds., *Fair Trade and Harmonization*, Cambridge, MA: MIT Press.

Winters, L. Alan, 1996, "Regionalism versus Multilateralism," Policy Research Working Paper 1687, World Bank, Washington, D.C.

Wonnacott, Paul, 1996, "Beyond NAFTA—The Design of the Free Trade Agreement of the Americas," in Jagdish Bhagwati and Arvind Panagariya, eds., *The Economics of Preferential Trade Agreements*, AEI Press, Washington, D.C.

Wonnacott, Paul and Lutz, Mark, 1989, "Is There a Case for Free Trade Areas?" in Schott, Jeffrey, *Free Trade Areas and U.S. Trade Policy*, Washington, D.C.: Institute for International Economics, 59-84.

World Trade Organization (WTO), 1996, "The Road Ahead: International Trade Policy in the Era of the WTO." Fourth Annual Sylvia Ostry Lecture, Ottawa, 28 May 1996. WTO Press/49, Geneva, 29 May 1996.

Yeats, Alexander J., 1996, 'Does Mercosur's Trade Performance Justify Concerns About the Effects of Regional Trade Arrangements? Yes!,' World Bank, mimeo.

Yi, Sang-Seung, 1996, "Endogenous Formation of Customs Unions under Imperfect Competition: Open Regionalism is Good," *Journal of International Economics* 41, 153-77.

2.   Preferential Trading Areas and Multilateralism: Strangers, Friends or Foes?

(with Jagdish Bhagwati)

2.1 Introduction

The question of Preferential Trading Areas, as we should call them in preference to Free Trade Areas (FTAs) and Customs Unions (CUs), phrases that
falsely equate them in the public mind and discourse with nonpreferential
free trade, has never been distant from international economists' thoughts
and concerns since the beginning of the postwar period when the architects
of the General Agreement on Tariffs and Trade (GATT) had to confront
them and accommodate them into the GATT via Article XXIV.[25]

Originally published, as chapter 1, in the *Economics of Preferential Trade Agreements*, ed.,
Jagdish Bhagwati and Arvind Panagariya (washington, DC: American Enterprise Institute,
1996), 1-78. The appendix, containing a list of the existing PTAs, has been deleted.

We thank Jeffrey Frankel, Philip Levy, T.N. Srinivasan, Robert Staiger and participants in
the CIE-AEI Conference, as well as Pravin Krishna for many helpful conversations and comments on an earlier draft of this paper. We have also benefitted from suggestions made at
seminars at Harvard and Osaka Universities, the University of Maryland and the Stockholm
School of Economics. Special thanks are due to Maria Pillinini of the Development Division
of the World Trade Organization for providing the list of PTAs (not included in this repro-
duction).

[25]The focus of our chapter will be on Article XXIV-sanctioned PTAs, rather than on every
kind of preferential arrangement among any subset of WTO members. PTAs, often grouped
together into a single category, actually fall into three different WTO categories: Article
XXIV arrangements involving FTAs and CUs, Enabling Clause arrangements limited to
developing countries and permitting partial preferences, and Generalized System of
Preferences (GSP) arrangements permitted via a grant of an exception to Article I.

Their wisdom became a center of analytical attention, especially at the time of the steps taken to form the European Community by the Treaty of Rome in 1957 and when, in what Bhagwati (1991) has called the period of *First Regionalism*, other Article XXIV-sanctioned PTAs were considered and even attempted in other areas.[26] The Vinerian (1950) theory of PTAs, to which Meade (1955), Lipsey (1957)(1960) and other international economists at the time made important contributions, while preceding the formation of the European Community, developed more fully as a result of that singular event. The attempts at providing a more realistic rationale for the extension of such PTAs to developing countries, on the other hand, as a way of reducing the cost of any targeted level of industrialization, came from Cooper and Massell (1965a)(1965b), Johnson (1965) and Bhagwati (1968) at the time.[27]

It must be said that the First Regionalism was stillborn; beyond the European Community (and its offshoot, the European Free Trade Area) there was practically no successful emulation of the European developments elsewhere. At the same time, given the fact that it arose over the concerns that such PTAs were not the same as nondiscriminatory freeing of trade, the Vinerian Theory was "static," concerning itself simply with the issue as to when such PTAs would be trade-diverting or trade-creating, thus diminishing or increasing welfare.

The recent revival of interest in the theory of preferential trading areas, marking what Bhagwati (1991) has christened the *Second Regionalism*, has come instead from the conversion of the United States to preferential trading arrangements, starting with the Canada-US Free Trade Agreement (CUFTA) and the later extension to include Mexico under the North American Free Trade Agreement (NAFTA). This time around, the movement has extended equally to other areas, involving again developing countries on their own, as in the Southern Cone Common Market (MERCOSUR), but with success rather than failure.

---

[26] The reasons why these did not succeed are discussed in Bhagwati (1991).

[27] These different approaches, as also the later new approaches to the static theory of preferential trading areas such as by Kemp and Wan (1976) and by Brecher and Bhagwati (1981), have been distinguished and discussed in the graduate textbook by Bhagwati and Srinivasan (1983). The Cooper-Massell-Johnson-Bhagwati argument has also been formalized recently, using the Kemp-Wan approach and combining it with the theory of non-economic objectives, by Krishna and Bhagwati (1994).

In 1982, the United States could not get multilateral trade talks started at Geneva and, hence, turned to ever-expanding PTAs as an alternative way of getting eventually to worldwide free trade. This has given the theory of PTAs a "dynamic time-path" dimension (Bhagwati 1993a): when would such an approach lead to a progressive freeing of trade barriers through expanding membership (and/or accelerating multilateral trade negotiations in a benign symbiosis)? This is also a political-economy-theoretic question, fitting nicely into the modern preoccupation of economic theorists with questions relating to what policies emerge (that is, with "public choice") rather than what they should be (that is, with "social choice").

From a policy viewpoint also, this revival of PTAs is an important development. It was fed (if not led) by the US-centered NAFTA and its proposed extension to Chile and beyond, and by Asia Pacific Economic Cooperation (APEC) which some in the US would like to see turn into another PTA, and by the call of European politicians such as Mr. Klaus Kinkel of Germany at the outset, and by many others subsequently, to form TAFTA (a Transatlantic Free Trade Area). With GATT jumpstarted and multilateralism functioning, the theoretical and policy questions then must be confronted: should these proposals for proliferating PTAs, especially when inclusive of hegemonic powers such as the United States, be encouraged by economists?

In this paper, we undertake the following tasks. After reviewing key phrases and concepts in Section 2.2, we extend the "static" analysis of PTAs in Section 2.3. This enables us to examine several recent claims in favor of PTAs and persuades us to discard them as unpersuasive.

Specifically, our analysis enables us to examine and reject the much-cited claim that it is wrong to worry about trade diversion and that PTAs are generally as good as nonpreferential trade liberalization.

Our analysis also gives added insight into why the usual argument made these days is mistaken. This is the argument that, when countries joining a PTA have large shares of their trade with one another and are thus "natural trading partners", they need not fear losses. The nonhegemonic countries that are liberalizing with a hegemon that is generally open and offering few new reductions of trade barriers, as is the case with Mexico and with other potential NAFTA members outside of the United States and Canada, could face the prospect of significant "static" welfare losses.

Next, we turn to the dynamic time-path question. In the policy context, this necessitates our considering arguments as to why a proliferation of

PTAs, despite their creating a harmful *spaghetti-bowl phenomenon* in the world economy, may be beneficial because of their helpful consequences for the progressive freeing of trade and moving the world economy to worldwide free trade.

We systematize the current analytical contributions on this problem in Section 2.4 and evaluate the current policy developments in Section 2.5.[28] It is our policy judgment that PTAs that are hegemon-centered, as NAFTA is, are not the desirable way to advance the cause of worldwide freeing of trade barriers and that it is better to focus on World Trade Organization (WTO)-centered MFN trade liberalization. By contrast, we will consider intra-developing-country, nonhegemon-centered PTAs, such as MERCOSUR, in a more favorable light.

2.2 Phrases and Concepts

Two phrases are frequently used: PTAs and regionalism. The two significant concepts are, first, trade creation and trade diversion and, second, stumbling blocks and building blocks.

2.2.1 Phrases
We first define PTAs and regionalism.

Preferential Trade Areas
By Preferential Trading Areas, we will mean Free Trade Areas, Customs Unions (which also have a common external tariff) and Common Markets (which additionally have freedom of internal factor movement within the area defined by member states). All these arrangements fall within the purview of GATT Article XXIV. Lesser forms have traditionally been permitted for developing countries and come under Economic Cooperation among Developing Countries (ECDC) and we will have something to say about that too though this chapter will be almost exclusively focused on Article XXIV-sanctioned PTAs, and within that category, on FTAs in particular.

---

[28] The analytical synthesis in Section 2.4 draws on Bhagwati, Krishna and Panagariya (1996) and also on our paper for the 1996 American Economic Association meetings in San Francisco, Bhagwati and Panagariya (1996).

Regionalism

The phrase Regionalism is loosely used by many, including us, as synonymous with PTAs. However, strictly speaking, Regionalism refers to PTAs defined by a geographic region. There is a school of thought (to which Summers and Krugman have subscribed) that considers regional PTAs to be a priori less likely to lead to static trade diversion than nonregional PTAs and such regional PTAs to be therefore ipso facto acceptable. This is a substantive issue that we will consider, as did Bhagwati (1993a) in a preliminary way. Our focus in the chapter will, however, be on PTAs, not regional PTAs.

2.2.2 Concepts

As just noted, two sets of concepts are central to our subsequent discussion: trade creation versus trade diversion and stumbling blocks versus building blocks.

Trade Creation and Trade Diversion (Viner)

The phraseology, and conceptualization, of trade creation and trade diversion as two possibilities that define the second-best nature of the static analysis of PTAs goes back to Viner (1950), of course. While there are various ways in which these two concepts have subsequently been defined, we will use them (in the theoretical analysis below) in the original Vinerian sense to mean a shift of imports from an efficient to an inefficient source under trade diversion, and a shift from an inefficient to an efficient source under trade creation.[29]

"Stumbling Blocks" and "Building Blocks" (Bhagwati)

The phraseology and conceptualization of PTAs that, in a dynamic time-path sense, contribute to the multilateral freeing of trade either by progressively adding new members (down the PTA path to worldwide free trade) or by prompting accelerated multilateral trade negotiations and are thus *building blocks* towards the multilateral freeing of trade and those that do the opposite and hence are *stumbling blocks* to the goal of worldwide, multilateral freeing

---

[29] In Viner's analysis, reproduced in Figure 2.1, with constant costs everywhere, the concepts translates immediately into a shift of imports from the outside to the partner country as trade diversion and a shift from the home country production to imports from the partner country as trade creation. This translation does not hold fully in Figure 2.3, for example.

of trade, owes to Bhagwati (1991, p. 77) and has been adopted by Lawrence (1991) and others.[30] Insofar as Viner's "trade creation" and "trade diversion" concepts were designed to divide PTAs into those that were "good" and those that were "bad" in the static sense, Bhagwati's "building block" and "stumbling block" concepts are designed to divide PTAs into those that are "good" and those that are "bad" in the dynamic, time-path sense.

2.3 Rethinking Static Welfare Analysis

We now begin with the static analysis. Frankly, so much has been written on the static analysis since Viner's pioneering 1950 contribution, indeed by virtually every important international economist, that one may think that there is little to add.

2.3.1 The Issues Examined

Yet, there is something to be gained by another, close look at the conventional static analysis in view of several presuppositions, mostly favorable to PTAs, which have recently been made by policy analysts. We consider two sets of issues.

1. It has been forcefully argued by Larry Summers (1991) in an influential paper that international economists should not be preoccupied by trade diversion: "I find it surprising that this issue is taken so seriously—in most other situations, economists laugh off second best considerations and focus on direct impacts."

Our first reaction is to deny the premise of his analogy: economists, faced with a second best problem, typically *do* worry about that aspect of the problem. Indeed, if the world was first best, market prices would reflect social opportunity costs and there would be no need for cost-benefit analysis for projects. The World Bank that Summers served with distinction, would then have to close down most of its project-lending research and analysis

---

[30] In a generous introductory footnote to his article entitled "Emerging Regional Arrangements: Building Blocks or Stumbling Blocks?," Lawrence's (1991) writes "I owe this phrase to Jagdish Bhagwati." Bhagwati (1991, 77) refers to the expansion of membership as a test of PTAs serving as "building blocks" for worldwide freeing of trade: this concept is illustrated in Figure 2.9, reproduced from Bhagwati (1993a). Evidently, if going down the PTA path can trigger multilateral negotiations and their successful conclusion that too can be a way in which PTAs may serve as building blocks, as discussed here.

aimed at determining the shadow prices to be used in judging the acceptability of projects.

Second, the problem of preferential trade liberalization is indeed an inherently second best problem since nondiscriminatory trade liberalization is being ruled out. Ignoring this aspect is unwarranted.

Third, one should not confuse "second best" with primary impact." "First best" problems also are characterized by primary and total effects.

Fourth, if Summers implies that trade-diverting PTAs are a minor nuisance, he is misled presumably by the fact that efficiency losses are Harberger triangles and "small." But such PTAs impose losses on member countries also through tariff-revenue-*redistribution* and these can be large: these are rectangles while the efficiency effects are triangles.

2. Next, we consider the contention in the recent policy debate that countries which trade with each other in larger volume than with other nations are "natural" trading partners and hence that PTAs among them are likely to be welfare enhancing to their members for that reason.

This contention is further linked with the argument that "regional" PTAs are *desirable* (in the sense of being more likely to create welfare gains for their members) because geographically contiguous countries (particularly if they share common borders) have larger volumes of trade with one another than with others.

Our analysis here serves to challenge the premise that large volumes of initial trade mean that the likelihood of loss from PTAs is less. This also undermines therefore the contention that regional PTAs are more desirable.

We also question the alternative but related "natural trading partners" hypothesis that regional PTAs are likely to improve welfare by conserving on transport costs. We show that transport costs by themselves do not provide a reason for discriminatory PTAs.[31]

---

[31] The "natural trading partners" hypothesis comes therefore in two forms. In the first form, the emphasis is on a large initial volume of trade that may result, *inter alia,* from geographical proximity. In the second form, the emphasis is on transport costs that are assumed to be low between countries within the same region. We have been reminded by Paul Wonnacott that the term "natural trading partner" originated in Wonnacott and Lutz (1989). Many authors have attributed the term instead to Krugman (1991a) who, along with Summers, should nevertheless be credited with popularizing it.

2.3.2 The Theoretical Analysis

We may recall that, since Viner's (1950) classic work, PTAs have been considered to be harmful both to member countries whose imports are the subject of the trade diversion and to the world under trade diversion and welfare-enhancing under trade creation. This ambiguity of outcomes, depending on the relative strengths of the two effects when a PTA is formed, has been the principal reason for the debate among economists as to whether a specific PTA is desirable.

We will begin the theoretical analysis below by showing, however, that the conventional trade creation and trade diversion are not the entire story in deciding on the welfare outcome for an *individual* member of a PTA. Even if trade creation effects are larger than trade diversion effects so that the union as a whole benefits, an individual member could lose on account of adverse income distribution effects arising from tariff revenue redistribution.

The redistribution of tariff revenue between member countries arises, of course, due to a shift in the terms of trade within the union. When a member country lowers its tariff on the partner without lowering it on the rest of the world, within-union terms of trade shift in favor of the partner (for both existing and new imports from it). The extent of the unfavorable redistributive effect on a member country is obviously determined by the degree of preferential access it gives to the partner country in relation to the preferential access it receives from the latter: the greater the margin of preference the country gives the more it stands to lose. This implies that when a country with a high degree of protection forms a PTA with a country with relatively open markets, as in the case of Mexico and U.S.A., the former may well be faced with a net welfare loss. We develop this theme and its ramifications, in the following analysis, using simple models from the literature and distinguishing clearly among the effects on member country and world welfare.

i. The Viner Model: Constant Costs

The natural starting point for explaining the economics of regional integration is Viner's partial equilibrium model. This model does not fully capture the effects noted above but is, nevertheless, an important step towards understanding them. Assume that there are three countries, A, B and C such that A and B are potential union partners and C represents the rest of the world. In Figure 2.1, panels a and b, let $M_A M_A$ represent A's import demand for a specific product and $P_B E_B$ and $P_C E_C$ the (export) supplies of the same product available from B and C, respectively. Following Viner, it is assumed that the supply prices of B and C are constant at P_B and P_C, respectively. In panel a, the supply price of C exceeds that of B and in panel b the opposite is true.

In panel a illustrating the case of a *trade creating* union, with an initial nondiscriminatory *specific* tariff t, A imports OM_0 quantity of the good.[32] All imports come from B so that A raises areas 1 and 2 in tariff revenue. If A now forms an FTA with B, imports from B expand from OM_0 to OM_{FTA}. The tariff revenue disappears but the price facing consumers declines by t; A's consumers capture the entire revenue in the form of increased surplus. Because B is the lower-cost source of the product, there is positive trade creation and no trade diversion.[33] Working like nondiscriminatory free trade, the FTA yields to A and to the union a net gain represented by areas 3 and 4.[34]

Panel b illustrates the case of a *trade diverting* union. Here B is the higher-cost source of the product with the result that, given a nondiscriminatory tariff in A, all imports come from C. A imports OM_0 and collects areas 1 and 2 in tariff revenue. If A and B now form an FTA, imports expand to OM_{FTA}, but the source of their supply switches from C to B. Though the reduction in A's domestic price leads to some trade creation— increased imports lead to a displacement of some inefficient domestic production and increase in consumption in A—, the switch to the higher-cost source, B, leads to a large trade diversion of OM_0 quantity of imports from C to B. Thus, panel b shows a case where the union diverts trade from C, but also has some trade creation. The gains to A are given by area 3 and the losses by area 2. The loss of area 2 results from a deterioration in A's terms of trade from P_C to P_B and takes the form of the excess of the loss of tariff revenue (1+2) over that which is captured partially (area 1) by A's consumers. Area 2 goes to pay for the higher cost of production in B than in C.

Note now that, unless cost differences between B and C are small, areas similar to area 2 will be large in relation to the triangular areas of gain. The

---

[32]We assume a specific rather than an ad valorem tariff for geometric simplicity when supply curves are rising. Nothing in the analysis hangs on it.

[33]Because imports expand, some of the inefficient domestic production is replaced by imports from B. A also gains from an increase in the consumers' surplus in excess of the tariff revenue.

[34] B gains nothing and C loses nothing, given the constant-cost assumptions on their supply curves in trade.

Figure 2.1: Vinerian Analysis with Constant Costs

Panel A. Trade-creating Union of A and B

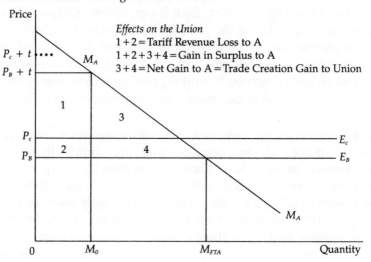

Panel B. Trade-Diverting Union of A and B

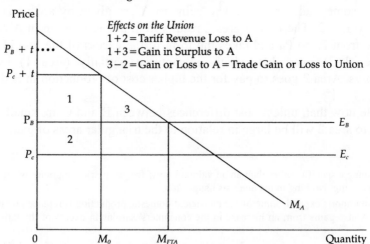

Figure 2.1 (continued): General Equilibrium

Panel C. General Equilibrium Analysis: Viner-Lipsey Model of Trade-Diverting Union

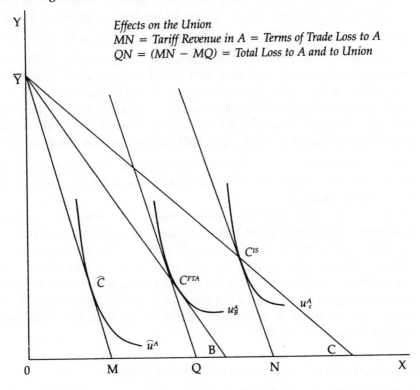

welfare loss to A due to the loss of revenue on diverted imports applies to the *entire* initial quantity of imports whereas the gain applies only to the *change* in the quantity of imports. The FTA will be associated with trade creation in some sectors and trade diversion in others. But since losses are likely to be large in cases involving trade diversion, trade diversion in even a small number of sectors can more than offset the gains arising from trade creation in a large number of sectors.

The trade-diverting case of panel b can also be illustrated in general equilibrium by using the Lipsey version of the Viner analysis as in panel c. There, the economy of A is specialized in producing at $\overline{Y}$, with $\overline{Y}C$ and $\overline{Y}B$ the given, fixed terms of trade with C and B respectively. With an initial nondiscriminating tariff, A trades with C and consumes at C^{IS}, winding up with welfare at U_C^A. With the FTA between A and B, the trade shifts to B. A winds up consuming at C^{FTA} and its welfare is reduced to U_B^A. The welfare loss QN can then be seen as the difference between the tariff-revenue or terms-of-trade loss MN and the gain MQ that comes from the ability to shift consumption from $\hat{C}$ to C^{FTA}.[35] (OM is the income at domestic prices in the initial situation and tariff revenue is MN, the sums of the two yielding ON as national expenditure.)

A final and obvious point may be stressed, concerning nondiscriminatory trade liberalization by country A. In both the cases shown in Figure 2.1, A obtains maximum trade gains and its welfare is improved relative to the initial as well as the FTA equilibrium by a nondiscriminatory liberalization. Such liberalization leads to the same equilibrium in the trade-creating union in panel a (as a limiting case) and eliminates trade diversion in the case in panel b, amounting to free trade with the most efficient supplier for each commodity.

ii. Partner Country's Supply Curve is Upward Sloped

Because of the assumption that the export-supply curves of both B and C are perfectly elastic, however, the model in Figure 2.1 leads to at least two unre-

---

[35] The measure used is the conventional Hicksian equivalent variation: keeping the initial non-discriminatory tariff, how much income can A withdraw so as to yield the same welfare loss as the FTA imposes?

alistic outcomes. [36] First, imports into A come from either B or C but not both. Second, in the trade diversion case, the losses of A represented by area 2 are used up entirely to finance B's higher costs of production: the partner country B makes no gain whatsoever. The model thus captures only one side of the possibly "mercantilist" nature of trade-diverting FTAs: A can lose from its own (discriminatory) trade liberalization but B does not gain from it.

A more realistic model allows the supply curve of one or both countries B and C to slope upward. In the interest of simplicity, we will allow for an upward-sloped supply curve for only one country at a time. Figure 2.2 takes up the case when the partner country B's supply curve slopes upward and that of the outside country C is horizontal. This case captures the essence of the more general model in which the outside country's supply curve also slopes upward but is more elastic than the partner's. Figure 2.3 considers instead the case when the union is between A and C so that the partner country's supply curve is more elastic than that of the outside world.

In both Figures 2.2 and 2.3, as before, we then let $M_A M_A$ represent the import demand for a product imported by A. The supply curve of the product available from B is upward sloped and is represented by DE_B. Country C's export supply curve, represented by $P_C E_C$, is horizontal. The tariff continues to be specific. Consider then Figure 2.2, taking successively three cases: (1) an initial nondiscriminatory tariff; (2) free trade; and (3) an FTA.

(1) Under a *nondiscriminatory tariff* at rate t per unit, supplies from B and C, as perceived by buyers in A, are given by $VE_B{}^t$ and $P_C{}'E_C{}^t$, respectively. Total imports into A equal OQ_3 of which OQ_1 come from B and $Q_1 Q_3$ from C. A collects tariff revenue equivalent to rectangle GHNS. The gains from trade for A amount to the area under the import-demand curve and above the domestic price plus the tariff revenue, that is, triangle KSG plus rectangle GHNS. For country B, the gains from trade equal the area above EBEB and below the net price received, PC, that is, area HUD.

---

[36] Many of the points in this and the following subsection have been made earlier in Panagariya (1995a, 1995b). The tariff-revenue-transfer effect that is central to our analysis is normally present in all models characterized by flexible terms of trade. Thus, see the three-good, three-country general-equilibrium analyses of Berglas (1979) and Riezman (1979) which are neatly summarized within a unified framework by Lloyd (1982). Both Berglas and Riezman find, as we do, that when intra-union terms of trade are flexible, a large volume of imports from the partner country is inversely related to the welfare effect of a preferential liberalization. Neither of these authors makes many of the points made below or looks at the problem as we do, however.

Country C neither gains nor loses from trade. Table 2.1 summarizes this information in column 1.

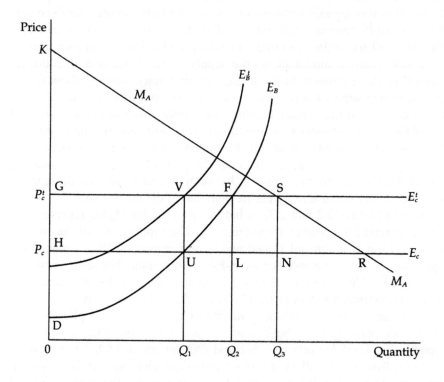

Figure 2.2: Effects of Union (A+B) with Rising Costs from the Partner Country

(2) Suppose now that A decides to adopt a policy of *free trade* by eliminating the tariff on a nondiscriminatory basis. The price in A declines to P_C, imports from B do not change, and imports from C rise by NR. Tariff revenue disappears but the gains from trade rise to KGS+GHNS+RSN: there is a net welfare gain to A of RSN. The extra gain comes from increased benefits to consumers and producers in A. The gains to country B remain unchanged at HDU. Because of the perfectly elastic supply, country C neither gains nor loses from trade before or after trade liberalization by A. Therefore, the world as a whole benefits by area RSN. These changes are summarized in column 2 of Table 2.1.

Table 2.1: The Welfare Effects of Unilateral Liberalization and Free Trade Area
between A and B

(This table relates to Figure 2.2 in the text. Relative to the initial
situation, world welfare falls by FLU after FTA. Relative to FT, it falls by
FLU+RSN under FTA.)

Country	Nondiscriminatory Tariff (Initial Situation)	Free Trade	FTA between A and B
A	KGS + GHNS	KGS + GHNS + RSN (A gains)	KGS + GHNS—GFLH (A loses)
B	HDU	HDU (no change)	HDU + GFLH—FLU (B gains)
C	0	0	0 (no change)
World	KGSD + GHNS + HDU	KGS + GHNS + HDU + RSN (world gains)	KGS + GHNS + HDU—FLU (world loses)

(3) Next, assume that A forms an FTA with B by eliminating entirely
the tariff on B but retaining it on C. Imports from B rise to OQ_2 and those
from C decline to Q_2Q_3. Now, B gains from the FTA due to an improvement
in its terms of trade. The net price received by the exporters of B increases
from P_C to P_C^t and the gains from trade to B rise to HDU+GFUH. Country B
gains from A's liberalization.

Because imports continue to come from C before as well as after the
FTA and C's supply is perfectly elastic, the price in A is unchanged. But now
that there is no tariff revenue on goods coming from B, A's gains from trade
decline by GFLH. Stated differently, A's within-union terms of trade worsen
by the full amount of the tariff liberalization: A loses from its own
liberalization. Because the FTA diverts imports Q_1Q_2 from the more efficient

C to the less efficient B, A's loss exceeds B's gain by the area FLU. The world as a whole loses by the same area FLU. The last column in Table 2.1 shows these changes.

Three conclusions follow immediately.

(1) Summers' earlier-cited argument that international economists should embrace PTAs because second best "trade diversion" worries are "laughable," and that primary effects must be considered to be dominant, is misplaced when impacts on the welfare of specific countries are considered. The loss to A from its own preferential liberalization arises primarily from the primary effect of the FTA. If we assume that the initial imports from the union partner are large, the loss to A in this wholly trade-diverting union is substantial.[37] It reflects the tariff revenues lost on the original [plus the new (diverted)] imports from the partner country B.

Clearly FTAs can give rise to large redistributive effects (on original imports) between countries. That the amount of trade diverted (Q_1Q_2) may be small, and that the loss to the union from this trade diversion is small because it is a triangle, has really no relevance to this conclusion.

(2) Our analysis also casts doubt on the recent presumption in the policy debate that countries that trade with each other in large volume are "natural" trading partners and regional arrangements among them must therefore be beneficial to them. It is not clear from the literature what it means to be "natural" trading partners.[38] A quotation from Summers (1991) should help:

> Are trading blocs likely to divert large amounts of trade? In answering this question, the issue of natural trading blocs is crucial because to the extent that blocs are created between countries that already trade disproportionately, the risk of large amounts of trade diversion is reduced.[39]

We consider this entire question of natural trading partners and their desirability in subsection vii below at length. But we can say immediately that our analysis so far already provides a devastating critique of the

---

[37] There is no trade creation in the example as the FTA leaves the domestic price and therefore total imports into A unchanged.

[38] We deal with the natural trading partners hypothesis in the alternative context of transport costs later in the paper.

[39] In a similar vein, Krugman (1991a, p. 21) notes, "To reemphasize why this matters: if a disproportionate share of world trade would take place within trading blocs even in the absence of any preferential trading arrangement, then the gains from trade creation within blocs are likely to outweigh any possible losses from external trade diversion."

presumption advanced in favor of such natural trading blocs. It is evident from Figure 2.2 that the larger the initial quantity of imports from a trading partner, the greater (*not* smaller) the loss to the country liberalizing preferentially, *ceteris paribus*. That is to say, the more natural the trading partner according to Summers' definition, the larger the loss from a discriminatory trade liberalization with it!

(3) Finally, it has been frequently argued that, given today's low levels of trade restrictions, preferential trading arrangements are unlikely to be harmful: trade creation effects should dominate the outcome, making PTAs as good as FT (free trade). But this argument, plausible as it sounds, is contradicted by our analysis. Thus in Figure 2.2, if the initial nondiscriminatory tariff is sufficiently high, an FTA between A and B can eliminate C as a supplier of the product. In this case, the FTA lowers the internal price in A and gives rise to trade creation. Under some (admittedly strong) conditions, this trade creation can outweigh the tariff-revenue loss and may improve welfare. By contrast, if the initial tariff is low, the chances are poor that the formation of the FTA will eliminate imports from C and lower the internal price.

iii. The Outside Country's Supply Curve is Upward Sloped

The conclusion that A's preferential liberalization hurts itself and benefits its union partner has been derived under the assumption that the supply of B is less than perfectly elastic and that of C is perfectly elastic. In this setting, the union partner is a less efficient supplier of the product than the outside world. What will happen if the situation was reversed such that B's supply curve was perfectly elastic and C's less than perfectly elastic?

This case can be analyzed by letting A form a union with C rather than B. In this case, analyzed in Figure 2.3, an FTA lowers the price in A to P_C. Though there is no gain to the union partner, A's gain from the FTA (= RSN + HWYZ) exceeds that under nondiscriminatory liberalization (that is, free trade) by the amount of tariff revenue (= HWYZ) collected on imports from the outside country.[40] This case brings us back to the conventional presumption that A's liberalization should benefit it (though, the presumption that others should gain from the liberalization does not carry through for the

---

[40] *Ceteris paribus*, the less A trades with the outside country, the less tariff revenue it collects and the less is its gain. Thus, in the spirit of the previous subsection, a high proportion of trade with the partner implies smaller gains from preferential liberalization.

outsider country B that loses). The precise welfare results, based on analysis
of Figure 2.3, are drawn together in Table 2.2.

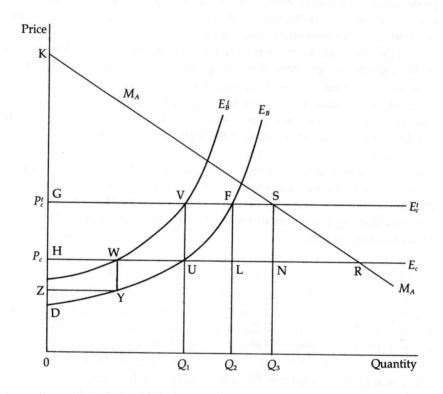

Figure 2.3: Effect of Union (A+C) with Rising Costs from Outside Country

This case clearly undercuts the arguments about the dangers of PTAs to
country A that were made in the previous section. Therefore, it is important
to ask how relevant it is empirically. It is perhaps reasonable to assert that a
union partner is likely to resemble B for some products and C in other
products and, therefore, the effect of the FTA will be ambiguous in general.

In the specific case of NAFTA, a common claim has been that, on net, it
is likely to gain because the United States is very large and, *therefore*, the

most efficient supplier of a majority of Mexico's products. There are, however, at least two reasons why this conclusion is unwarranted. First, given that the outside world includes the EU, Japan, China, Korea, Hong Kong and numerous other outward-oriented and highly competitive countries, the conclusion that the United States and Canada are the most efficient suppliers of a large majority of Mexico's products is highly suspect. Indeed, if it were true, we would be hard-pressed to explain the persistent demands for anti-dumping and other forms of protection in the United States.[41] Second, recall that if the union partner is a large supplier of imports, the tariff-redistribution losses to A in the case of trade diversion are large. Therefore, even if the union partner is the most efficient supplier of the majority of A's imports, losses may outweigh any gains. In the case of NAFTA, the United States does account for a sufficiently large proportion of Mexico's imports for us to conjecture plausibly that the tariff-redistribution losses in trade-diversion cases could outweigh the gains in trade-creation cases.

This analysis has an important qualification that will be discussed in the next section. Before doing so, we mention two additional possibilities which are worthy of brief consideration: (a) export-supply curves are upward sloped for both B and C and (b) the products of A, B and C are imperfect substitutes. In either of these cases, the small-country and small-union assumptions are violated and a complete elimination of the tariff by A, whether on a discriminatory or nondiscriminatory basis, is not the optimal policy.[42] Below, we will look at case (b) in detail.

But here we note that our conclusions remain valid under the following circumstances. In case (a), if the elasticity of supply of the outside country is high in relation to that of the union partner, a discriminatory tariff reduction by A is likely to hurt itself while benefiting B. In case (b), analyzed in subsection v below, if B's goods are poor substitutes for A's goods but not C's, as seems entirely plausible, discriminatory liberalization by A will hurt itself and benefit the union partner even at constant terms of trade, whereas the terms of trade effects will reinforce this outcome. Before we present this

---

[41] In addition, a fraction of the large imports from the US could well be a result of preferential policies rather than competitiveness.

[42] It is a common practice in the computable general equilibrium (CGE) models to differentiate goods by the country of origin and yet impose the small-country assumption. To a general-equilibrium theorist, this is not correct. If a country is the sole producer of its exports, it necessarily has market power.

analysis in detail, an important qualification to Figures 2.2 and 2.3 must be noted.

Table 2.2: The Welfare Effects of a Free Trade Area between A and C
(This table refers to Figure 2.3 in the text.)

Country	Nondiscriminatory Tariff (1)	FTA between A and C (2)
A	KGS + GHNS	KGS + GHNS + RSN + HWYZ (A gains)
B	HDU	ZYD = HDU—WYU—HWYZ (B loses)
C	0	0 (no change)
World	KGS + GHNS + HDU	KGS + GHNS + HDU + RSN—WYU (world may gain or lose according as RSN >< WYU)

iv. A Qualification and Modification

Figures 2.2 and 2.3 capture the essence of a large body of the literature on regional arrangements that emerged in 1950s and 1960s. But these figures have an important limitation that has been ignored entirely in the literature until recently. They implicitly assumes that either (i) the partner country maintains the same tariff as A on the product under consideration (that is, the arrangement is a customs union) or (ii) the product is not consumed in the partner country. Let us explain why.

Consider first the case depicted in Figure 2.2. The common practice in the literature, as in our foregoing analysis, has been to assume that post-FTA prices in a member country are determined by the price in the outside country, C, plus the country's own tariff. As Richardson (1994) has noted recently, however, this assumption is incorrect in general. For it implies that, if tariffs in A and B are different, producer as well as consumer prices in A and B are different. But given duty-free movement of goods *produced within the union*, producer prices between A and B must equalize under an FTA.

Assume that the tariff on the product under consideration is lower in B than in A, violating condition (i) above. In Figure 2.2, recall that DE_B is B's supply curve for exports, that is, output supply net of domestic consumption. Under a nondiscriminatory tariff in A, B's producers sell OQ_1 in A. Because the net price received by exporters on sales in A is P_C, the domestic price in B will also be P_C. If A and B now form an FTA and the price in A remains P_C^t, producers in B have no incentive to sell anything in their domestic market unless the price there also rises to P_C^t. But given that the tariff in B is lower than that in A, the price in B cannot rise to P_C^t, and the entire quantity of the product previously sold in B is diverted to A. The rules of origin can forbid the diversion of goods *imported* from C to A but not of goods *produced* in B.[43] Unless domestic consumption of the product in B is zero (assumption (ii) above), B's export-supply curve shifts to the right by the quantities demanded in B at each price, that is, B's export supply curve coincides with its output-supply curve.

Figure 2.4 lays out how the allowance for the diversion of B's domestic sales to A after the formation of the FTA affects our conclusions. It reproduces Figure 2.2, omitting VE_B^t. In the initial equilibrium, with a nondiscriminatory tariff in A, imports from B are OQ_1 as in Figure 2.2. After the FTA is formed, the expansion of exports is larger than that given by point F. How much larger it is will depend on where B's total supply curve lies. There are three possibilities.[44]

---

[43] Rules of origin can and do, of course, restrict trade in other ways. For a recent analysis of how rules of origin can lead to welfare-worsening outcomes, see Krueger (1993, 1995).

[44] See Grossman and Helpman (1995) in this context.

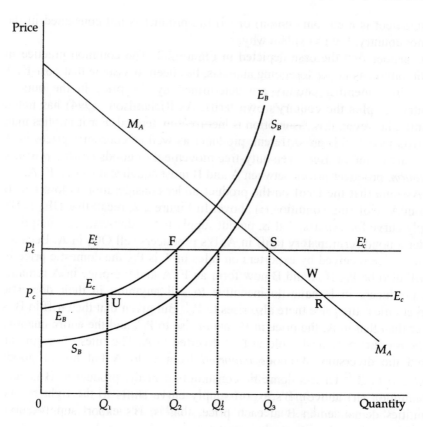

Figure 2.4: The Consequences of Differing External Tariff Rates in Member
Countries of a Free Trade Area

First, if the total supply curve intersects M_AM_A above point S as shown
by S_BS_B, the results of the previous subsection hold with vengeance.[45]
Exports from B now expand more than in Figure 2.2 and losses to A due to
the transfer of tariff revenue are larger. In this case, B's producers sell all of
their output in A and receive the same price as A's producers, namely, P_C^t.
The entire quantity consumed in B is imported from C, with consumers
paying a price lower than P_C^t. A imports from both B and C.

---

[45] Note that the horizontal difference between E_BE_B and S_BS_B declines as price rises. This is
because the demand in B must fall with a rise in the price.

Second, suppose that B's supply curve intersects $M_A M_A$ between S and W were the height of W is P_C plus the tariff in B. In this case, the price in A is determined by the height of the point of intersection of B's supply curve and $M_A M_A$. Because this price is below P_C^t, a part of the lost tariff revenue is now captured by A's consumers. But we still have a tariff-revenue transfer to firms in B. The transfer is larger the closer the intersection point of the two curves to S. Producers in B sell all their output in A, A does not import anything from C, and B imports everything from C.

Finally, if B's supply curve intersects $M_A M_A$ below point W, the price in A drops to the tariff-inclusive price in B given by the height of point W. All of A's imports come from B with producers in B selling in A as well as B. Both consumer and producer prices equalize between A and B. In this case, the redistributive effect is a declining function of the tariff in B. In the limit, if the external tariff in B is zero, the FTA leads to free trade in A (just as in B).

The case depicted in Figure 2.3 is also modified along the lines of Figure 2.4 if the good in question is consumed in the partner country (C) and the latter levies a tariff lower than that of A. To illustrate, assume that the tariff in C is zero and the demand for the product in C at P_C is larger than B's supply at that price. Then, B can sell all it wants to export at P_C to C. In the post-FTA equilibrium, A's imports come entirely from C while B sells all its exports to C. The tariff revenue raised by A on imports from B in Figure 2.3 is no longer available and A's gains from the FTA with C are reduced, to triangle RSN, the same as under unilateral, nondiscriminatory liberalization.

v. An Imperfect-Substitutes Model

An unrealistic implication of the model just explored is that, under an FTA, either producers of B must sell all their output in A and none in their domestic market (the first two cases) or consumers in A must import everything from B and none from C (the last case). This conclusion does not require a complete FTA; it holds true even in the presence of a small tariff preference as long as external tariffs in the two countries are different. A quick examination of the direction of trade data of member countries of preferential trading arrangements such as the ASEAN and NAFTA shows that this outcome is inconsistent with reality.

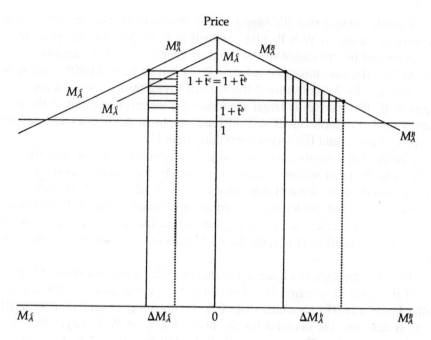

Figure 2.5: The Effect of a Tariff Preference in an Imperfect-Substitutes Model

Note: Starting with equal tariffs, $\bar{t}_b = \bar{t}_c$, the tariff on product b is reduced by a small amount. Assuming all goods (including the exportable) to be substitutes, this change increases the imports of product b, reduces those of product c, and increases exports, all measured at world prices that are set equal to 1 by appropriate choice of units. The increase in imports of b, ΔM_A^b, leads to a welfare gain measured by the vertically shaded area while the decrease in imports of c, ΔM_A^c, leads to a welfare loss measured by the horizontally shaded area. For small changes in the tariff, both of these areas are approximated by rectangles formed by the change in in imports and the height of the initial tariff. This means that the rectangle with the larger base is bigger. Because exports rise, the trade balance condition implies that there is net expansion of imports. Thus, ΔM_A^b is larger than ΔM_A^c, leading to the conclusion that the vertically shaded area is bigger than the horizontally shaded area.

A natural way to avoid these extreme results is to cast the analysis in terms of a model with product differentiation. A fully satisfactory model of this type requires the introduction of economies of scale and monopolistic competition or oligopoly. Such an elaborate model is beyond the scope of this paper. But taking recourse to the Armington structure whereby products are distinguished by the country of origin and drawing on the Meade (1955) model, we take a first stab at the problem.

An important point to note at the outset is that when products are differentiated by the country of origin, the small-country or small-union assumption must be abandoned.[46] If the product originating in a country is not produced anywhere else, by definition, the country is a monopolist for that product and cannot be a price taker in the world market.[47] Our approach below is to first consider the implications of FTAs at constant border prices and then bring in the effects of changes in the terms of trade.

Assume that there are three products denoted a, b and c. Countries A, B and C specialize in and export a, b and c, respectively. Choose the units of each product such that its international price is unity in the initial equilibrium. Focus as before on country A's welfare. In the initial equilibrium, let A impose a uniform tariff t per unit on imports from B and C.

In Figure 2.5, we measure A's consumption of b to the right and that of c to the left of the origin, O. Because b and c are not produced in A, the demand curves also represent import demands. Given the tariff t on b and c, (import) demand curves are represented by $M_A^b M_A^b$ and $M_A^c M_A^c$. The demand curve for each product is drawn given the tariff rate on the other product. Assuming substitutability, a reduction in the tariff on one product shifts the demand curve for the other product towards the vertical axis.

Let us now introduce preferential trading through a small reduction in the tariff on imports from B. Imports from B expand and generate a gain equal to $t^b \Delta M_A^b$ and approximated by the vertically shaded area in Figure 2.5. This is trade creation. But the reduction in the tariff on b also causes an inward shift in the demand curve for c as shown by the dotted curve. There

---

[46] This simple point seems to have escaped a number of CGE-modelers of NAFTA who distinguish products by the country of origin and continue to impose the small-country assumption.

[47] The same will also hold true if we were to use a monopolistic-competition or oligopoly model.

is trade diversion and a corresponding loss equal to $t^c \Delta M_A^c$ and approximated by the horizontally shaded area.[48]

Is there a net gain or loss to A? The answer depends on the relative sizes of the two shaded areas. For a small change in the tariff, these areas are approximated by rectangles whose height equals t. Therefore, the gain is larger than the loss if and only if the increase in the value of imports of b at world prices is larger than the reduction in the value of imports of c.[49] If we now assume that the partner country's good, b, and A's export good, a, are substitutes in A's demand, the preferential reduction in the tariff lowers the consumption of good a and allows an expansion of exports. Working through the trade balance condition, we can see that the expansion of exports must expand total imports valued at world prices. That is to say, imports of b expand more than imports of c contract. The area associated with trade creation in Figure 2.5 exceeds the area associated with trade diversion; the *introduction* of preferential trading is beneficial.

This result is due to Lipsey (1958) and hinges critically on substitutability between demands for partner country's goods and exportables and constancy of the terms of trade. For the moment, let us make these assumptions and ask what happens as we continue to lower the tariff on good b, holding that on good c unchanged. For each successive reduction in the tariff, the height of the rectangle associated with trade creation declines but that of the rectangle associated with trade diversion remains unchanged. Sooner or later, before the tariff on b goes to zero, the gain from extra trade creation becomes smaller than the loss from extra trade diversion. Further reductions in the tariff lead to a *reduction* in welfare.[50]

In sum, assuming constant terms of trade and substitutability between imports from B and exports, a preferential reduction in the tariff on B's

---

[48] In a small, open economy with tariffs as the only distortion, the change in welfare (real income) due to an infinitesimally small change in any set of tariffs equals the change in tariff revenue evaluated at initial tariff rates (Eaton and Panagariya 1979). For an infinitesimally small change in the tariff on B, the vertically shaded area in Figure 2.5 is the increase and horizontally shaded area the decrease in tariff revenue measured at the original tariff rates.

[49] Observe that the world price of each product is unity. Therefore, the base of the rectangle represents both the quantity and value of imports at world prices.

[50] To make this point another way, start with a zero tariff on good b and a positive tariff on c. The introduction of a small tariff on b will not lead to an efficiency loss in the b market but will generate an efficiency cost in the c market.

goods first improves welfare and then lowers it. This relationship is shown in Figure 2.6. As drawn, the level of welfare with a complete FTA is lower than that in the initial equilibrium. But in general, we cannot tell whether welfare rises or falls upon the establishment of an FTA.

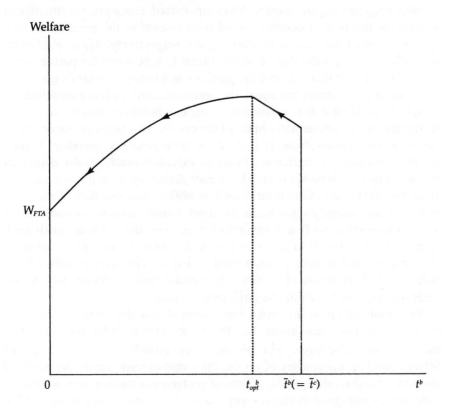

Figure 2.6: Preferential Tariff Reduction and Welfare

The natural question then is whether we can establish a presumption one way or the other. To answer it, let us examine the second-best optimum tariff on B's goods given the tariff on C's goods. As shown in Panagariya (1996a), this tariff can be written as

$$\frac{t_{opt}^b}{1 + t_{opt}^b} = \frac{\bar{t}^c}{1+\bar{t}^c} \cdot \frac{1}{1 + \dfrac{\eta_{ba}}{\eta_{bc}}} \qquad (1)$$

where η_{ba} and η_{bc} are country A's compensated, cross-price elasticities of demand for the partner country's good with respect to the price of its own good and that of the outside country's good, respectively. These elasticities respectively measure the degree of substitutability between the partner's and A's own goods and that between the partner's and outside country's goods.

If the two elasticities are equal, the optimum tariff on b is approximately half of the tariff on c. It is reasonable to expect, however, that the degree of substitutability is substantially higher between the two types of imports than that between imports from B and A's exportables. For instance, Chile's imports from North America are likely to exhibit a much greater degree of substitutability with goods from EU or East Asia than with its own exports. Given this fact, the optimum tariff on b is higher than one half of the tariff on the outside country's goods. In the limit, if the elasticity of substitution between imports from B and exports of A is zero, the optimum tariff on b equals the initial tariff! In terms of Figure 2.5, exports do not change at all when preferential trading is introduced and trade diversion exactly offsets trade creation. In terms of Figure 2.6, welfare falls monotonically as we lower the tariff on b holding the tariff on c constant.

The analysis up to this point has assumed that the terms of trade are constant and does not allow for the tariff-revenue-redistribution effect discussed in subsections i-iii above.[51] As already noted, with goods differentiated by the country of origin, the terms of trade cannot be assumed constant. The derivation of the effects of preferential trading on the terms of trade in the three-good model is complicated. Fortunately, in a neglected but important paper, these effects were worked out by Mundell (1964). To quote him,

(1) A discriminatory tariff reduction by a member country improves the terms of trade of the partner country with respect to both the tariff reducing country and the rest of the world, but the terms of trade of the tariff-reducing country might rise or fall with respect to third countries.

---

[51] The effects shown in Figure 2.5 do not arise in the partial-equilibrium model of Figures 2.2 and 2.3. Because these effects require the presence of at least two importables, they do not arise even in a two-good general equilibrium model.

(2) The degree of improvement in the terms of trade of the partner country is likely to be larger the greater is the member's tariff reduction; this establishes the presumption that a member's gain from a free-trade area will be larger the higher are initial tariffs of partner countries. (Mundell 1964, 8)

Not surprisingly, once the terms-of-trade changes are brought back into the analysis, the "mercantilist" bias in results noted earlier (that is, that A loses from its own liberalization) comes back even in the Meade model.[52] We are once again driven to the conclusion that a high-protection country (Mexico) forming an FTA with a low-protection country (U.S.A.) is likely to lose from the FTA. Observe that the terms-of-trade effects are in addition to the likely losses from second-best considerations at fixed terms of trade as discussed in Figures 2.5 and 2.6.

vi. Revenue Seeking

The conclusion that a country is likely to lose from its own preferential liberalization can break down in the presence of 100 percent, perfectly competitive, resource-using revenue-seeking activities. [53] Given this type of revenue seeking, each dollar's worth of tariff revenue will be matched by a dollar's worth of real resources used unproductively. The tariff revenue is represented by the rectangle GHNS in Figure 2.2, where A and B form the FTA. This revenue is now lost in revenue seeking and will not contribute to the country's welfare. The introduction of preferential trading will then lead to a loss of tariff revenue in the amount GFLH, but will generate an exactly equivalent gain due to a release of resources employed in revenue seeking, leaving A's welfare unchanged. For the union as a whole, however, the reduced revenue seeking will generate a net gain equal to GFLH. A large part of this gain, trapezium GFUH, will go to the partner country B while the re-

---

[52] Recall that in Figures 2.1 and 2.2, the *internal* terms of trade are variable. A's terms of trade with respect to B deteriorate by the full amount of the tariff reduction. But due to the small-union assumption, the external terms of trade do not change there.

[53] One hundred percent revenue seeking means that the entire revenue is available for those who wish to seek it. Perfectly competitive revenue-seeking leads to a dollar worth of resource loss for a dollar of revenue sought. The two assumptions together imply that the resources used up in revenue seeking equal the tariff revenues in equilibrium. For rent seeking, see Krueger (1974) and for revenue seeking, see Bhagwati and Srinivasan (1980).

maining part, triangle UFL, pays for the cost of trade diversion. In sum, country A's welfare does not change while that of B rises.

Next, consider the case in Figure 2.3 where A and C have the FTA instead. Once again, the rectangle GSNH now will not contribute to the country's welfare in the initial equilibrium. But when preferential liberalization is introduced, the internal price of A falls to the level shown by point R and the rectangle (plus triangle SNR) becomes a part of the consumers' surplus and hence A's welfare rises. Country B's welfare does not change.

Combining the two cases, we obtain the conclusion that, in the presence of 100 percent perfectly competitive revenue seeking, each partner benefits unambiguously (or at least does not lose) from preferential trading. This conclusion undermines our argument that preferential liberalization by a country with respect to its major trading partner is likely to hurt itself and benefit the latter.

We suggest, however, that there are at least two reasons why we should not take this conclusion seriously. First, even though revenue seeking is an important phenomenon in certain contexts and worthy of analysis in its own right, it is hardly invoked when making major policy decisions. We are not aware of a single reference to revenue seeking as a major reason for NAFTA in the public debate in either Mexico or the United States and Canada preceding its approval. Indeed, if we are to take revenue seeking seriously, we should take it and other types of directly unproductive profit seeking (DUP) activities arising from all other polices into account as well. Second, the twin assumptions of 100 percent and perfectly competitive revenue seeking are unrealistic. Empirically, revenue seeking is likely for several reasons to be a small fraction of the total revenue. In particular, the operation of the "Brother-in-Law Theorem" and of settled rules for allocation of revenues will often turn potential DUP activities into transfers.

vii. "Natural Trading Partners" Hypothesis and Regional PTAs

We now turn to the question of "natural trading partners."[54] As we noted earlier, the "natural trading partners" phrasing and hypothesis (that PTAs among them are more likely to be beneficial) originated in Wonnacott and Lutz (1989). Based on the work of Viner (1950), Lipsey (1960) and Johnson

---

[54] A detailed, general-equilibrium analysis of this issue is provided in Panagariya (1996a, 1996b).

(1962), these authors provided detailed criteria for determining whether or not a given set of countries constituted natural trading partners:

> Trade creation is likely to be great, and trade diversion small, if the prospective members of an FTA are natural trading partners. Several points are relevant:

- Are the prospective members already major trading partners? If so, the FTA will be reinforcing natural trading partners, not artificially diverting them.
- Are the prospective members close geographically? Groupings of distant nations may be economically inefficient because of the high transportation costs.

Wonnacott and Lutz offered two further criteria, one based on complementarity vs. competitiveness of the economies and the other on the countries' relative levels of economic development. They noted, however, that these characteristics are "much more difficult to evaluate." Because subsequent advocates of FTAs have not included these criteria in defining natural trading partners, we will not discuss them.

For clarity, we will refer to the first two criteria spelled out in the above passage from Wonnacott and Lutz as the "volume-of-trade" and "transport-cost" criteria and examine them in turn.

vii.1 The Volume-of-Trade Criterion

The volume-of-trade criterion for choosing natural trading partners and treating them as likely therefore to be welfare-enhancing to their members, seems plausible at first glance but is, in fact, treacherous for several reasons.

First, the criterion is neither symmetric nor transitive. A lack of symmetry implies that country A may be a natural trading partner of country B, but the reverse may not hold true. A lack of transitivity implies that even if A is a natural trading partner of B, and B is a natural trading partner of C, A may not be a natural trading partner of C. Lest this be viewed as a purely academic point, we note that the United States is the largest trading partner of both Canada and Mexico, but Canada and Mexico have little trade with each other.

Second, the volume-of-trade criterion is premised on the view that a larger initial volume of trade between potential partners implies a lower likelihood of loss due to trade diversion. In terms of Figure 2.2, this implies that the larger is OQ_1, the smaller is Q_1Q_2.

This is, however, an unsupported inference from the fact that, for any given volume of initial imports (OQ_3), the higher is the partner country's initial share, the lower is the outside country's share and hence the smaller is the *scope* for diverting trade. For what one needs to determine is how likely is the *actual* trade diversion. [Thus, for example, between two alternate situations, one where Q_1Q_3 (the scope for trade diversion) is twice as large as in the other, Q_1Q_2 (the actual trade diversion) could still be half as much.]

The underlying model that defines the trade volumes in different equilibria may well imply then that the relationship between the initial volume of imports from the partner country and the trade to be diverted to it may be altogether tenuous.

Thus, consider the Lipsey (1958) analysis of the question, based on the small-union version of the Meade model discussed in subsection v.[55] Lipsey, as Bhagwati recalled in his earlier critique of the volume-of-trade criterion, focused not on the initial volume of imports but "on the relative sizes of imports from each source *vis-a-vis* expenditure on domestic goods as the key and decisive factor in determining the size of losses and gains from preferential cuts in trade barriers" (Bhagwati 1993a, 34). Of course, on the basis of equation (1) and the discussion of it, we can also conclude that, in general in this model, the higher is the compensated crossprice elasticity of its demand for the partner's good with respect to the price of its own good, *relative* to the crossprice elasticity of its demand for the good with respect to the price of the outside country's good, the higher is the likelihood that an FTA improves a country's welfare. This general conclusion reducing to the Lipsey argument when the liberalizing country's preferences are of the CES variety.[56]

---

[55] In subsection v, we assumed that each country is the sole producer of its export good. This assumption necessarily makes the terms of trade variable. In the conventional analysis, as also in the present discussion, the outside country is assumed to produce all goods and is large. The terms of trade are then determined in the outside country and the only effects that arise are those depicted in Figure 2.5. In arriving at the conclusions discussed in this paragraph, Lipsey also assumed that preferences are Cobb-Douglas. For further details, see Panagariya (1996a).

[56] As quoted in footnote 12 of Bhagwati (1993a), according to Lipsey, "...the larger are purchases of domestic commodities and the smaller are purchases from the outside world, the more likely is it that the union will bring gain." If the liberalizing country's preferences are of the CES variety, the cross-price elasticity of its demand for the partner's good with respect the price of its own good reduces to the product of the expenditure share of its own good and the elasticity of substitution. A similar statement applies to the cross-price elasticity of the country's demand for the partner's good with respect to the price of the outside country's good.

For a country such as Mexico joining the NAFTA with the United States, we may well expect in fact the former elasticity to be lower than the latter so that the welfare presumption for this "natural trading partner" of the United States from NAFTA is ironically likely to be in favor of trade diversion effects dominating the outcome.

There is a further subtle point to be noted. In Figure 2.6, starting from a nondiscriminatory tariff, as country A lowers the tariff on B, trade share shifts in favor of B at the expense of country C. That is, A and B become more natural trading partners according to the volume-of-trade criterion. Yet, once the tariff on B attains the second-best optimum, t^b_{opt}, further preferential liberalization is accompanied by a *reduction* in the welfare of A. Thus, to the left of t^b_{opt}, A and B are more natural trading partners than to the right of it, but preferential tariff reductions in that range reduce welfare

Third, even this conclusion understates the folly of focusing on a large initial volume of imports as a benign phenomenon. For it ignores the crucial tariff-revenue-redistribution effect which we have highlighted. We have already argued that, in FTAs involving countries with asymmetric levels of protection and a high volume of trade initially, the country with higher protection is likely to lose even if trade creation effects dominate trade diversion effects. For, under such circumstances, the net gain from trade creation and trade diversion effects could likely be swamped by the loss from the tariff-revenue-redistribution effect. The case for Mexico gaining from joining NAFTA thus looks dismal on this account as well.

While, therefore, the volume-of-trade criterion for judging FTAs to be benign is clearly to be rejected, we must also add that linking it to *regionalism* and thus declaring *regional* FTAs to be more benign than nonregional FTAs is additionally wrong because there is no evidence at all

that pairs of contiguous countries, or countries with common borders, have larger volumes of trade with each other than pairs that are not so situated or that trade volumes of pairs of countries, arranged by distance between the countries in the pair, will show distance to be inversely related to trade volumes.[57]

Thus, under CES preferences, our condition in the text reduces to Lipsey's. As noted in the previous footnote, Lipsey himself had relied on Cobb-Douglas preferences to derive the conclusion quoted at the beginning of this footnote.

[57] This would not be generally true even if we were to take the measure just for one individual country with every other country instead of pooling all possible pairs together.

Table 2.3: Direction of Exports by Major Regions, 1980, 1985 and 1990

EXPORTER	YEAR	NORTH AMERICA	W. EUROPE	EUROPE	EAST ASIA*	LATIN AMERICA	AFRICA	MIDDLE EAST	SOUTH ASIA
N. AMERICA	1980	33.5	25.2	27.4	15.8	8.9	3.3	4.2	1.0
	1985	44.4	19.3	21.0	15.5	5.9	2.5	3.2	1.0
	1990	41.9	22.3	23.4	20.4	5.0	1.7	2.6	0.8
W. EUROPE	1980	6.7	67.1	71.9	2.9	2.4	7.2	5.5	0.7
	1985	11.3	64.9	68.9	3.6	1.6	5.2	5.0	0.9
	1990	8.3	71.0	74.4	5.3	1.1	3.3	3.3	0.7
EUROPE	1980	6.3	63.7	72.7	2.7	2.3	6.9	5.5	0.7
	1985	11.0	63.5	69.2	3.4	1.6	5.1	5.0	0.9
	1990	8.2	70.6	74.5	5.2	1.1	3.3	3.3	0.7

E. ASIA	1980	26.0	16.8	18.9	29.9	4.1	4.4	7.4	1.8
	1985	37.8	13.6	15.5	25.3	2.8	2.2	5.1	2.0
	1990	31.9	19.8	20.7	32.3	1.9	1.6	3.0	1.5
L. AMERICA	1980	27.9	26.5	35.1	5.4	16.6	2.7	1.9	0.5
	1985	35.8	25.9	30.4	7.1	12.1	3.7	3.0	0.7
	1990	22.9	25.3	27.6	10.3	14.0	2.1	2.4	0.4
AFRICA	1980	27.4	43.6	46.1	4.3	3.2	1.8	1.7	0.3
	1985	14.8	64.9	69.3	1.8	4.2	5.1	2.2	0.7
	1990	3.0	66.0	68.0	4.6	0.6	12.8	4.4	3.6
M. EAST	1980	11.5	40.3	41.5	28.7	5.0	1.5	4.1	2.5
	1985	6.2	15.0	17.7	1.5	0.3	1.4	8.7	0.4
	1990	17.8	48.6	53.0	9.1	1.2	3.6	8.5	0.9
S. ASIA	1980	10.9	24.6	39.4	14.5	0.5	6.8	14.5	5.6
	1985	18.4	20.8	37.0	16.4	0.4	4.6	11.0	4.4
	1990	17.1	30.1	46.6	18.3	0.3	2.7	6.5	3.2

*East Asia does not include China

Source: Panagariya (1993). Constructed from the United Nations Commodity Trade Statistics.

Note: The table broadly underlines the point that *total* trade volume that matters does not show any relationship to proximity of countries geographically.

This is evident from the somewhat aggregated destination-wise trade volume statistics for major regions in 1980, 1985 and 1990 in Table 2.3.[58] Then again, take just one telling example.[59] Thus, Chile shares a common border with Argentina but, in 1993, shipped only 6.2% of exports to, and received only 5% of its imports from her [Panagariya (1995b, Tables 3 and 4)].

By contrast, the United States does not have a common border with Chile but accounted for 16.2% of her exports and 24.9% of her imports in 1993. The volume-of-trade criterion then would make the United States, *not* Argentina, the natural trading partner of Chile, clearly controverting the claim that the volume-of-trade criterion translates into a regional criterion.

Thus, as contended by Bhagwati (1993a), the equation of the two concepts of volume of trade and regionalism (whether of the distance or the common border or contiguity variety) by Krugman (1991) and Summers (1991) is simply wrong.

Nonetheless, Frankel and Wei (1995) have recently argued otherwise, claiming that their empirical work favors the Krugman-Summers assertion.

They use the gravity model as their basic tool to conclude that "proximity is in general an important determinant of bilateral trade around the world, notwithstanding exceptions like India-Pakistan and other cases."

But this misses the point at issue. What is at stake is *not* whether distance, interpreted through the gravity model and/or common border modeled through a dummy, matters.[60] There does seem to be a *partial* correlation between distance, proximity, common border, and so on, on the one hand and trade volumes on the other.[61] But what we have to look at is

---

[58] Thus, intra-African exports were only 12.8% of total African exports in 1990.

[59] There are countless other examples. For example, Bhagwati (1993a) cites India-Pakistan versus India-U.K. and India-USSR as an example.

[60] Although Frankel and Wei find that a common border increases trade volumes, Dhar and Panagariya (1994), who estimate the gravity equation on a country-by-country basis for 22 countries, find the common-border effect to be negative in 6 cases. This conflict of results underlies the serious reservations we have about the use of these gravity models to infer "trade diversion" and so on: the coefficients vary considerably depending on the data set and sometimes the signs do as well.

[61] We note, however, that the recent critique of gravity models by Jacques J. Polak (1996) casts serious doubt on even this conclusion. Polak estimates a gravity equation for total estimates as a function of income, population, and a location index measuring how favorably a country is located for purposes of international trade. He finds that, for 1960 trade data, the

the *total* initial volume of trade: and this does not correlate simply with distance as the right-hand side variable, as required by the "natural trading partners" assertion of the volume-of-trade criterion for forming PTAs.

Next, we have the difficult problem of endogeneity of initial trade volumes with respect to preferences. If the large volumes are themselves attributable, in significant degree, to preferences granted earlier, then they are not "natural" nor is it proper to think that additional preferences are "therefore" harmless. The point is best understood by thinking of high trade barriers by a country leading to a larger within-country trade. To deduce therefore that added barriers are harmless is to compound the harm done by existing barriers that are, of course, preferences in favor of trade within the country.

This is not an idle question. Offshore assembly provisions between the United States and Mexico and the longstanding GATT-sanctioned free trade regime in autos between Canada and the US are certainly not negligible factors in pre-NAFTA US trade with these NAFTA members. Again, remember that, in granting preferences under the Generalized System of Preferences, the US, EC and Japan have all concentrated on their regions. Thus, the partial correlation between distance and trade volumes (in gravity models) may be a result of preferences granted to proximate neighbors, rather than a "natural" phenomenon justifying (new) preferences.[62]

Finally, we also need to raise a different objection to the argument that a high initial volume of imports from a partner country will work to protect oneself against trade diversion. Quite aside from the fact that aggregate volumes shift significantly in practice over time, the comparative advantage in specific goods and services often changes in different locations.[63] This means that, consistent with a given aggregate trade volume, its composition may shift so as to yield greater trade diversion when a PTA is present. Thus, consider a case, based on constant costs for simplicity, in which the United States imports a product from Canada under a nondiscriminatory tariff. If a

---

location index yields a statistically significant effect, as in Frankel-Wei regressions. But for the 1990 sample used by Frankel and Wei, the effect is statistically insignificant.

[62] Of course, even if the relationship was "natural", it does not justify preferences as argued already by us.

[63] Bhagwati, in several writings, for example, Bhagwati and Dehejia (1994) and Bhagwati (1996), has argued that comparative advantage has become "kaleidoscopic," that is, thin and volatile, as technical know-how has converged, multinationals have become global, interest rates are closer across nations and access to different capital markets is more open. Ever more industries are thus footloose.

PTA is formed between the two countries, the product will continue to be imported from Canada. But suppose that, on a future date, Canada loses its comparative advantage to Taiwan ever so slightly that the preferential advantage enjoyed by her outweighs this loss. There will be trade diversion and imports into the United States will continue to come from Canada with the volume of trade remaining unchanged.[64] Observe that there is an asymmetry here between a shift in comparative advantage away from the partner and that towards it. If Canada experiences a reduction in the cost of production of a product imported by the United States from Taiwan under a PTA, there can still be trade diversion. Due to the preference, Canada will replace Taiwan as the supplier of this product even before her costs fall below those of the latter. The volume of trade will rise and, at the same time, there will be trade diversion.[65] The proponents of the complacent "high volume of imports" thesis are thus trapped in a static view of comparative advantage that is particularly at odds with today's volatile, "kaleidoscopic" comparative advantage in the global economy.

vii.2. Transport-Cost Criterion

But if the volume-of-trade criterion is conceptually inappropriate and must be summarily rejected, what about the transport-cost criterion?

This criterion, of course, maps directly into distance and hence into regionalism. However, the question to be analyzed is: should PTA partners be chosen on the basis of lower transport costs, and hence greater proximity, to maximize gains to members or to minimize losses to them?

The earliest reference to transport costs in the context of trade liberalization that we could find is due to Johnson (1962). He remarked that: "If the separate markets of various members are divided by serious geographical barriers which require high transport costs to overcome them, the enlargement of the market may be more apparent than real;..." All he seemed to be arguing was that trade liberalization may be meaningless if high transport costs prevented trade from breaking out.

---

[64] In this paragraph, we abstract from the demand effects. The inclusion of demand effects will modify the discussion but not the fundamental point.

[65] And if costs indeed fall below those of Taiwan, there is no extra gain from the PTA since in that case Canada would have replaced Taiwan as the supplier even under a nondiscriminatory tariff.

But the natural trading partners hypothesis is altogether different and incorrect. There is, in fact, no reason to think that greater proximity increases the likelihood of gain for members in a PTA. This can be seen by simply constructing a counterexample, below, where a union with a country (C) which is more distant produces more gain (for A) than a union with the country (B) which is less distant but otherwise identical (to C).

First note immediately that as long as country A in Figure 2.2 imports the good from both B and C in the pre- and post-FTA equilibrium, the presence of transportation costs has no effect whatsoever on the analysis based on that figure. All we need to do is to imagine that the supply price of C is inclusive of transport costs while such costs are absent for the partner, B. This introduction of transport costs leaves the remainder of the analysis entirely unchanged.

To construct the counterexample noted above, however, consider a world consisting of three countries A, B and C. Country A has the option to form an FTA with either B or C. B and C are identical in all respects except that the latter is located farther. If the supply curves of B and C were horizontal, we would be in a world represented in panel a of Figure 2.1 with (P_C- P_B) representing transportation costs from C to A. Technically, in this case an FTA with the geographically proximate B improves A's welfare. But recall the limitation of such an FTA: (i) A does not trade with C before or after the union is formed; and (ii) in the post-FTA equilibrium, the external tariff does not matter so that the FTA is really equivalent to nondiscriminatory free trade.

To make the example substantive, we must therefore assume that supply curves of B and C are upward sloped.[66] In Figure 2.7, we draw three panels. In the first two panels, we show the export supply curves of C and B as ECEC and EBEB, respectively. In the third panel, we have their combined supply obtained by summing horizontally the individual supplies from the first two panels. The supply curves of C and B are identical in all respects except that C's supply price includes a constant per-unit transportation cost. Thus, for each quantity, C's supply price exceed that of B by the per-unit transportation cost.[67]

---

[66] This makes the analysis complicated because the countries now wield market power and unilateral free trade is no longer optimal.

[67] The point can also be made under "iceberg" type transport costs that are frequently employed in international trade literature. In this formulation, a constant fraction of the good melts away in transit.

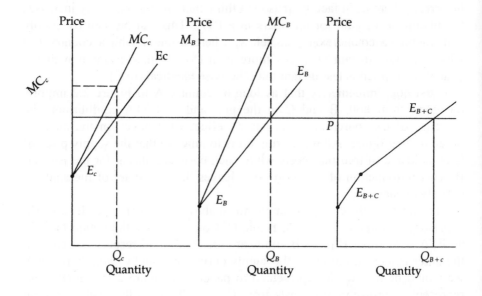

Figure 2.7: A Union with the Distant Partner is Superior to that with the Proximate Partner

To avoid clutter, we do not draw A's demand curve. Instead, imagine that there is an arbitrary nondiscriminatory tariff initially which yields the total demand for imports as represented by point Q_{B+C}. The price paid for this quantity to B and C is P*. Individual supplies of B and C can be obtained by intersecting their supply curves with P* and are shown by Q_B and Q_C. Not surprisingly, imports are larger from the geographically proximate country B than C.

Now consider the introduction of preferential trading. To see which way preferences should be given, draw the *marginal* cost curve associated with each supply curve. These are shown by MC_B and MC_C. It is then immediate that, at the initial nondiscriminatory tariff, the marginal cost of imports is higher on imports from B than C. We then obtain the dramatic conclusion that if A wants to give a tariff preference, it should opt for the distant partner C rather than the proximate B! The transport-cost criterion for choosing partners in a PTA is exactly wrong in this instance.

The explanation of this result is straightforward. The discriminating monopsonist model says that for any quantity of total purchases, the supplier with higher elasticity should be paid a higher price. In the present problem, this prescription translates into a lower tax on the supplier with higher elasticity. And transportation costs make C's supply curve more elastic than that of B.

viii. Endogenous Tariffs on the Outside Country

So far, we have assumed that when an FTA is formed, the tariff on the out-side country is held at its original level. But this may not always be true. When an FTA begins to take a bite, lobbies representing declining domestic industries may be able to reassert themselves. Because the FTA ties the authorities' hands with respect to the union partner, they will have to respond by raising protection against outside countries. This, indeed, happened recently following the Mexican crisis when the country raised external tariffs on 502 products from 20% or less to 35%!

This possibility had been anticipated by Bhagwati (1993a) who argued,

Imagine that the United States begins to eliminate (by out competing) an inefficient Mexican industry once the FTA goes into effect. Even though the most efficient producer is Taiwan, if the next efficient United States out competes the least efficient Mexico, that would be desirable trade creation...

But what would the Mexicans be likely to do? They would probably start AD actions against Taiwan...

This possibility raises the questions whether, once we allow for endogenous policy response, welfare may actually decline relative to the FTA and, indeed, to the initial equilibrium. Answers to both questions are in the affirmative.

A simple example demonstrating welfare deterioration relative to the FTA can be given as follows. For a zero tariff on B, calculate A's optimum tariff on C. Suppose that A sets the initial, nondiscriminatory tariff on B and C at this level. Then, by construction, an FTA with B, holding C's tariff unchanged, not only improves A's welfare but actually maximizes it. If now lobbying pressure leads to a rise in the external tariff, A's welfare will necessarily fall.

The more interesting is the possibility that A's welfare can decline relative to the initial, pre-FTA equilibrium. To demonstrate it, note that A's welfare can be written as

$$W = CS + PS + t_B P_B^* M_B + t_C P_C^* M_C$$
$$= CS + PS + (P-P_B^*)M_B + (P-P_C^*)M_C$$
$$= CS + PS + P(M_B+M_C)-(P_B^* M_B+P_C^* M_C)$$

where CS denotes A's consumers' surplus, PS its producers' surplus, P domestic price, P_i^* (i = B, C) border price on imports from i, t_i the *ad valorem* tariff on imports from i, and M_i imports from i. The last two terms in these equalities represent tariff revenue on imports. Given a non-discriminatory tariff initially, $P_B^* = P_C^*$.

Take the case favorable to an FTA with B by assuming that at each world price, B's supply is more elastic than C's. Assume further that the initial, nondiscriminatory tariff is sufficiently high that the FTA with no change in the tariff on C is welfare improving for A.[68] We will now show that if, because of lobbying pressure, the FTA is accompanied by a rise in the tariff on C such that *total* imports are unchanged, it is possible for its welfare to decline. Given that the FTA with no change in the tariff on C is welfare improving, this result shows that the endogenous tariff response can turn a welfare-improving FTA into a welfare-reducing proposition.

With no change in imports, the domestic price in A does not change and neither do CS and PS. From the above equation, it is then clear that welfare will rise or fall as the cost of imports, represented by the last term in the last equality, falls or rises. This property allows us to analyze the impact of the endogenous choice of the tariff by focusing on imports supplies from B and C only.

In Figure 2.8, as assumed, B's export-supply curve is more elastic than that of C at each price. This means that under a nondiscriminatory tariff, A's

---

[68] If the initial tariff is above the optimum tariff, given the elasticity assumption, a small preferential reduction in the tariff on B is welfare improving. For a complete removal of the tariff on B to be welfare improving, the initial tariff must be substantially higher than the optimum tariff.

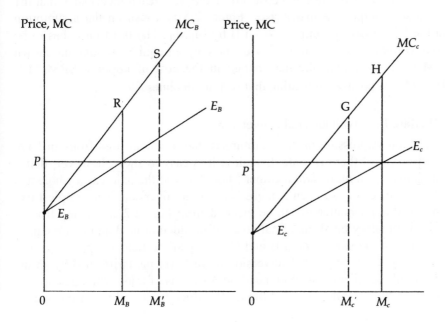

Figure 2.8: Welfare Loss from Endogenous Increase in External Tariff After
Formation of a Free Trade Area

private marginal cost of obtaining imports from B is lower than that from C.
Therefore, *at the margin*, A benefits by switching imports from C to B.

Initially, with a nondiscriminatory tariff, A buys the product at P* per-
unit from both B and C. Imports from the two countries are given by M_B and
M_C, respectively. The marginal cost of obtaining imports from B is less
than that from C, $RM_B < HM_C$. As noted in the previous paragraph, at the
margin, switching imports from C to B is beneficial to A: a small reduction
in the tariff on B and increase in tariff that on C which keeps total imports
unchanged is welfare improving. But the FTA requires taking the tariff on B
all the way to 0. As that is done, the marginal cost of obtaining imports from
B rises and, as we correspondingly raise the tariff on C to keep the total

imports unchanged, the marginal cost of imports from C falls. It is entirely possible that the two marginal costs cross and then reach levels such that the total cost of imports actually rises. Figure 2.8 is drawn on the assumption that the FTA increases imports from B by $M_B M_B'$. The tariff on C has to be raised to reduce imports from that country by an equivalent amount shown by $M_C M_C'$. As drawn, the net change in the cost of imports, $SRM_B M_B'$-$GHM_C M_C'$, is positive indicating that welfare declines.[69]

ix. Welfare Loss without Trade Diversion

The general impression in the literature is that a welfare loss from an FTA can arise only if there is trade diversion. It is easy to show, however, that a welfare loss to an *individual* member (though not to the union as a whole nor to the world) can arise even if there is no trade diversion. The simplest example of this phenomenon can be gleaned from Figure 2.2. Starting from a nondiscriminatory tariff, marginal costs of production in B and C are equal. Given that *at the margin* both B and C are equally efficient suppliers of the product, there can be no trade diversion if we lower the tariff on B by an infinitesimally small amount. Yet, because A's terms of trade with respect to B deteriorate by the full amount of the tariff reduction, it will lose from such a change.

In Figure 2.2, because the domestic price does not change after the introduction of preferential trading, there is no trade creation. But if we allow C's supply curve to slope upward, the introduction of a small tariff preference for B will also generate a trade creation effect. This is because the preference improves A's terms of trade with respect to C, lowers the domestic price and displaces some inefficient domestic production. For reasons explained in the previous paragraph, there is no trade diversion, however. Yet, it is possible for the loss due to the accompanying deterioration in the terms of trade vis-a-vis B to more than offset the gain from trade creation as well as the improvement in the terms of trade vis-a-vis C (a result which can be derived algebraically, of course).

---

[69] Melo, Panagariya and Rodrik (1993) note a similar possibility when the country faces a revenue constraint.

x. Concluding against PTAs.

Our analysis of the static effects of PTAs is then far less sanguine than is customarily assumed by several policy economists, bureaucrats and politicians today. It also challenges and undermines the validity of the claims made in behalf of "regional" PTAs, whether the regions are defined in terms of countries with relatively high intraregional trade or in terms of proximity with or without common borders.

Therefore, if we were to assume that PTAs result from a variety of noneconomic factors, we need not be complacent about the possibility of their resulting in harmful effects.[70] Nor would there be any good reason to be complacent even if those PTAs were to be essentially regional in scope, when "regional" means geographic proximity or higher volumes of trade among members rather than with outside countries.

We add three final observations. First, the common usage by journalists and politicians of the word "regional" frequently includes "common-ocean" arrangements such as APEC. Remember that APEC includes both South Korea and Chile, countries whose mutual trade is characterized by smallness of volume *and* largeness of distance, so that neither of the two criteria of distance or volume of trade for sanctifying PTAs as desirable, inappropriate as we have shown it to be, holds for every member of APEC vis-a-vis every other.

Second, is the presence of common waters a new criterion for nations to form a PTA (the Pacific Ocean in the case of APEC)? We should not forget that the major oceans, and hence most of the trading nations of the world, are united by the world's water, and even more readily thanks to the Suez and Panama Canals! In fact, the fullest-bodied common-waters "regional" area is clearly approximated by the membership of the WTO, as would have been appreciated by Ferdinand Magellan who, starting out from San Lucar in 1519, sailed from the Atlantic into the Pacific, an ocean unknown at the time.[71]

---

[70] We discuss these noneconomic factors in Section 2.5 below. Our analysis, which has focused mainly on the effects on the member countries, and has not addressed adequately the issue of the effects on nonmembers. However, there is a revival of interest in that issue as well. See, in particular, Srinivasan (1995) and Winters (1995a) (1995b).

[71] The common-water definition, of course, excludes land-locked countries such as Nepal and countries with shores only on land-locked seas such as the Caspian. These, however, add up to only a small fraction of world trade.

Third, the phrase "continental" trading arrangements has also been frequently used by Wei and Frankel (1995) who argue that "many [trading blocs] are along continental lines".[72] But this is, at best, misleading and, at worst, incorrect. Even if we confine ourselves to Article 24-sanctioned arrangements, we still must distinguish among PTAs which are continentwide and hence "continental" and those that consist of members entirely *within*, but are not extended to *all* countries in, a continent and hence must be called "subcontinental".

Geographers and earth scientists divide the earth traditionally into four oceans (Arctic, Indian, Atlantic and Pacific) and seven continents: Europe, Asia, Africa, Australia, North America, South America and Antarctica. Only NAFTA and the PTA between Australia and New Zealand can then qualify as continental. And, the major new Article 24-sanctioned PTAs, which have been proposed by different groups in recent years (NAFTA extension into South America, APEC and TAFTA) and which would clearly dwarf the continental PTAs clearly cut across continents.[73] Then again, MERCOSUR and ASEAN are clearly subcontinental. Of course, if one adds all the non-Article 24 preferential trading arrangements, the matter looks even worse for those who claim that "many" of today's "trade blocs" are "continental".

2.4 Theoretical Analyses of the Dynamic Time-Path Question

Our analysis of the economics of PTAs would be seriously incomplete if, having analyzed the static effects, we did not go on to analyze the dynmaic time-path question.

2.4.1 Formulating the Time-Path Question

Essentially, this question relates, not to whether the immediate (static) effect of a PTA is good or bad, but whether the (dynamic) effect of the PTA is to accelerate or decelerate the continued reduction of trade barriers towards the

---

[72] Also see Frankel, Stein and Wei (1995a, 1995b). Interestingly, Haberler (1943) appears to have been the first to use the term *continental blocs*.

[73] As matters stand currently, however, APEC and TAFTA are extremely unlikely to become Article 24-sanctioned PTAs, despite the US obsession with PTAs, whereas the extension of NAFTA to the south looks like a long-term process.

goal of reducing them worldwide. This question may be formulated analytically in two separate ways:

Question I: Assume that the time-path of MTN (multilateral trade negotiations) and the time-path of PTAs are separable and do not influence each other, so that the two policies are "strangers" to (that is, independent of) one another: neither hurts nor helps the other. Will then the PTA time-path be characterized by stagnant or negligible expansion of membership; or will we have expanding membership, with this even turning eventually into worldwide membership as in the WTO, thus arriving at nondiscriminatory free trade for all? A similar question can, of course, be raised for the MTN time-path. And the analysis can be extended to a comparison of the two time-paths, ranking the efficacy of the two methods of reducing trade barriers to achieve the goal of worldwide free trade for all.

Question II: Assume instead, as is more sensible, that if both the MTN and the PTA time-paths are embraced simultaneously, they will interact. In particular, the policy of undertaking PTAs will have a malign impact on (that is, be a "foe" of) the progress along the MTN time-path or have a benign effect on (that is, be a "friend" of) the MTN time-path.[74]

Question I can be illustrated with the aid of Figure 2.9 which portrays a sample of possibilities for the time-paths in question. World (rather than individual member) welfare is put on the vertical axis and time along the horizontal axis. For the PTA time-paths drawn, an upward movement along the path implies growing membership; for the MTN (or what are described as "process-multilateralism") time-paths, it implies nondiscriminatory lowering of trade barriers among the nearly worldwide WTO membership instead. The PTA and MTN time-paths are assumed to be independent of each other, not allowing for the PTA time-path to either accelerate or decelerate the course of MTN (thus ruling out Question II-type issues). The goal can be treated as reaching U^*, the worldwide freeing of trade barriers on a nondiscriminatory basis, at a specified time.

Question I can be illustrated by reference to the PTA paths I-IV. Thus, PTAs may improve welfare immediately, in the static sense, from U^0 to U_p^2 or reduce it to U_p^1. In either case, the time-path could then be stagnant (as with time-paths II and III), implying a fragmentation of the world economy through no further expansion of the initial PTA. Else, it can lead (as in time-paths I and IV) to multilateral free trade for all at U^* through continued

---

[74] Similarly, the MTN path may facilitate or obstruct the expansion of PTA membership, so that the interaction between the two paths may be mutual.

expansion and coagulation of the PTAs. Under "process multilateralism", that is, MTN as a multilateral process of reducing trade barriers as distinct from multilateralism as the goal desired, the time-path may fail to reach U* and instead fall short at U_m because of free-rider problems.

As indicated, if the PTA and MTN time-paths are interdependent, we can address Question II. In that case, the MTN time-path becomes a function of whether the PTA time-path is traveled simultaneously.

2.4.2 Question Originating in Policy

The dynamic time-path question has arisen, just as the static one did, in policy concerns and political decisions that ran ahead of the theory. The static question coincided, more or less, with the movement that eventually created the European Community through the Treaty of Rome in 1957. The dynamic time-path question has arisen in the context of the US failure to get an MTN Round started at the GATT Ministerial in 1982 and the US decision to finally abandon its studied avoidance of Article XXIV-sanctioned PTAs. The policy choice made was really Hobson's choice: if the MTN could not be used to continue lowering trade barriers, then PTAs would be used instead. If the turnpike could not be used, one had no option except to use the dirt road.

But, for several reasons that have been systematically explored in Bhagwati (1993b), the United States wound up becoming committed to "walking on both legs", embracing both the PTA and the MTN paths. Indeed, the United States has now become an active proponent of this view, continuing to do so even after the Uruguay Round of MTN had been successfully conducted and the WTO launched. And, in doing so, its spokesmen have frequently implied that PTAs will have a benign, beneficial impact on the worldwide lowering of trade barriers through induced acceleration of MTN.

The questions that we have distinguished above spring therefore from this shift in US policy which has been manifest for several years, starting from the Bush administration and articulated as a distinct policy in the Clinton administration. In Bhagwati (`1991)(1993), the challenge to international trade theorists to analyze these questions was identified and a preliminary set of arguments offered. We recapitulate briefly those arguments (in subsection 2.4.4 below) and then proceed to systematize the theoretical literature that has been developing since then on the dynamic time-path questions.

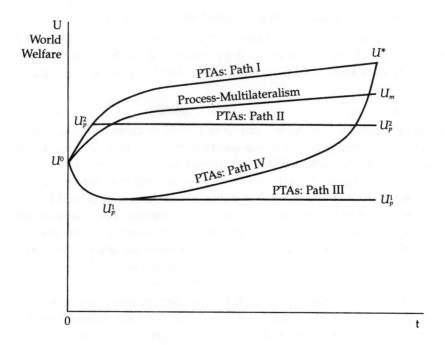

Figure 2.9: Alternative Paths under Multilateralism and under PTAs

Note: This figure illustrates the "building blocks" and "stumbling blocks" concepts in the context of the question whether the regionalism (that is, PTA) dynamic time-path will show increasing or stagnant membership. The PTA may improve welfare immediately, from U^0 to U_p^2 or (because trade diversion dominates) reduce it to U_p^1. The time-path with PTA, in either case, could then be stagnant (paths II and III), implying a fragmentation of the world economy through no further expansion of the initial trading bloc. Or, it could lead (paths I and IV) to multilateral free trade for all at U^* through continued expansion and coagulation of the PTA. Under "process multilateralism", the time-path may fail to reach U^* and instead fall short at U_m because of free-rider problems. Or it may overcome them and reach U^*. This diagram assumes that the time-paths are independent: embarking on the PTA path does not affect the process-multilateralism path. This independence is discussed in the text.

Source: Adapted from Bhagwati (1993a).

2.4.3 *"Exogenously-determined" Time-Paths: A Diversion*

First, however, it is necessary to consider and to turn aside certain theoretical approaches which are not meaningful for thinking about the dynamic time-path questions at hand, even though they have often been mistaken to be so.

Kemp-Wan

The seminal approach of Kemp and Wan (1976) to customs union theory seems to be the most pertinent to our questions but is, in fact, not. In contrast to the Vinerian approach, which we explored in the static analysis above, Kemp and Wan made the external tariff structure (of the customs union) endogenously chosen so that each member country's welfare would be improved while that of the nonmembers was left unchanged. The beauty of this approach was that it restored, as it were, the commonsense intuition prior to Viner that a CU should be welfare improving for members and for the world. This is, of course, a "possibility" theorem, no more and no less.[75]

It is then immediately apparent that the PTA time-path to U* in Figure 2.9 can be made monotonic, provided expanding membership of a PTA always satisfies the Kemp-Wan rule for forming a customs union. But what this argument does *not* say, and indeed cannot say, is that the PTA will necessarily expand and, if so, in this Kemp-Wan fashion.

For *that* answer, to what is obviously Question I above, we must turn to the *incentive structure* that any CU/PTA provides, through interests, ideology and institutions, for expansion or stagnation of its membership.

Krugman

The same argument applies to the theoretical approach to the question of PTAs recently introduced by Paul Krugman (1991a) (1991b) (1993). Again, the expansion of membership is treated as exogenously specified, as in Viner, and the welfare consequences of the world mechanically dividing into a steadily increasing number of symmetric blocs—clearly demarcated countries are then not even the natural constituents of these "blobs"-cum-blocs—are considered and, for particular specifications, the monotonicity of world welfare examined, including even calculations concerning the "optimal" number of such symmetric PTAs/blocs! This, in turn, has led to critiques, as

---

[75] Christopher Bliss (1994) has tried to put some structure on the argument; and, more recently, T.N. Srinivasan (1995) has also done so in the context of examining the question of the impact on nonmember welfare.

of the symmetry assumption by Srinivasan (1993), who essentially shows that the specific Krugman conclusions are easily reversed by abandoning symmetry, and to further variations by a few others.[76] Yet, it is hard to see the analytical interest of this approach or, more important, its relevance to the compelling (incentive-structure) questions today concerning the membership expansion of PTAs. In short, it fails to throw light on the analysis of the dynamic time-path questions of the type introduced above. For that analysis, which is currently, quite correctly, on the top of the theoretical agenda, we must turn elsewhere.

2.4.4 Incentive Structure Arguments

At the April 1992 World Bank Conference on Regional Integration, Bhagwati (1993a), having reiterated the need to analyze the dynamic time-path question, advanced several arguments concerning the incentive structure within specific PTAs, once formed, to expand or to stagnate. Before we proceed to discuss immediately below the subsequent theoretical modeling of such ideas that is now available, by Baldwin (1993), Krishna (1995) and Levy (1995), among others, it is worth recapitulating the principal arguments distinguished by Bhagwati.[77]

We need to recognize, of course, that the incentives may be political rather than (narrowly) economic. A PTA may be formed, and even expanded, to seek political allies by using trade as foreign policy and to target the benefits of trade to politically favored nations.[78] Politics is not a negligible factor in the discriminatory trade arrangements implemented by the EU via Association Agreements with the smaller countries on its periphery and beyond; and it certainly cannot be ignored in the transformation of the original Canada-US Free Trade Agreement into NAFTA with Mexico and then into the Enterprise of Americas Initiative.

But that is clearly not the whole story and we can learn much by thinking carefully about the incentive structure for membership expansion in

---

[76] See Deardorff and Stern (1994).

[77] Bhagwati (1993a, pp. 40-44) also discussed skeptically the claims that PTA formation is quicker, more efficient and more certain than MTN.

[78] For an early analysis of the political factors underlying the formation of PTAs, see the work by the political scientist, Edward Mansfield, cited and discussed in Bhagwati (1993a). Other political scientists such as Miles Kahler and Joseph Grieco have also written in this area recently.

political-economy-theoretic terms. To do this, Bhagwati (1993a) distinguished among three different types of "agents", and offered the following analysis:

1. Governments of Member Countries

PTAs will be under pressure not to expand because governments may feel that "we already have a large market, so what do we stand to gain by going through the hassle of adding more members?" This is the "our market is large enough" syndrome, emphasized by Martin Wolf who has often noted that large countries have tended to opt for inward-looking trade and investment strategies while the small ones have gone the outward-looking route.

2. Interest Groups in Member Countries

The interest groups in member countries may be for or against new members. The internationally-oriented exporting firms may be expected to endorse new members whose markets then become preferentially available to them vis-a-vis nonmember exporters to these new members.[79] On the other hand, the firms that are profiting from access to preferential markets in the member (partner) countries will not want new members whose firms are also exporters of the same or similar products in the member markets. Both incentives reflect, of course, the preferential nature of the PTAs.

The former incentive was clear in the NAFTA debate in the United States and reflected in many pronouncements, including that of pro-NAFTA economists (and even President Clinton who played the Japanophobic card that the US would have preferential access to Mexico vis-a-vis Japan). It is also evident in the statement of Signor Agnelli of Fiat: "The single market must first offer an advantage to European companies. This is a message we must insist on without hesitation."

---

[79] In comparing incentives for export-oriented firms, for lobbying for a PTA (for example, NAFTA) as against MTN (for example, the Uruguay Round), a dollar's worth of lobbying would go a longer way in the former case because any preferential opening of the Mexican market would be better for the US exporter than such an opening on an MFN basis that yields the benefits equally to US rivals in Japan, EU and elsewhere. This argument applies only to the extent that the MTN process simultaneously does not equally open other markets to the US exporter on a reciprocal basis.

3. Interest Groups in Nonmember Countries

The third set of agents is in the nonmember countries. Here, the example of a PTA may lead others to emulate, even to seek entry. Otherwise, the fear of trade diversion may also induce outsiders to seek entry.[80]

2.4.5 Recent Theoretical Analyses

Subsequently, the analysis of the dynamic time-path question has moved into formal political-economy-theoretic modeling. We provide here a synoptic review of the few significant contributions to date, organizing the literature analytically in light of the two questions distinguished above and also in terms of whether the analysis models the incentives of nonmembers to join or those of the members to expand.[81]

Question I:

The single contribution that focuses on Question I, that is, the incentive to add members to a PTA, is by Richard Baldwin (1993), who concentrates, in turn, on the incentive of nonmembers to join the PTA. He constructs a model to demonstrate that this incentive will be positive: the PTA will create a "domino" effect, with outsiders wanting to become insiders on an escalator. The argument is basically driven by the fact that the PTA implies a loss of cost-competitiveness by imperfectly-competitive nonmember firms whose profits in the PTA markets decline because they must face the tariffs that member countries' firms do not have to pay. These firms then lobby for entry, tilting the political equilibrium at the margin towards entry demands in

---

[80] Bhagwati (1993a) cites Irwin's (1993) study of the historical experience with trade liberalization in the 19th century, which shows that the Anglo-French Treaty may well have served this purpose. Richard Baldwin's (1993) subsequent formalization of this basic idea in what he calls the "domino" theory of PTA expansion is discussed below.

[81] In this review, we do not include the important contributions to the political-economy-theoretic analysis of PTAs that do not directly address either of the two dynamic time-path questions at issue in the text. For example, Grossman and Helpman (1995) have modeled the formation of PTAs, demonstrating the critical role played by the possibility of trade diversion in the outcome, a conclusion also arrived at independently by Pravin Krishna (1995) in a different model. Similarly, Panagariya and Findlay (1996) have formalized the endogeneity argument that reduced protection between members in a PTA can lead to increased protection against nonmembers. Using a political process consisting of lobbying by owners of specific factors, they also investigate the external tariffs that emerge under an FTA and a CU. For answers to a similar set of questions, but under the assumption of a welfare-maximizing government, see our discussion of Bagwell and Staiger (1993) below.

their countries. The countries closest to the margin will then enter the bloc, assuming that the members have open entry, thus enlarging the market and thereby increasing the cost of nonmembership and pulling in countries at the next margin. Given the assumptions, including continuity, this domino model can take the PTA time-path to U* in Figure 2.9.

While Baldwin formalizes the incentive of nonmembers to get inside the PTA, interestingly there is no formalization of the incentives of members to add or reject new members that have been discussed in the literature, as by Bhagwati (1993a). Indeed, the Baldwin model itself shows, on the flip side, that member firms will gain from the cost advantage that they enjoy vis-a-vis the nonmember firms and hence will have an opposed interest in not admitting the nonmembers to the PTA: a full analysis of the political economy of both members and nonmembers in the Baldwin model could then lead to specific equilibrium outcomes that leave the PTA expansion imperiled.

Question II:

The rest of the theoretical contributions address Question II, that is, whether the PTA possibility and/or time-path helps or harms the MTN time-path. Here, the two major analyses to date, addressed directly and quite aptly to this question, by Pravin Krishna (1994) and Philip Levy (1994), reach the "malign-impact" conclusion, unfavorable to the exhortation to "walk on both legs".

Krishna, models the political process in the fashion of the government acting in response to implicit lobbying by firms as what Bhagwati (1990) has called a "clearinghouse"-government assumption where the government is passive as in Findlay and Wellisz (1982). Krishna shows in his oligopolistic-competition model that the bilateral PTA between two member countries reduces the incentive of the member countries to liberalize tariffs reciprocally with the nonmember world and that, with sufficient trade diversion, this incentive could be so reduced as to make impossible an initially feasible multilateral trade liberalization.

Levy models the political process instead in a median-voter model a la Mayer (1984); the government is not what Bhagwati (1990) has christened as "self-willed" with its own objectives but acts again as a clearinghouse. Using a richer model with scale economies and product variety, Levy demonstrates that bilateral FTAs can undermine political support for multilateral free trade. At the same time, a benign impact is impossible in this model: if a multilateral free trade proposal is not feasible under autarky, the same multilateral proposal cannot be rendered feasible under any bilateral FTA.

The Krishna and Levy models therefore throw light on the incentive-structure questions at hand when the agents are the lobbying groups and interests that are affected by different policy options. However, we might also note that there are contributions that take the more conventional view of governments, which act as agents maximizing social welfare (so that they may be regarded as acting as the custodians of the "general interest" as defined by economists), but then ask whether the effect of allowing PTAs to form affects outcomes concerning trade policy relating to the multilateral system. Thus, Rodney Ludema (1993) has analyzed the effect of PTAs on multilateral bargaining outcomes, arguing plausibly that the PTAs give strategic advantage to their members, whereas Kyle Bagwell and Robert Staiger (1994) have analyzed as to how the formation of a PTA—distinguishing between an FTA and a CU, as they yield different answers—will affect the (unbound) tariffs of the members countries on the existing multilateral (that is, external) tariffs on nonmembers.

2.4.6 The Sequential Bargaining Argument

In conclusion, we may note that a different kind of model is implied, though not yet formalized, by the recent argument of Bhagwati (1994) which combines three separate notions:

The first is that even though a multilateral bargain *simultaneously* with a group of nonhegemonic powers is profitable and hence possible, a hegemonic power will gain a greater payoff by bargaining *sequentially* with them, using bilateral and plurilateral PTA approaches, picking the countries that are most vulnerable and then moving onto the next one and so on.[82]

The second is that this insight has now been appreciated by several lobbies (for example, the intellectual property protection lobby, the environmental and labor standard groups) which are piggybacking on to

---

[82] As noted in Bhagwati (1993a) (1994), this is exactly what the United States achieved, in terms of intellectual property protection and even concessions on environmental and labor standards enforcement, by getting President Salinas into a one-on-one bargaining situation in NAFTA. And now Chile is poised to accept these obligations as the price of getting into NAFTA. On the other hand, as the virtually unanimous developing country objections to labor standards demands at the WTO show, neither Mexico nor Chile would have agreed to these demands in the purely WTO context.

trade liberalization and trade institutions to secure their maximalist objectives and which see that the PTA approach (which may be seen as an "incentive" strategy), combined with the occasional use of aggressive unilateralism a la punitive Section 301 actions (which may be seen as a "punishment" strategy), is more likely to procure their objectives at the WTO and multilaterally than if pursued directly there through MTN alone.

The third is that the two processes, the MTN and the PTA path, are to be traveled in tandem since the ultimate goal is indeed to arrive at multilateral, universal obligations in the areas desired by these lobbies by the nonhegemonic powers.

If this "model" indeed provides insight into the political process that is driving the legitimation of the PTA time-path, then no hegemonic power is likely to abandon the PTA path simply because the WTO exists and is jumpstarted. A "selfish hegemon", looking after its own narrowly-defined interests, reflecting its own lobbying-derived needs, will indeed want to "walk on both legs". But the multilateral outcome, so affected and determined, need not then be considered to have been affected in the socially optimal direction unless one makes the assumption, made effortlessly by hegemonic spokesmen in their policy pronouncements, that "what is good for the hegemon (and its lobbies) is good for the world trading system." Indeed, when we see that the intellectual property protections that were built into the WTO are almost certainly excessive according to the analytical and empirical argumentation of many of the best international economists today, it is hard to regard the ability of the hegemon to induce such outcomes with the aid of PTAs (and aggressive unilateralism) as creating a ?benign? effect of the PTAs on the MTN path.

2.5 Implications for Current Policy

The case for PTAs, whether on static or on dynamic grounds, appears far less compelling and attractive than many politicians and policymakers now believe. In fact, it is likely that most of them, misled by the inevitable confusion between free trade and free trade areas that some economists have wittingly or unwittingly encouraged, are not even aware that the scholarly scene is rife today with serious opposition to PTAs.[83]

2.5.1 The Politics of PTAs

The current preoccupation with PTAs reflects overriding political factors. Recall our earlier discussion of the sequential-bargaining advantage to hegemonic powers, discussed at the end of the preceding Section. Or consider the fact that the leaders of the smaller, nonhegemonic powers get to play a more prominent role, with better photo-opportunities, with smaller summits, especially when a hegemonic power such as the United States features its own president, than would ever be the case at the WTO. Or consider that where the PTAs are regional, as is MERCOSUR (among Argentina, Brazil, Paraguay and Uruguay), the discriminatory trade agreement can be depicted politically as an act of foreign policy statesmanship. Or consider simply the operation of Gresham's Law: PTAs by some encourage PTAs by others, especially when they are being continually misportrayed by other politicians and countries as statesmanlike moves to free trade. And, of course, there are always the amateur geopoliticians and geoeconomists. Like little boys playing Nintendo games on their computer screens, they think of playing the game of "trade blocs" to indulge their pet prejudices against Europe or Japan. Some want to make the APEC into a PTA to play off against a "protectionist" Europe while others think of TAFTA as a weapon to play off against the "unfairly-trading" Japan.[84]

---

[83] This was stated to be the case for Washington by a wellplaced trade economist in the Clinton administration, at a recent conference on the subject of PTAs. The first author, at a Stockholm conference on WTO issues this summer, organised by the Swedish trade minister, Mats Hellstrom, found a similar unawareness among some of the trade ministers and bureaucrats present, even as the response of the attending economists as also of yet other well-known politicians wedded to the MFN principle to the critical remarks about the current obsession with PTAs was enthusiastic.

[84] And then there are also those who think that the APEC, turned into a PTA that excludes the extension of trade barrier reductions to Europe, will prompt Europe to its own tariff cuts in a benign outcome. This viewpoint, ascribed in the media to C.F. Bergsten, is premised on his view that the Seattle APEC summit pushed the Europeans into settling the Uruguay Round. This view is entirely unpersuasive since, in the end, it was the United States administration that decided to accept the advice of many to close the Round with whatever it could get and to proceed to build on that in future negotiations. For a critique of similar, special pleading to justify NAFTA, see Bhagwati (1995, pp.11-12).

2.5.2 The "Spaghetti Bowl" Phenomenon

Our view, for reasons explored fully in this chapter, is that the spread of PTAs is deplorable except when two justifications do not obtain: you are building a Common Market, with full-scale integration of factor markets and even political harmonization; or the multilateral MFN, MTN process is not working. As we argued earlier, neither rationale is operative today.

In fact, the proliferation of PTAs today poses the danger, in fact the certainty, that a veritable "spaghetti bowl" phenomenon, as Bhagwati has called it, will emerge where trade barriers, including duties, will vary depending on origin, and complex and protection-accommodating rules of origin will find their way into practice.[85] And this too at a time when multinationals are getting truly global and the identification of "local content" and hence origin of traded goods and services is becoming increasingly meaningless and hence subject to inevitable arbitrariness. PTAs are just one, and indeed a gigantic, step backwards from this viewpoint: the need today is to intensify the commitment to the basic principle of nondiscrimination that the architects of GATT correctly saw as a principal virtue, not to undermine it.

2.5.3 PTAs with and among Hegemons

We would therefore suggest that Article 24-sanctioned PTAs which involve hegemonic powers be actively discouraged. They involve NAFTA extension southwards or overseas, EU free-trade-area agreements with non-EU countries, APEC's transformation into a PTA, and TAFTA.

Such a self-denial would appear anti-free-trade, given the current state of confused thinking and the political capital invested by many in the cause of the PTAs. But it would be speaking to a far more compelling, and truer, version of free trade. It would also require true statesmanship on the part of the leaders of the hegemonic powers, as against the political advantages of opting for what is an inefficient and indeed harmful option.

2.5.4 PTAs among the Nonhegemons

Our view of PTAs among the nonhegemons, principally developing countries, is just a trifle less critical, however.

---

[85] For a detailed statement of this critique, see Bhagwati (1995).

To begin with, what MERCOSUR does, for example, has only a fraction of the significance that US and EU have individually. The trade policy choices of the nonhegemons have comparatively more consequences for themselves than for the world. This contrast is sufficient to regard what the nonhegemons are doing with a less fiercely critical eye than that directed at the hegemons.

Remember again that the impact on their own welfare of PTAs is not benign. Especially, when these countries get into a PTA with hegemonic powers (for example, Mexico joining the US in NAFTA), the outcomes for them may well be welfare-worsening (in the static sense) because of the tariff-revenue-redistribution effect we introduced in Section 2.3, among other reasons. Failure to understand the differential economics of PTAs, as contrasted with that of free trade, underlies many of the favorable assessments often advanced in behalf of the developing countries that seek to join such PTAs with the hegemonic powers.[86] A similar caveat could be relevant to PTAs among the nonhegemons themselves.

We may still consider these PTAs, such as MERCOSUR, with some favor, although nondiscriminatory free trade is the best option. Afterall, the acceptance of Article 24 discipline (imperfect as it is) can still be considered to be an improvement over protectionism or over the utterly chaotic and arbitrary ECDC (economic cooperation among developing countries) at the GATT under which these countries were free from such discipline and could indulge in any level and kind of preferences among themselves.

2.6 Concluding Remarks

At present, the spread of hegemonic PTAs has been halted. The Osaka meeting of APEC in November 1995 witnessed the Asian members of APEC reaffirming their desire to stick to MFN and hence implicitly to reject the PTA approach even though the US position on the issue has apparently remained problematic and ambiguous (with several pro-PTA proponents in the administration). Equally, at Madrid, the idea of TAFTA has been deflected

---

[86] Unfortunately, this comment also applies to many of the numerical, including the computable-general-equilibrium models, estimating the gains from PTAs, as discussed by Panagariya in a forthcoming essay. And then there are the more elementary conceptual errors that afflict the numerical estimates of gains in *employment* from NAFTA, which were widely reported by the media at the time.

away from an Article XXIV agreement to the New Trans-Atlantic Agenda that merely seeks, and in a presumably nondiscriminatory fashion, the lowering of trade and investment barriers in the area. For the time being, the extension of NAFTA to the South has also been halted, for reasons that may not hold for long beyond the presidential election in 1996.

All this yields enough time to take a closer look at the dangerous drift to PTAs, aided by the unfortunate conversion of the United States to the thesis that any trade liberalization is as good as any other. Perhaps, as often happens in economic policy, what presently looks like a politically irreversible trend will yield to economic wisdom. We will see.

References

Bagwell, Kyle and Robert Staiger, 1993, "Multilateral Cooperation During the Formation of Free Trade Areas," NBER Working Paper No. 4364.

Baldwin, Richard, 1993, "A Domino Theory of Regionalism," CEPR Working Paper No. 857, November.

Berglas, Eitan, 1979, "Preferential Trading: The n Commodity Case," *Journal of Political Economy* 87, No. 21, 315-331.

Bhagwati, Jagdish, 1968, "Trade Liberalization Among LDCs, Trade Theory and GATT Rules," in Wolf, J.N., ed., *Value, Capital, and Growth: Papers in Honor of J.R. Hicks*, Oxford: Oxford University Press.

Bhagwati, Jagdish, 1990, "The Theory of Political economy, Economic Policy, and Foreign Investment," in Scott, M. and D. Lal (eds.) *Public Policy and Economic Development*, Essays in Honour of I.M.D. Little, Oxford: Clarendon Press, pp. 217-230.

Bhagwati, Jagdish, 1991, *The World Trading System at Risk*, Princeton: Princeton University and Harvester Wheatsheaf.

Bhagwati, Jagdish, 1993a, "Regionalism and Multilateralism: An Overview," in Melo and Panagariya, (ed.).

Bhagwati, Jagdish, 1993b, "Beyond NAFTA: Clinton's trading Choices," *Foreign Policy*, Summer, 155-62.

Bhagwati, Jagdish, 1994, "Threats to the World trading System: Income Distribution and the Selfish Hegemon," *Journal of International Affairs*, Spring.

Bhagwati, Jagdish, 1995, "U.S. Trade Policy: The Infatuation with Free Trade Areas," in Bhagwati, J. and Krueger Anne O., eds.

Bhagwati, J., 1996, Trade and Wages: A Malign Relationship?" in Collins, Susan, ed., *The American Worker: Exports, Imports and Jobs*, Brookings Institution: Washington, D.C., forthcoming.

Bhagwati, Jagdish and Dehejia, V., 1994, "Trade and Wages: Is Marx Striking Again?" in Bhagwati, J, and M. Kosters, eds., *Trade and Wages: Leveling Down?*, American Enterprise Institute: Washington, D.C.

Bhagwati, Jagdish, Krishna, Pravin, and Panagariya, Arvind, 1996, "Introduction," in Jagdish Bhagwati and Pravin Krishna (eds.), *Contributions to the Theory of Preferential Trading Areas*, MIT Press, (forthcoming).

Bhagwati, Jagdish and Krueger, A.O, ed., 1995, *The Dangerous Drift to Preferential Trade Agreements*, Washington, D.C.: American Enterprise Institute for Public Policy Research.

Bhagwati, Jagdish and Panagariya, Arvind, 1996, "The Theoretical Analyses of Preferential trading Areas," paper presented at the American Economic Association Meetings, San Francisco, January 5-7, 1996; to appear in the *American Economic Review. Papers and Proceedings*, May.

Bhagwati, Jagdish and Srinivasan, T.N., 1980, "Revenue Seeking: A Generalization of the Theory of Tariffs," *Journal of Political Economy* 88, December, 1069-87.

Bhagwati, Jagdish and Srinivasan, T.N., 1983, *Lectures in Trade Theory*, Cambridge, MA: MIT Press.

Bliss, Christopher, 1994, *Economic Theory and Policy for Trading Blocks*, Manchester and New York: Manchester University Press.

Brecher, Richard and Bhagwati, Jagdish, 1981, "Foreign Ownership and the Theory of Trade and Welfare," *Journal of Political Economy* 89, No. 3, June, 497-511.

Cooper, C.A. and Massell, B.F., 1965a, "A New Look at Customs Union Theory," *Economic Journal* 75, 742-747.

Cooper, C.A. and Massell, B.F., 1965b, "Towards a General Theory of Customs Unions for Developing Countries," *Journal of Political Economy* 73, No. 5, 461-76.

Deardorff, Alan V. and Stern, Robert M, 1994, "Multilateral Trade Negotiations and Preferential Trading Arrangements," in Deardorff, Alan V. and Stern, Robert M., *Analytical and Negotiating Issues in the Global Trading System*, Ann Arbor: University of Michigan Press.

Dhar, Sumana and Panagariya, Arvind, 1994, "Is East Asia Less Open than North America and the European Economic Community? No." Policy Research Working Paper #1370, World Bank.

Eaton, Jonathan and Panagariya, Arvind, 1979, "Gains from Trade under Variable Returns to Scale, Commodity Taxation, Tariffs and Factor Market Distortions," *Journal of International Economics* 9, 481-501.

Frankel, Jeffrey and Wei, Sheng-Jin, 1995, "The New Regionalism and Asia: Impact and Options," presented at the Asian Development Bank Conference on Emerging Global Trading Environment and Developing Asia, May 29-30, 1995.

Frankel, J., Stein, E. and Wei, S., 1995a, "Trading Blocs and the Americas: The Natural, the Unnatural and the Supernatural," *Journal of Development Economics*, forthcoming.

Frankel, J., Stein, E. and Wei, S., 1995b, "Continental Trading Blocs: Are They natural or Super-Natural," NBER Working Paper No. 4588.

Grossman, Gene and Helpman, Elhanan, 1995, "The Politics of Free Trade Agreements," *American Economic Review*, September, 667-690.

Haberler, Gottfried, 1943, "The Political Economy of Regional or Continental Blocs," in Harris, Seymour, E., ed., *Postwar Economic Problems*, New York.

Irwin, Douglas, 1993, "Multilateral and Bilateral Trade Policies in the world Trading System: An Historical Perspective," in Melo and Panagariya (eds.)

Johnson, Harry, 1962, *Money, Trade and Economic growth*, Cambridge, Mass.: Harvard University Press.

Johnson, Harry, 1965, "An Economic Theory of Protectionism, Tariff Bargaining, and the Formation of Customs Unions," *Journal of Political Economy* 73 (June), 256-83.

Kemp, Murray C. and Wan, Henry, 1976, "An Elementary Proposition Concerning the Formation of Customs Unions," *Journal of International Economics* 6 (February), 95-8.

Krishna, Pravin, 1995, "Regionalism and Multilateralism: A Political Economy Approach," mimeo., Economics Department, Columbia University, December; presented to the NBER Universities Research Conference on *International Trade and Regulations*, Cambridge, Mass., 1993.

Krishna, Pravin and Bhagwati, Jagdish, 1994, "Necessarily Welfare-enhancing Customs Unions with industrialization Constraints: A Proof of the Cooper-Massell-Johnson-Bhagwati Conjecture," Columbia University Working Papers, April.

Krueger, Anne O., 1974, "The Political-Economy of the Rent Seeking Society," *American Economic Review* 69, No. 3, 291-303.

Krueger, Anne O., 1993, "Rules of Origin as Protectionist Devices," NBER Working Paper No. 4352, April. Forthcoming in Melvin, J., Moore, J. and Riezman, R., *International trade Theory*, eds., MIT Press, Cambridge, MA.

Krueger, Anne O., 1995, "Free Trade Agreements Versus Customs Unions," NBER Working Paper No. 5084, April.

Krugman, P., 1991a, "The Move to Free Trade Zones," in Symposium Sponsored by the Federal Reserve Bank of Kansas City, *Policy Implications of Trade and Currency Zones*.

Krugman, P., 1991b, "Is Bilateralism Bad?" in E. Helpman and A. Razin (eds.), *International Trade and Trade Policy*, Cambridge, Mass.: MIT Press.

Krugman, P., 1993, "Regionalism versus Multilateralism: Analytical Notes," in Melo and Panagariya (eds.)

Lawrence, Robert Z., 1991, "Emerging Regional Arrangements: Building Blocks or Stumbling Blocks?" In Richard O'Brien (ed.), *Finance and the International Economy*, Amex Bank Prize Essays, Oxford University Press for the Amex Bank Review.

Levy, Philip, 1994, "A Political Economic Analysis of Free Trade Agreements," Economic Growth Center, Yale University, Center Discussion Paper No. 718.

Lipsey, Richard, 1957, "The Theory of Customs Unions: Trade Diversion and Welfare," *Economica* 24, 40-46.

Lipsey, Richard, 1958, *The Theory of Customs Unions: A General Equilibrium Analysis*, University of London, Ph.D. thesis.

Lipsey, Richard, 1960, "The Theory of Customs Unions: A General Survey," *Economic Journal* 70, 498-513.

Lloyd, Peter J., 1982, "3x3 Theory of Customs Unions," *Journal of International Economics* 12, 41-63.

Ludema, Rodney, 1993, "On the Value of Preferential trade Agreements in Multilateral Negotiations," mimeo.

Meade, James, E., 1955, *The Theory of Customs Unions*, Amsterdam: North-Holland.

Melo, Jaime de, Panagariya, Arvind and Rodrik, Dani, 1993, "The New Regionalism: A Country Perspective," in Melo and Panagariya, ch. 6.

Melo, Jaime de and Panagariya, Arvind, ed., 1993, *New Dimensions in Regional Integration*, Cambridge, Great Britain: Cambridge University Press.

Mundell, Robert A., 1964, "Tariff Preferences and the Terms of Trade," *Manchester School of Economic and Social Studies*, 1-13.

Panagariya, Arvind, 1993, "Should East Asia Go Regional? No, No and Maybe." WPS 1209, World Bank, Washington, D.C. (Chapter 3, this volume)

Panagariya, Arvind, 1994, "East Asia and the New Regionalism," *World Economy* 17, No. 6, November, 817-39.

Panagariya, Arvind, 1995a, "Rethinking the New Regionalism." Paper presented at the Trade Expansion Program Conference of the UNDP and World Bank, January 1995.

Panagariya, Arvind, 1995b, "The Free Trade Area of the Americas: Good for Latin America?" Center for International Economics, University of Maryland, Working paper #12. (Chapter 5, this volume)

Panagariya, Arvind, 1996, "The Meade Model of Preferential trading: History, Analytics and Policy Implications," mimeo, University of Maryland, Department of Economics.

Panagariya, Arvind and Findlay, Ronald, 1996, "A Political Economy Analysis of Free Trade Areas and Customs Unions," Robert Feenstra, Douglas Irwin and Gene Grossman, eds., *The Political Economy of Trade Reform*, Essays in Honor of Jagdish Bhagwati, MIT Press, forthcoming.

Richardson, M. 1994. "Why a Free Trade Area? The Tariff Also Rises," *Economics & Politics* 6, no. 1, March, 79-95.

Riezman, Raymond, 1979, "A 3x3 Model of Customs Unions, *Journal of International Economics* 9, 341-354.

Srinivasan, T.N., 1993, "Discussion," in Melo, Jaime de and Panagariya, Arvind.

Srinivasan, T.N., 1995, "Common External Tariffs of a Customs Union: The Case of Identical Cobb-Douglas Tastes," mimeo., Yale University.

Summers, Lawrence, 1991, "Regionalism and the World Trading System," Symposium Sponsored by the Federal Reserve Bank of Kansas City, *Policy Implications of Trade and Currency Zones*.

Viner, Jacob, 1950, *The Customs Union Issue*, New York: Carnegie Endowment for International Peace.

Wei, S. and Frankel, Jeffrey, 1995, "Open Regionalism in a World of Continental Trade Blocs," revised version of NBER Working Paper No. 5272, November.

Winters, L.A., 1995a, "Regionalism and the Rest of the World: The Irrelevance of the Kemp-Wan Theorem," mimeo., The World Bank.

Winters, L.A., 1995b, "European Integration and Economic Welfare in the Rest of the World," mimeo., The World Bank.

Wonnacott, Paul and Lutz, Mark, 1989, "Is There a Case for Free Trade Areas?" in Schott, Jeffrey, *Free Trade Areas and U.S. Trade Policy*, Washington, D.C.: Institute for International Economics, 59-84.

PART II EAST ASIA

3.   Should East Asia Go Regional?

3.1 Introduction

By June 1, 1995, the World Trade Organization (WTO)—the successor institution to General Agreement on Tariffs and Trade (GATT)—had been notified of more than 130 regional arrangements (Bhagwati and Panagariya 1996). Today, with the exception of Hong Kong and Japan, every WTO member boasts of a membership in at least one regional arrangement.[87] Neither the successful completion of the Uruguay Round nor the recent peso crisis in Mexico has been able to reverse the rising tide of regionalism. Having already concluded Free Trade Area (FTA) agreements with its neighbors in Eastern and Central Europe, the European Union (EU) is now beginning to bring the countries in North Africa into its fold. The United States, on the other hand, has set a target date of 2005 for the creation of the Free Trade Area of the Americas (FTAA) consisting of the entire Western Hemisphere. Germany has even made overtures for a Trans-Atlantic Free Trade Area (TAFTA) between the United States and the EU.

Originally published, as chapter 4, in *Economic Development and Cooperation in the Pacific Basin*, ed. Hiro Lee and David W. Roland-Holst (Cambridge, U.K.: Cambridge University Press, 1998), 119-154. An earlier version of this paper was circulated as the World Bank's Policy Research Working Paper #1209. A shorter paper based on that version appeared in the November 1994 issue of the *World Economy* under the title "East Asia and the New Regionalism." I thank Hiro Lee for comments and Sumana Dhar for excellent research assistance. The original version of the paper was written as a part of the Regional Integration Initiative Study of the East Asia Region of the World Bank and of RPO 677-86. Findings, interpretations, and conclusions in this paper are entirely those of the author and should not be attributed in any manner to the World Bank, its affiliated organizations, or to members of its Board of Executive Directors or the countries they represent.

[87]. Not all of these countries belong to regional arrangements under Article XXIV of GATT. Many developing countries belong exclusively to south-south arrangements under the Enabling Clause of GATT.

Historically, East Asia has not been enthusiastic towards preferential trading. Till recently, the only functioning preferential trading scheme in the region was the Association of South-East Asian Nations (ASEAN) Preferential Trading Area (APTA) and was very limited in scope.[88] Starting in 1989, the rise of regionalism in North America and Europe led to some rethinking in the region. In 1989, the forum for Asia Pacific Economic Cooperation (APEC) was created to bring the Uruguay Round to a speedy conclusion and to promote liberalization of trade and investment policies at the regional level. APEC, which has eighteen members currently, includes not only countries from East Asia but also the Americas.[89] In 1990, Prime Minister Mahathir of Malaysia announced the formation of the exclusively Asian East Asian Economic Group (EAEG) which, under U.S. pressure, was later recast as the East Asian Economic Caucus (EAEC).[90] In January 1992, members of ASEAN signed an agreement to turn the APTA into ASEAN Free Trade Area (AFTA) by the year 2007, a date that was subsequently moved up to 2003. In 1994, at its Bogor meeting, APEC members agreed to establish free trade by the year 2010 in the developed member countries and by 2020 in the developing member countries.

In the light of these developments, it is timely to ask whether regionalism should assume a more central role in East Asia. If yes, in what form and, if not, why not. And what are the implications of the APEC process in general and Bogor agreement in particular? In the present chapter, I subject these important issues to a systematic analysis. In Section 3.2, I subject the literature on regional integration to a critical examination. I argue that, from the viewpoint of small countries willing to liberalize trade unilaterally, a clear economic justification for regional arrangements is difficult to find. In Section 3.3, I consider the case for exclusively East Asian regional integration schemes. Cases for three possible forms of integration are evaluated: sub-regional groupings such as ASEAN, an region-wide trading bloc, and region-wide nondiscriminatory liberalization. I argue that

---

[88.] The original membership of ASEAN included Brunei, Singapore and ASEAN 4, namely, Indonesia, Malaysia, the Philippines and Thailand.

[89.] APEC membership includes the six original members of ASEAN, Korea, China, Hong Kong, Taiwan, Mexico, Chile, Papua New Guinea, Japan, Canada, Australia, New Zealand and the United States.

[90.] The proposed membership of the EAEG included ASEAN, NIEs, China and Japan. But US was opposed to the idea and "persuaded" Japan to stay out of the group. When the EAEG was recast as EAEC, Vietnam was also became a member.

the first of these is undesirable, the second is infeasible, and the third holds some promise though the case for it is far from clear-cut. In Section 3.4, I discuss the implications of the APEC process for the region. Because APEC includes the United States, its implications are more complicated than of exclusively Asian arrangements discussed in Section 3.3. In Section 3.5, brief concluding remarks are offered.

3.2 The Economics of Discriminatory Liberalization[91]

The term regional integration has been used traditionally to refer to discriminatory trade liberalization whereby two or more countries lower trade barriers against one another relative to the rest of the world. Because such liberalization makes the participating countries more open to each other but possibly less open to outside countries, its effects on economic efficiency are ambiguous in general. This fact has made regional integration a highly contentious issue.

In this section, I summarize the broad implications of discriminatory liberalization by a pair of countries. The analysis is essentially applicable to more than two countries. The discussion begins with an exposition of the influential concepts of trade creation and trade diversion introduced by Viner (1950) in his classic work *The Customs Union Issue*. This is followed by a comparison between a free trade area and nondiscriminatory, unilateral trade liberalization. The section is concluded with a discussion of why countries find regional integration an attractive option today.

3.2.1 Trade Creation and Trade Diversion

Let us begin with the standard, static analysis of a discriminatory liberalization by a pair of countries. Imagine that starting from a nondiscriminatory tariff, Japan and Indonesia form an FTA. For simplicity, focus on the market for VCRs. Assume that VCRs are a homogeneous good and that Indonesia is a net importer of them. At $200 per VCR, Korea is the cheapest supplier of

---

[91.] Some of the points made in this section can be found in Melo and Panagariya (1992) which, in turn, is based on Melo and Panagariya (1993). For a summary of theoretical developments, see Bhagwati and Panagariya (1996a).

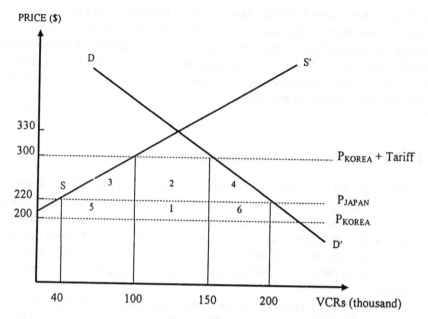

Figure 3.1: Welfare Effects of a Free Trade Area

the product in the world.[92] Japan supplies the product at a per-unit price of $220. Unit costs and, hence, the selling prices of Korea and Japan are constant.

Assume that initially Indonesia imposes a 50% tariff on all imported VCRs. This makes the tariff-inclusive price of VCRs from Korea $300 and those from Japan $330. All imports come from Korea and the price of VCRs in Indonesia settles at $300. At this price, suppose that Indonesians buy a total of 150,000 VCRs. Of these, Indonesian sellers, who produce VCRs at increasing marginal costs, supply 100,000. The remaining 50,000 units come from Korea. Indonesia collects $5,000,000 in import duties.

Now suppose that Indonesia forms a free trade area with Japan. The two countries drop tariffs on each other but retain them on outside countries including Korea. Because there is no tariff on VCRs from Japan any longer, these latter can be sold in Indonesia at $220 while Korean VCRs are priced

---

[92.] Note that we deliberately assume that Japan is not the cheapest source of VCRs. If it were, a free trade area in VCRs will be vacuous in that, given constant costs, the outcome will be unaffected by whether liberalization is preferential or nondiscriminatory.

at $300. All imported VCRs now come from Japan and the price of VCRs in Indonesia declines to $220. From an efficiency standpoint, assuming for now a fixed total demand of 150,000 VCRs in Indonesia, two effects can be identified.

First, the original imports of 50,000 VCRs that came from the lowest-cost supplier, Korea, now come from the higher-cost partner, Japan. In Vinerian terms, this is "trade diversion" and is associated with a loss for Indonesia. The loss is manifest in the disappearance of tariff revenue, which is recaptured only partially by consumers in the form of a lower price of VCRs. The remainder of tariff revenue goes to pay for less efficiently produced VCRs of the partner country. Second, because VCRs are produced under increasing marginal costs in Indonesia, the output there declines with the decline in price. VCRs produced at a marginal cost higher than $220 in Indonesia are replaced by cheaper imports. This "trade creation" improves efficiency by replacing higher-cost Indonesian production by lower-cost imports from Japan.[93]

Trade diversion reduces efficiency while trade creation improves it. Therefore, the net effect of an FTA is ambiguous in general. *Ceteris paribus, the higher the initial tariff, the lower the difference between the prices of the two suppliers of imports, and the larger the economic size of the union, the more likely that the FTA will improve efficiency.* A high initial tariff means that the potential gains from liberalizing the domestic industry even on a discriminatory basis are large or, equivalently, the trade creation effect is likely to dominate. A small difference between the prices of the partner and the outside source means that the term of trade deterioration from switching to the partner is small or, equivalently, the trade diversion effect is small. Finally, the larger the union, the more likely that the lowest-cost source of supply will be within the union. For instance, in our example, if Korea was also included in the union, there will be no trade diversion in the VCR market and welfare will rise unambiguously.

As an anchor for future discussion, it is useful to summarize this analysis graphically. In Figure 3.1, DD' and SS', respectively, represent Indonesia's demand for and supply of VCRs of a given quality. The vertical axis shows

---

[93.] Observe that as noted before, resources released from VCR industry in Indonesia are assumed to be reallocated to other sectors which are more productive. In the transition, there is likely to be unemployment. Moreover, reallocation of resources may involve training and other adjustment costs. These costs are not incorporated into the analysis in the text. If we could measure these costs satisfactorily, however, the analysis can be modified to take them into consideration without harm to the basic conclusions.

the price of an VCR in U.S. dollars and the horizontal axis the quantity in thousand VCRs. Under a nondiscriminatory tariff of 50%, the price in Indonesia is $300 and quantities consumed, produced and imported are 150,000, 100,000, and 50,000, respectively. All imports come from Korea at a border price of $200. Import duties sum to areas 1 plus 2.

An FTA between Indonesia and Japan lowers the price in Indonesia to $220 per VCR and all imports now come from Japan. Of the original 150,000 VCRs bought earlier, 40,000 are now produced domestically and 110,000 imported from Japan. The 60,000 additional imported units replace higher-cost domestic units. This is trade creation and yields a gain of area 3 for Indonesia. The other 50,000 units replace cheaper Korean units. This is trade diversion and leads to a loss of area 1 for Indonesia.[94]

There is one more source of efficiency effects which, in the spirit of Viner, we have not identified so far.[95] The reduction in price from $300 to $220 per VCR expands the consumption of VCRs and brings the marginal benefit from consumption closer to the marginal cost of it. This generates a further welfare gain represented by area 4. The net effect of the FTA is positive or negative as the sum of areas 3 and 4 is larger or smaller than area 1.

3.2.2 A Puzzle: Why form an FTA when Nondiscriminatory, Unilateral Liberalization is Superior?

In the small-country context we have chosen in the previous subsection, it is easy to see that Indonesia can improve its welfare unambiguously relative to the initial as well as the post-FTA equilibrium by liberalizing trade unilaterally on a nondiscriminatory basis. For example, if Indonesia lowers its tariff on both Japan and Korea to 10%, Korea continues to outcompete Japan. The tariff inclusive price of Korean VCRs is now $220; we obtain the same equilibrium as under FTA but without any trade diversion. Indonesia is able to collect import duties represented by areas 1, 5, and 6 in addition to the efficiency gains represented by areas 3 and 4 in Figure 3.1; the country gains relative to the initial as well as FTA equilibrium.

[94.] Observe that all of tariff revenue represented by areas 1 and 2 disappears. But area 1 is recaptured by consumers via a lower price of VCRs.

[95.] Viner implicitly assumed a completely inelastic demand. This practice is surprisingly common in policy analyses, which often ignore the changes in demand.

The proposition that unilateral, nondiscriminatory liberalization is superior to an FTA is robust to a variety of modifications provided we continue to make the "small union" assumption (i.e., the countries forming the union are too small to influence the terms of trade in the outside world). Three such modifications may be mentioned. First, in the Indonesia-Japan example above, suppose we introduce increasing marginal costs of production in Japan. In this case, Indonesia is likely to import VCRs from both Japan and Korea before as well as after the FTA. This will not change our conclusion, however. Indonesia's welfare under a nondiscriminatory liberalization will remain unambiguously higher than under a FTA. Moreover, the gains from Indonesia's preferential liberalization will accrue largely to Japan.

Second, suppose we now recognize the fact that as a part of the FTA, Japan also lowers its tariffs on Indonesian goods. This will surely create benefits for Indonesia, which are not available through unilateral liberalization. While this is true, we also know from our earlier analysis that the gains to Japan from lowering its tariff are higher if it does so on a nondiscriminatory basis. Indeed, it can be shown that the extra gains to Indonesia from preferential liberalization by Japan are less than the extra benefits to Japan from a nondiscriminatory liberalization. Put differently, though one country can enjoy a higher real income under an FTA than under a nondiscriminatory liberalization, the *combined* income of the partners will be lower under the former scenario. The country benefiting more from an FTA than nondiscriminatory liberalization cannot afford to bribe the other country into forming an FTA.

Third, suppose there are scale economies. Here again, as long as we maintain the small union assumption, nondiscriminatory liberalization dominates. The simple point is that, with declining costs, if it is profitable for the country to produce the good subject to economies of scale, it should expand production all the way to the minimum cost point, consume what it can consume domestically, and export the residual to the outside world. To exploit scale economies, one does not need a "partner country's" market when the world market is there.

3.2.3 The Attraction of Regionalism: Some Answers?

In spite of this dominance of unilateral, nondiscriminatory liberalization, how do we explain the attraction of regionalism today? The literature offers a number of explanations though, as I will argue later, none of them is persuasive.[96]

(i) The small union assumption may not be valid. Thus, in our Japan-Indonesia example, the price at which Korea sells VCRs to Indonesia may depend on the number of VCRs sold. In response to a switch in demand from Korea to Japan due to preferential liberalization, Korea may lower its price to remain competitive in the Indonesian market. The terms of trade for Indonesia improve. Likewise, the price paid by Japan to extra-union suppliers may decline in response to the preferential access offered by it to Indonesia. This improvement in the terms of trade yields benefits not available through nondiscriminatory, unilateral liberalization.[97]

(ii) There is the closely related issue of access to the world markets. In a world infested with voluntary export restraints, administered protection, and a strong tendency for the formation of trading blocs, the difference between discriminatory and nondiscriminatory liberalization may be blurred. In the limit, we can imagine an outside world that does not trade externally at all. Then trade restrictions on the outside world are vacuous and it does not matter whether liberalization is discriminatory or nondiscriminatory. What is important is that liberalization be undertaken on a region wide basis and for this regional integration may be a powerful instrument. By bringing countries together to liberalize *simultaneously*, the regional approach can help solve the same prisoners' dilemma at the regional level that the GATT helps solve at the multilateral level.

(iii) Once we admit the limits on access to the world market, large gains from regional integration are possible if scale economies are present. Mutual liberalization by countries in the region will then provide room for expanded scale of operation, specialization, and plant rationalization. Regional opening may also offer gains from increased product variety.

(iv) Even when the rest of the world is open, there may be goods which are tradable only regionally. For these goods, a simultaneous liberalization

---

[96.] For a detailed critique of discriminatory liberalization, see Bhagwati (1985), Bhagwati and Panagariya (1996b) and Panagariya (1996).

[97.] In the same vein, if the union is not small, it can benefit by exploiting the economies od scale more effectively. In a three-country model, if each country restricts imports from the other, each may produce the good subject to scale economies and fail to take full advantage of declining costs. If two of the countries form a regional arrangement with one country becoming the exporter and the other the importer of the product, the union as a whole can benefit. The difficulty with this argument, however, is that with the U.S., European and Japanese markets being relatively open, market size is not a major constraint for most countries.

through a regional approach can bestow gains for the same reasons as multilateral trade liberalization. Trade in electricity between neighboring countries is one such example. Under a broad interpretation, we can include cooperation on projects of regional interest—development of roads, dams, and water resources—in this category. A concrete example is the recent agreement, signed in 1991, under which Singapore will cooperate with Indonesia to develop water resources in the latter's province of Riau in return for guaranteed water supply for 50 years.

(v) For smaller economies of the region, a regional arrangement with Japan can guarantee future access to a large, developed-country market. Under normal circumstances, this may not be important but in the event the EU and Americas continue to travel down the road leading to inward-looking blocs, such access may be crucial. From the viewpoint of entire East Asia, the threat of a regional arrangement may also serve to deter the EU and Americas from turning more inward.

(vi) Unilateral liberalization, even if superior to the regional route in principle, may be politically infeasible. At political levels, there is a strong mercantilist bias in trade-policy thinking. Any reduction in trade barriers is viewed as a concession given to foreigners. Under this mind set, unilateral import liberalization is a free gift to the world while liberalization via the regional route brings concessions from partners. In practice, This factor seems to become particularly important when the level of protection is not wildly high. Mexico and Chile have been able to liberalize imports unilaterally to a considerable degree but further liberalization seems to require a regional context. In East Asia, countries such as Malaysia, Thailand, Korea and Philippines have also been successful in unilateral liberalization up to a degree but may require a regional context for further import liberalization.

(vii) Regional integration can go far beyond trade liberalization. In East Asia, intra-regional labor mobility, direct foreign investment, and financial-capital flows will play an increasingly important role in the forthcoming years. To the extent that harmonization of policies across countries can help facilitate such movements, regional integration can offer gains not available through either unilateral or global actions.[98]

[98.] Melo, Panagariya, and Rodrik (1993) develop a formal model in which regional integration leads to "trade" in institutions between partner countries. Among other things, they show that this type of integration may serve to dilute the power of lobbies and help create superior institutions.

(viii) For a small developing country, a regional arrangement with a large, developed country may be an effective instrument of making its trade reform credible. Even if future governments happen to be more protectionist, they cannot reverse liberalization undertaken via an international treaty with a large developed country. Credibility will, in turn, induce investment from both domestic and foreign sources and stimulate growth.

(ix) Finally, regional integration may be an instrument of promoting peace and harmony among participating countries. The most dramatic example of this is the EC, which has united two former enemies—France and Germany—, in such a tight economic union that another war between them is unthinkable. In East Asia also, a regional arrangement can help reduce political tensions and promote political harmony among former enemies (e.g., China and Japan; China and Taiwan; Republic of Korea and Japan; and North Korea and the Republic of Korea).

Let us examine each of these arguments critically.

The first of these arguments relies on the member countries' ability to exploit monopoly power over outside countries. If the outside countries do not retaliate and initial structure of tariffs in member countries is such that it permits each member to obtain approximately as much preferential access to other member countries' markets as it gives them to its own, a discriminatory arrangement may benefit all members.[99] But this is the traditional optimum-tariff argument which economists generally do not recommend.

Arguments (ii)-(iv) are all correct but they do not require *discriminatory* liberalization. It is important to guard against these arguments because they often get used to promote discriminatory liberalization. Argument (v) is examined in detail below. I conclude that it cannot serve as the basis of a discriminatory bloc in Asia. Argument (vi) has at least two flaws. First, it assumes that when tariffs are very low, discriminatory liberalization is a welfare-improving proposition. We saw even within the restrictive case depicted in Figure 3.1 that the possibility of a gain from discriminatory liberalization declines sharply if the level of initial tariffs is low. In general, ruling out the optimum-tariff argument and assuming that the union is small, discriminatory liberalization is welfare worsening. Second, due to lobbying pressures, removal of tariffs on the union partner can lead to an increase in

---

[99] The second condition is not fulfilled by the North American Free Trade Agreement (NAFTA) because the initial protection in Mexico is much higher than in the United States and canada. As a result, Mexico receives a much lower margin of preference than it receives. This means a deterioration of Mexico's intra-union terms of trade.

tariffs on nonmembers. This was illustrated recently by the Mexican experience. In the wake of the macroeconomic crisis, because Mexico was unable to raise tariffs against the United States, she raised tariffs on 502 products on outside countries from 20% or less to as much as 35%. If Mexico's hands had not been tied against the United States, the required tariff increase would have been much smaller. Argument (vii) assumes once again that harmonization of domestic policies is desirable. A strong case can be made that optimum domestic policies for countries with different per-capita income levels are likely to be quite different and that harmonization under such circumstances is likely to be harmful, not beneficial.[100] Argument (viii) was used widely to support NAFTA from Mexico's viewpoint. A critique of this argument requires more space than is available here and the reader is referred to Bhagwati (1995), Panagariya (1996a) and Bhagwati and Panagariya (1996b) for a detailed discussion. Here it suffices to note that if the country is serious about its trade reform, it can do so credibly by binding its tariff with the WTO.

The last argument, (ix), has some validity but its significance is greatly exaggerated. There are innumerable examples of former enemies living in peace in the absence of a regional arrangement. During the last 50 years, Japan has lived in peace with China, Korea and other Asian neighbors without a regional arrangement. We give much credit to the EC for keeping peace between Germany and France. But in the Second World War, Germany also fought against Austria, Czechoslovakia, Hungary and Poland and has lived in peace with these latter since 1945. With U.S. troops stationed in both Japan and Germany, it is inconceivable that these countries could have gone to a war against their former enemies even if there had been no EC. And we cannot rule out the possibility that the GATT process would have led to the (nondiscriminatory) integration of the EC countries independently of the EC. Recall that till the beginning of the Tokyo Round, there were only six countries in the EC/EU. But this did not hamper the integration of the non-EC countries into the world economy and with each other.

In the end, unless regional arrangements are designed to enhance and exploit the member countries' monopoly power, one must seek the explanation for their existence in their underlying political economy. Attraction to regionalism today is not unlike the attraction to import-

---

[100.] For example, it is easy to show in a reasonable model that the optimal level of pollution-abatement policy for China is lower than that for Japan.

substitution policies in developing countries in the 1950s through 1970s. Like import-substitution policies in those days, regionalism is being embraced today despite its inferiority to alternative policies.

3.3 Should East Asia Go Regional?

Having discussed different aspects of regionalism, we are now in a position to confront directly the central question of this chapter: Should East Asia go regional? Not surprisingly, I will argue in this section that both economics and politics are against a discriminatory bloc in East Asia. Historically, East Asia has benefited greatly from an open world trading system. The region's future interests will continue to be served best by a strategy, which ensure an open world trading system.

In the following, I evaluate the role of regionalism at three levels. First, I examine closely the only serious attempts at preferential trading, the ASEAN which has recently announced plans to form the ASEAN Free Trade Area (AFTA). I suggest that the costs of such sub-regional schemes far outweigh their expected benefits. Second, I evaluate the case for a formal East Asian bloc along the lines of the EC or North America and conclude that though the *threat* of such a bloc may serve some purpose, its actual execution is a highly risky proposition. Finally, I evaluate the case for *simultaneous*, MFN style, nondiscriminatory liberalization on a *region-wide* basis. I argue that a case for such a regional approach is at best weak.[101]

3.3.1 Sub-Regional Groupings? No

I divide the discussion in this sub-section into three parts. Sections 3.3.1.1 and 3.3.1.2 *describe* the evolution of ASEAN in trade area and plans for the AFTA, respectively. Section3.3.1.3 evaluates the case for discriminatory liberalization in the sub-region.

[101.] Lee and Woodall (1995) offer an analysis of static welfare effects of some of these possibilities using a computable general equilibrium model.

3.3.1.1 ASEAN: The Disappointing Past[102]

Major developments in ASEAN are associated with four Summits attended by the heads of states of the member nations. The First Summit, held in August 1967, created the association through the ASEAN Declaration. The Second Summit produced the ASEAN Concord of February 24, 1976 which paved the way for economic cooperation among member nations. The Third Summit attempted to strengthen the cooperation through Manila Declaration of December 15, 1987. Finally, the Fourth Summit concluded with the Singapore Declaration of January 28, 1992, which announced plans for an ASEAN Free Trade Area (AFTA). In-between, numerous ministerial meetings have taken place to give shape to the broad intentions in the declarations signed at the summits.

Areas of economic cooperation in ASEAN are wide ranging. They include trade, industry, energy, tourism, forestry, minerals, food and agriculture, and finance. In the following, I will focus primarily on three programs which fall in areas of trade and industry and are designed to promote preferential trade and investment within the region. These are, (i) Preferential Trading Arrangements (PTA) introduced in 1977; (ii) ASEAN Industrial Joint Ventures (AIJVS); and (iii) ASEAN Industrial Complementation (AIC) schemes.

(i) Preferential Trading Arrangements (PTA). The PTA provides for tariff preferences, referred to as the margin of preference, for intra-ASEAN trade.[103] Till the announcement of AFTA, the rules of origin required that the ASEAN content of a product be 50% or more to qualify for tariff preference. On a case by case basis, this limit could be reduced to 35%. Initially, items for tariff preferences were negotiated on a product by product basis. In 1980, an across the board minimum margin of preference was introduced for imports above a certain value but, because countries were allowed to have exclusion lists, the provision had little effect.

In 1987, preferences actually granted under the PTA were minimal. Based on the 50% (or 35% if agreeable) ASEAN content requirement, there

---

[102.] For details on ASEAN until 1987, see Sopiee, See and Jin (1987). For more recent developments, see Pangestu, Soesastro and Ahmed (1992) and Ariff and Tan (1992). In the following, I draw freely on Pangestu et al.

[103.] The PTA was introduced initially thorough the Agreement on ASEAN Preferential Trading Arrangements (APTA) signed in Manila on February 24, 1977 and strengthened later in the Protocol on Improvements on Extension of Tariff Preferences under the ASEAN Preferential Trading Arrangements, signed in Manila on December 15, 1987.

were 12,783 items on the PTA list. Out of these eligible items, only 337 or 2.6% items were actually granted tariff preferences. Furthermore, only 19% of the total value of imports of these items enjoyed the preferential tariff.

At the Manila Summit in 1987, the member countries adopted changes aimed at strengthening tariff preferences. The countries agreed to shorten the exclusion list to 10% of the eligible items on the PTA list by 1992 (1994 in the case of Indonesia and Philippines). They agreed to reduce the value of imports on the exclusion list to 50% or less of intra-ASEAN trade by the same date. There was also an agreement to freeze the level of nontariff barriers and to negotiate reductions in them.

Systematic data on the progress towards achieving these goals is not available. But from what is available, progress appears to have been less than sparkling. Thus, the share of Indonesia's exports to ASEAN, which benefited from tariff preferences, rose from 1.4% in 1987 to 3.5% in 1989. Similarly, Indonesia's imports entering under preferential tariffs as a proportion of its total imports from other ASEAN countries rose from 1.2% in 1987 to 1.6% in 1989.

(ii) ASEAN Industrial Joint Ventures. Introduced in 1983, the AIJV program is aimed at promoting intra-ASEAN investment among private investors. The main incentive is a tariff preference. The countries participating in an AIJV project charge only 10% of their prevailing tariff (i.e., give a 90% margin of preference) on goods produced by and imported from the latter. There have to be at least two ASEAN countries participating in the project. Foreign participation in equity is allowed but ASEAN participants must own at least 40% of the equity.

To receive the tariff preference, the product must be first included in the list of AIJV products. The process of getting a new product included in the list is cumbersome. To-date, only 26 products have been granted the AIJV status. These include automotive components and parts, mechanical power rack and steering systems, chemicals, enamel, food products, etc.

It is not clear how much *extra* investment has been generated by this scheme. There is only one AIJV having equity participation by all ASEAN countries. Most AIJVs have foreign equity participation. Projects under the scheme are concentrated largely in Malaysia and Thailand. In some cases, AIJVs have experienced difficulties in getting tariff preferences from participating countries. Sometimes, participating countries want a quid pro quo under which they ask the project to import goods from them.

(iii) ASEAN Industrial Complementation (AIC) Scheme. The AIC scheme was introduced in 1981 with the objective of dividing different production stages of an industry among ASEAN countries. The idea was to avoid duplication and take advantage of scale economies. The first AIC scheme, involving automotive parts and components, was a failure due to differences in brands and types of vehicles among the ASEAN countries. Intra-ASEAN trade under the scheme remained minimal.

Recognizing the brand incompatibility problem in the first scheme, The second AIC scheme was based on Brand to Brand Complementation (BBC) in the automotive sector. The scheme lets the private sector determine the division of production across member countries. Products of the BBC firms automatically receive a 50% tariff preference provided they satisfy the PTA's rules of origin. In 1991, the BBC was extended to non-automotive products.

Brunei, Indonesia and Singapore chose to stay out of the BBC scheme. Brunei and Singapore do not have an automotive industry while Indonesia wanted to protect its own automotive industry. To-date progress under the BBC scheme has consisted of approval of eight packages involving Mitsubishi, Volvo, Mercedes Benz, Nissan, Toyota, DAF group from Belgium, and Renault.

3.3.1.2 AFTA: Time for Serious Business?

Negotiations for the NAFTA and for a Single European Market in early 1990s swung the ASEAN members into action. At the Fourth ASEAN Summit in Singapore, on January 28, 1992, the member nations signed a framework agreement to establish and participate in the ASEAN Free Trade Area within 15 years, i.e., by the year 2007. Though the "framework" agreement is less binding than a treaty, member nations expect it to serve as an instrument of speeding up the integration process in the region.

The key vehicle for implementation of the AFTA is the Common Effective Preferential Tariff (CEPT) which will be applied to goods originating from ASEAN member States. The difference between the CEPT and PTA is that the former is slightly more encompassing. Only the nominating country grants the margin of preference under the PTA whereas all members grant that under the CEPT. The ASEAN content for qualifying for the CEPT is 40%, lower than the PTA's 50%.

The AFTA covers all manufactured products, including capital goods, processed agricultural products and those products falling outside the definition of agricultural products, in the CEPT scheme. Products for the

CEPT scheme are identified on a HS 6-digit sectoral level. Exceptions at the HS 8/9-digit level are permitted. The Third AFTA Council, held on December 11, 1992, identified a total of 38,680 items for inclusion in the CEPT. These items represent an average of 88% of the total tariff lines of the ASEAN member states. The coverage ranges from 80% to 98% among the six member countries. A total of 3,321 items have been identified for exclusion on a temporary basis. These items are to be reviewed at the end of eight years.

The Third AFTA Council also drew detailed schedules of reductions in CEPTs for all member countries. The Framework Agreement had identified 15 products as *Fast Track* products for a more speedy liberalization.[104] For these products, tariffs above 20% are to be reduced to 0-5% by January 1, 2003 while those at or below 20% are to be reduced to 0-5% by January 1, 2000. The remaining products are on the *Normal Track*. Products in this category with tariff rates 20% or less are to be reduced to 0-5% by January 2003 while those with tariff rates above 20% are to be first reduced to 20% by 2003 and then to 0-5% by 2007. According to the schedules drawn by the Third AFTA Council, except Malaysia, no member plans any tariff reductions in the first two years of AFTA and even reductions planned by Malaysia are very small.

The AFTA agreement also calls for a removal of quantitative restrictions on products as soon as they are subject to the CEPT. It also provides for the elimination of other non-tariff barriers over a period of five years after the product is brought under the CEPT. This provision is stronger than the PTA which allowed members to maintain their quantitative restrictions.

3.3.1.3 Evaluating AFTA: A Wrong Turn

The sudden upsurge in FTAs around the world notwithstanding, on balance, the AFTA is likely to contribute only marginally to prosperity in the region. Indeed, the net effect of it may well be negative. As a forum for promoting political and cultural harmony and as an instrument of encouraging cooperation on projects of regional interest, the ASEAN has served the member countries well. But the preferential trading and investment promoted by the

---

[104.] These products include vegetable oils, cement, chemicals, pharmaceutical, plastics, rubber products, leather products, pulp, textiles, ceramic and glass products, gems and jewelry, copper cathodes, electronics, and wooden and rattan furniture.

ASEAN and planned by the AFTA are likely to be counterproductive. Several points may be noted.

(i) Small Internal Markets. The case against the AFTA lies primarily in the small size of the regional market. Because Singapore already has complete, nondiscriminatory free trade, the AFTA can, by definition, involve no greater access to its market than what exists currently. Therefore, the gains from AFTA, if any, must come from integration of the remaining five countries' markets. But markets in these countries are quite small in relation to the world. The share of ASEAN 4 (the ASEAN exclusive of Singapore and Brunei) in the world GDP has declined from a low 1.5% in 1980 to 1.3% in 1990. The share in the world exports is bigger—2.4% in 1990—but not big by any stretch of imagination. If we include Singapore in our calculations, the 1990 shares of the ASEAN in the world GDP and exports, respectively, rise to 1.43% and 3.87%. These ratios are still quite small so that the possibility that the most efficient producers are located outside the region is high.

(ii) Low Levels of Intra-Regional Trade. An analysis of intra-regional trade flows tells us a similar story.[105] Tables 3.1 and 3.2, respectively, show destinations of exports and origins of imports of the ASEAN countries. Because Singapore is already a free-trading country, exports to that country are shown separately from the remaining ASEAN countries. Though intra-ASEAN trade has gone up between 1990 and 1995, it, nevertheless, remains small in relation to extra-ASEAN-4 trade. Given the lows share of ASEAN-4 countries in the world GDP, this should be hardly surprising.

The ASEAN-4 countries, taken as a whole, sent 4.2% of their exports to each other in 1990 and 5.6% in 1995. On the import side, these figures are 3.9% in 1990 and 5.4% in 1995. The rise in the share is largely due to the higher growth in income in these countries relative to that in the rest of the world. The redirection of trade has taken place for all ASEAN members. Remarkably, exports by ASEAN-4 countries to Singapore were more than twice of those to each other in both 1990 and 1995.

---

[105] As Bhagwati and Panagariya (1996b) have shown, the extent of trade creation and trade diversion cannot be inferred from intra-regional trade. The argument here is twofold. First, with a very large number of potential suppliers left outside the union, the probability of trade diversion is large. Second, a focus on a relatively small market detracts sellers from aiming the much larger world market.

Table 3.1: Direction of Exports: ASEAN-5 (as percentage of world exports)

Country	Year	ASEAN-4	Singapore	NIEs[a]	Japan	East Asia	EC-12	N. Africa	Other
ASEAN-4	1980	3.2	11.8	5.3	34.6	55.6	13.6	19.2	11.5
	1985	4.50	11.90	8.1	30.8	56.7	12.0	20.6	10.7
	1990[1]	4.10	12.20	9.7	24.7	52.8	16.0	20.1	11.1
	1990[2]	4.20	12.30	9.6	24.3	52.5	16.1	20.3	11.2
	1995[2]	5.60	13.50	11.2	17.9	51.1	14.7	21.0	13.1
Indonesia	1980	1.30	11.30	3.7	49.3	65.5	6.5	19.8	8.1
	1985	1.90	8.70	7.3	46.2	64.7	6.2	22.0	7.1
	1990	2.40	7.10	10.9	42.7	66.4	11.9	13.9	7.9
	1990[2]	2.30	7.40	11.0	42.5	66.6	11.8	13.6	8.0
	1995[2]	5.00	4.90	14.2	28.4	56.6	15.7	16.8	10.9

Country	Year								
Malaysia	1980	3.20	19.10	5.7	22.8	52.5	17.6	16.9	13.0
	1985	6.30	19.50	9.6	23.8	60.2	14.6	13.7	11.5
	1990	6.00	22.80	10.0	15.8	56.6	14.9	17.9	10.5
	1990²	6.00	23.00	10.0	15.3	564.0	15.0	17.7	11.0
	1995²	6.20	20.30	11.3	12.7	53.1	13.8	21.5	11.6
Thailand	1980	8.50	7.40	7.1	15.3	40.1	26.4	13.2	20.2
	1985	6.40	7.70	7.5	13.4	38.8	19.2	21.1	20.9
	1990	3.90	7.30	7.8	17.2	37.3	21.6	24.5	16.6
	1990²	3.90	7.40	7.7	17.2	37.3	21.6	24.0	17.1
	1995²	4.90	14.00	9.0	16.7	47.5	14.5	18.9	19.2
Singapore	1980	20.80	(15.0)	10.9	8.1	41.3	12.8	13.6	32.3
	1985	20.60	(15.5)	9.3	9.4	40.7	10.6	22.0	26.7
	1990	20.90	(13.0)	13.6	8.7	44.8	14.4	22.3	18.5
	1990²	22.80	(12.7)	12.0	8.5	44.8	14.1	21.6	19.5
	1995²	27.70	(18.9)	15.2	7.7	52.8	12.8	18.5	15.9
Philippines	1980	4.60	1.90	8.5	26.5	42.2	17.6	29.1	11.2
	1985	6.00	5.30	7.5	19.0	39.5	15.8	37.5	7.2
	1988	3.70	2.90	9.9	20.3	37.7	17.7	37.4	7.1
	1990²	4.20	2.90	9.4	19.8	37.1	18.0	39.4	5.5
	1995²	7.30	5.20	10.7	16.0	40.4	17.1	37.1	5.5

a: NIEs stands for Newly Industrialized Economies excluding Singapore
1: Data for the Philippines, used in this row relate to 1988. 2: Direction of Trade Statistics (IMF).
Source: United Nations Commodity Trade Data (except as noted in note #2).

Table 3.2: Direction of Imports: ASEAN-5 (as percentage of world imports)

Country	Year	Trading Partner							
		ASEAN-4	Singapore	NIEs[a]	Japan	East Asia	EC-12	N. Africa	Other
ASEAN-4	1980	6.00	7.40	6.10	24.10	445	13.40	17.80	24.30
	1985	3.00	9.70	6.80	23.40	48.70	14.40	17.60	19.30
	1990[1]	3.90	8.90	10.90	26.20	52.70	14.90	15.40	16.90
	1990[2]	3.90	8.80	10.90	25.70	51.80	15.20	15.20	17.80
	1995[2]	5.40	7.80	11.90	27.10	55.00	14.10	14.30	16.60
Indonesia	1980	3.80	8.60	7.40	31.50	53.20	13.60	14.00	19.20
	1985	1.20	8.20	5.30	25.80	42.90	17.6	18.80	20.70
	1990	2.60	5.80	11.90	24.30	47.60	18.60	13.70	20.10
	1990[2]	2.50	5.80	11.90	24.80	48.00	18.80	13.30	21.80
	1995[2]	4.80	5.90	15.50	26.20	56.10	17.70	10.10	16.10
Malaysia	1980	4.70	11.70	5.50	23.00	47.20	15.70	16.10	21.00
	1985	6.60	15.80	6.60	23.20	54.20	14.10	16.40	15.20
	1990	4.20	14.60	10.40	25.30	56.50	13.20	18.50	11.70
	1990[2]	4.00	14.80	100	24.20	54.90	14.70	17.90	12.40
	1995[2]	4.80	12.40	11.30	27.30	58.10	13.90	16.90	11.20
Philippines	1980	4.50	1.60	6.50	19.90	35.10	10.70	24.70	29.50
	1985	11.50	2.6	11.1	14.40	45.00	8.50	26.00	20.50
	1988	4.70	4.00	14.50	17.40	43.70	12.60	22.30	21.30
	1990[2]	4.90	3.90	14.70	18.40	43.40	11.2	21.00	24.50
	1995[2]	6.00	4.00	15.70	22.40	50.60	10.20	19.30	19.80

Thailand								
1980	3.10	6.30	5.10	20.70	39.50	13.00	18.20	29.30
1985	7.20	7.50	6.30	26.50	49.90	14.80	12.90	22.40
1990	4.30	7.50	9.60	30.60	55.30	14.50	12.20	18.00
1990[2]	4.30	7.40	9.50	30.40	54.90	14.80	11.90	18.40
1995[2]	6.10	5.60	9.00	29.20	52.70	13.70	12.10	21.40
Singapore								
1980	16.20	(13.9)	5.60	17.80	42.20	11.00	14.70	32.10
1985	17.20	(14.4)	6.80	17.00	49.60	11.30	15.60	23.50
1990	16.90	(13.7)	10.70	20.10	51.20	12.90	16.70	19.30
1990[2]	19.30	(13.1)	9.90	19.50	52.10	12.40	16.20	19.30
1995[2]	23.60	(15.1)	11.40	20.60	58.80	11.90	15.10	14.30

a: NIEs stands for Newly Industrialized Economies excluding Singapore.

1: Figures for the Philippines, used to calculate 1990 ASEAN-4 share, relate to 1988.

2: Direction of Trade Statistics (IMF) have been used to calculate the shares in this row.

Source: United Nations Commodity Trade Data (except as noted in note #2)

(iii) Higher levels of Protection in Bigger Countries. Within the ASEAN 4, Indonesia and Thailand together accounted for approximately 70% of the region's GDP and 56% of its imports from anywhere in 1990. These are also the countries which are most protected within the region. Gains from discriminatory liberalization, if any, must come primarily from liberalization in these countries. But they did not plan to offer any preference in the first two years of the AFTA. Therefore, the impact of the AFTA—positive or negative—in the first two years will be minimal. Indeed, in the case of Indonesia, nondiscriminatory liberalization through unilateral reforms—a superior strategy from its viewpoint—has outpaced preferential liberalization by a long shot.

Closely related to this point is the issue of distribution of gains from preferential liberalization when such liberalization is undertaken. It stands to reason that the arrangement will benefit Malaysia and Singapore at the expense of other countries. This is because Malaysia and Singapore have either no or low tariffs to begin with. Therefore, the potential for discriminatory liberalization by them is minimal. Much of the liberalization will have to come from the more protected Indonesia, Philippines, and Thailand. This means that the terms of trade for Malaysia and Singapore will improve. The tariff revenue collected on goods exported by these countries to Indonesia, Philippines and Thailand will disappear to the extent of liberalization and become a part of the former's profits on export. There will not be a corresponding gain for Indonesia, Philippines and Thailand on goods exported to Singapore and Malaysia because the latter have relatively few high tariffs to liberalize.

These lopsided distributional effects may well explain why the progress on *preferential* liberalization in the region has been outstripped by unilateral, nondiscriminatory liberalization. For example, while Indonesia and Philippines have lowered trade barriers substantially during the 1980s as a part of their trade reform policies, they have been generally reluctant to offer tariff preferences under the PTA. In July 1992, Indonesia announced a list of 250 tariff cuts but 90% of these were on different types of batik cloth produced in Indonesia only. The distributional conflict is illustrated well by a remark made by the former foreign minister of Indonesia, Dr. M. Kusumaatmadja, at a meeting in 1992 to celebrate the 25th anniversary of the ASEAN:[106]

[106.] See *Financial Times*, January 26, 1993.

"Singapore and Malaysia are always telling us to lower tariffs and duties and let their goods into the country. But in return, how about the free movement of labor? We will take your goods if you will take our surplus labor supply. When they hear this and think about all those Indonesians coming to work in their countries, then they say, `wait a minute, may be it's not such a good idea'."

In the past, to lengthen their lists, member countries have gone so far as to include snow ploughs among items to receive preferential tariffs! There are also instances of tariff preferences on zero-tariff goods. Most recently, the liberalization package announced by Indonesia lowers trade barriers on an MFN basis and does not offer any significant preferences to AFTA members.

Assuming net benefits from preferential liberalization, in principle, gainers could compensate the losers. But in practice, compensation schemes tend to be distortionary and the AFTA has been wise to stay away from them. Compensation schemes adopted by regional arrangements in Africa proved highly distortionary.[107] In NAFTA, the United States has offered no compensation to Mexico that, on conventional criteria, is likely to lose from the arrangement.[108] Only the EC has been successful in affecting large transfers to its poorer partners as a part of the Southern Enlargement. This has been largely due to a very strong commitment on the part of the original members to unify Europe into a single market.

3.3.2 An East Asian Trading Bloc? No.

There are two main issues that must be addressed in considering the case for a bloc consisting of all major players in East Asia: (i) Is the bloc economically desirable; and (ii) Is the bloc feasible? I will argue below that the answer to the first question is at best uncertain while that to the second one is negative.

[107.] For example, see Foroutan (1993).

[108.] To the extent that Mexico's tariffs are far higher than those in the United States, the NAFTA is likely to worsen its terms of trade. On top of that, Mexico must effectively raise its environmental and labor standards.

3.3.2.1 Is a Trading Bloc Economically Desirable?

The economic desirability of an East Asian bloc is difficult to assess. This is because the effects of such a bloc go well beyond simple efficiency effects discussed in Section 3.2. The region accounts for approximately one fifth of the world's GDP and exports. Any major actions in the area of international trade at the region wide level which discriminate against the rest of the world will lead to repercussions in and perhaps retaliation from the rest of the world. Without being able to predict those reactions, it is difficult to estimate the costs and benefits of forming a region wide bloc.

The paramount objective of East Asia's regional trade policy has to be to ensure an open world trading system. Despite some redirection of trade towards itself in recent years, East Asia trades more than half its exports and imports with the rest of the world (see Tables 3.3 and 3.4).[109] There is little doubt that the phenomenal growth of East Asia during the past three decades has been facilitated greatly by relatively open world markets. Almost without exception, studies of the NIEs draw a direct connection between growth in exports and that in the GDP. More recently, Indonesia, Malaysia, Thailand and China have been repeating the experience of the NIEs.

This suggests that the case for an East Asian bloc should be evaluated primarily, not on the basis of static gains including those arising from an improvement in the terms of trade, but in terms of its impact on the world trading system. If a regional approach is to be pursued, it should help keep the world markets open. There are two arguments in favor of a discriminatory regional bloc, which deserve a close scrutiny.

First, an East Asian bloc may serve as a deterrent to the formation of closed trading blocs around the world. According to this argument, the world is already dividing into blocs. To ensure that the blocs do not become overly protective of their own markets and limit East Asia's access to them, East Asia should be united and be in a position to retaliate. Unilateral actions such as those taken by the United States under its Super 301 provisions will also be harder to take if East Asia is united.

[109.] Data on the extent of intra-regional trade vary according to the source and definition of the region. My tables rely primarily on the United Nations Commodity Trade data which do not report data for China for the early part of 1980s. Therefore, in Tables 3.3 and 3.4, East Asia does not include China. According to Lee and Woodall (1998), the proportion of total trade of East Asian, where east Asia includes China, was 30.7% in 1970 and had grown to 46.5% in 1993. Based on these data, the redirection of trade has been considerably more than suggested by the data in the text.

Second, frustration with slow progress of the Uruguay Round led some proponents of the regional approach to argue that the free-rider problem associated with the multilateral process makes the multilateral approach unworkable. In the multilateral setting, trade concessions negotiated by large, developed countries become automatically available to smaller countries through the MFN clause of the GATT. Negotiations with the latter are difficult because their numbers are large and each of them is individually too small to make such negotiations worthwhile. Therefore, if the world can be first divided into a small number of blocs, it will be easier to organize future GATT/WTO negotiations.[110] Regional blocs could free up trade internally while the GATT process, once freed from the free-rider problem, can serve to bring down the barriers between blocs rapidly and with greater certainty.

Proponents of the argument suggest that one reason why the past GATT rounds were so successful is that the United States could deal with the EC as a single unit. According to this view, if East Asia is turned into a bloc and the Americas into another, they together with the EU can move the world towards free trade faster. Both of these arguments have some merit but are highly contentious. Regarding the first argument, critics note that countries organized into a bloc enjoy more market power than they do individually. Therefore, in principle, there is nothing to prevent blocs from *raising* rather than lowering trade barriers. The deterrence role of blocs is good only so long as the threat is not carried out. Once a threat is carried out and trade war breaks out, retaliatory actions are likely to be larger with than without blocs.

As for the second argument, critics note that the Uruguay Round has been successfully concluded and the small and developing countries have given major concessions through accepting the Trade-Related Intellectual Property Rights (TRIPs) Agreement of the Uruguay Round Agreement. Equally impotant, small numbers do not necessarily mean faster progress.[111] The EC process began in 1957 and is still working towards a "Single Market". In the meantime, the EC's nontariff barriers have proliferated: according to Winters (1993), the coverage of these trade restrictions has expanded five fold from 1966 to 1986. More importantly, this argument had some force at a time when the Uruguay Round negotiations were faltering.

---

[110]. The argument can be found in Summers (1991) and Krugman (1993).

[111]. For example see Bhagwati (1993) and Winters (1993). A summary of the debate can be found in Melo and Panagariya (1992).

Table 3.3: Direction of Exports (as percentage of world exports)

Country	Year	NIEs	ASEAN-4	China[a]	Japan	East Asia	EC-12	NA	Other
NIEs	1980	9.00	8.90	0.90	10.30	29.10	17.20	28.30	25.30
	1985	8.50	7.00	2.30	10.70	28.50	11.40	40.70	19.50
	1990	13.00	9.30	3.20	12.70	38.20	15.50	31.10	15.20
	1990[b]	12.40	8.70	8.00	11.30	40.40	14.50	29.30	15.80
	1995[b]	16.00	11.10	13.20	9.40	49.70	12.80	22.30	15.10
Hong Kong	1980	4.20	2.80	2.40	3.40	12.80	29.50	36.00	21.70
	1985	3.00	2.00	11.70	3.40	20.10	18.40	47.90	13.50
	1990	6.80	3.20	24.00	5.30	36.30	20.40	32.10	11.20
	1990[b]	9.70	4.00	24.80	5.70	44.20	14.30	26.30	15.20
	1995[b]	7.10	3.60	33.30	6.10	50.20	13.90	23.60	12.40
Korea	1980	7.40	4.90	0.0 (4.7)	17.30	29.60	15.60	28.60	26.20
	1985	7.40	3.40	0.0 (5.2)	15.00	25.80	10.70	39.80	23.70
	1990	10.40	5.00	0.0 (5.8)	19.40	34.80	13.70	33.50	18.10
	1990[b]	10.50	5.00	0.4 (5.8)	19.40	35.30	13.60	33.40	17.60
	1995[b]	16.90	7.80	7.3 (8.5)	13.60	45.70	11.60	21.50	21.10
Singapore	1980	10.90	20.80	1.60	8.10	41.30	12.80	13.60	32.30
	1985	9.30	20.60	1.50	9.40	40.70	10.60	22.00	26.70
	1990	13.60	20.90	1.50	8.70	44.80	14.40	22.30	18.50
	1990[b]	12.00	22.80	1.50	8.50	44.80	14.10	21.70	19.30
	1995[b]	15.20	27.70	2.30	7.70	52.80	12.80	18.60	15.80
Taiwan	1980	12.00	5.10	0.0 (7.9)	11.00	28.10	14.60	37.00	20.30
	1985	12.00	3.10	0.0 (8.3)	11.30	26.40	8.80	51.60	13.10
	1990	17.80	6.80	0.0 (12.8)	12.40	37.10	16.00	35.30	11.70
	1990[b]	17.80	6.80	0.1 (12.7)	12.40	37.10	16.10	35.10	11.70
	1995[b]	29.60	8.50	0.3 (23.4)	11.80	50.30	12.60	25.30	11.90
China	1980	N.A.	N.A.	N.A.	N.A.	N.A.	N.A.	N.A.	N.A.
	1984	31.50	3.00	(26.5)	20.60	55.10	9.00	10.30	25.60
	1990	48.60	2.80	(42.9)	14.50	65.90	9.10	9.20	15.80
	1990[b]	47.30	2.60	(43.2)	14.60	64.50	9.50	9.30	16.60
	1995[b]	32.30	3.00	(24.2)	19.10	54.40	12.40	17.70	15.50

Country	Year	NIEs	ASEAN-4	China[a]	Japan	East Asia	EC-12	NA	Other
					Trading Partner				
Japan	1980	14.80	7.00	3.90	...	25.70	13.90	27.30	33.10
	1985	12.80	4.20	7.10	...	24.10	12.00	40.70	23.30
	1990	19.70	7.70	2.10	...	29.60	18.80	348	16.80
	1990[b]	19.70	7.70	2.10	...	29.60	18.80	34.80	16.80
	1995[b]	25.10	12.10	5.00	...	42.10	14.90	28.90	14.10

Notes:
a: Figures in parentheses are exports to Hong Kong.
b: Direction of Trade Statistics (IMF).
Source: United Nations Commodity Trade Statistics (except as noted in b).

But that has changed with a successful completion of the Round and creation of the WTO.

3.3.2.2 Is a Trading Bloc Feasible?

Though the economic desirability of a trading bloc in East Asia is difficult to assess, its feasibility—or lack thereof—is more predictable. Both internal circumstances of the region and possible retaliatory actions from outside—particularly the United States—make the formation of an East Asian free trade area an unlikely event.

Internally, there are at least three inter-related factors at work against a region wide FTA. First, historically, the major players in the region have been political rivals. Though time, trade, and intra-regional investments have gone a long way towards bringing the former enemies closer, they still do not appear ready to form a free trade area with one another. In this respect, the situation in East Asia is fundamentally different than in Western Europe after the Second World War. Then, backed by the United States, for economic as well as geopolitical reasons, Europeans were able to move into treaties establishing first the European Coal and Steel Community and later the European Community. Today, there are no similar pressures on Japan. Nor are countries such as Korea and China expressing eagerness to form an FTA with Japan.

Table 3.4: Direction of Imports (as percentage of world imports)

Country	Year	NIEs	ASEAN-4	China[a]	Japan	East Asia	EC-12	NA	Other
NIEs	1980	6.90	8.20	5.70	23.40	44.20	9.80	18.90	27.10
	1985	8.30	8.10	9.20	22.70	48.30	10.70	18.20	22.80
	1990	10.60	7.40	12.20	22.60	52.80	11.70	18.60	16.90
	1990[b]	10.30	8.00	12.30	22.20	52.80	12.20	18.30	16.60
	1995[b]	11.70	9.60	15.10	21.10	57.50	11.90	16.40	14.30
Hong Kong	1980	15.80	3.90	20.00	23.30	63.00	12.50	12.80	11.70
	1985	17.50	2.80	25.50	23.10	68.80	11.60	9.90	9.70
	1990	17.50	3.60	36.80	16.10	74.00	9.80	8'.6	7.70
	1990[b]	17.50	3.60	36.80	16.10	74.00	10.10	8.60	7.40
	1995[b]	18.80	4.60	36.20	14.80	74.50	I0.1	8.50	6.90
Korea	1980	2.60	5.90	0.0 (0.4)	26.20	34.70	7.30	23.90	34.10
	1985	3.50	7.10	0.0 (1.6)	24.20	34.80	9.80	23.30	32.10
	1990	4.30	5.60	0.0 (0.9)	26.70	36.60	12.10	26.80	24.50
	1990[b]	4.20	5.60	0.6 (0.9)	26.60	37.10	12.00	26.70	24.20
	1995[b]	4.10	5.50	5.5 (0.6)	24.10	39.20	12.10	24.60	24.10
Singapore	1980	5.60	16.20	2.60	17.80	42.20	11.00	14.70	32.10
	1985	6.80	17.20	8.60	17.00	49.60	11.30	15.60	23.50
	1990	10.70	16.90	3.40	20.10	51.20	12.90	16.70	19.30
	1990[b]	9.90	19.30	3.30	19.50	52.10	12.40	16.20	19.20
	1995[b]	11.40	23.60	3.20	20.60	58.80	11.90	15.20	14.10
Taiwan	1980	3.40	5.90	0.0 (1.3)	27.20	36.50	8.20	25.20	30.20
	1985	3.90	5.70	0.0 (1.6)	27.50	37.20	10.20	25.90	26.40
	1990	8.10	4.90	0.0 (2.3)	30.00	42.90	13.00	25.40	18.60
	1990[b]	7.60	4.70	0.6 (2.6)	29.10	42.00	15.40	24.70	17.90
	1995[b]	8.80	7.00	3.0 (1.8)	29.20	48.00	14.90	21.90	15.30
China	1980	N.A.	N.A.	N.A.	N.A.	N.A.	N.A.	N.A.	N.A.
	1984	11.50	2.60	(10.9)	31.30	45.40	12.70	19.10	22.80
	1990	33.60	3.90	(26.5)	14.20	51.80	15.00	15.20	18.00
	1990[b]	33.20	4.00	(27.0)	14.20	51.40	11.20	15.20	22.20
	1995[b]	28.10	4.50	(6.5)	22.00	54.60	14.40	14.10	16.90

Country	Year	NIEs	ASEAN-4	China[a]	Japan	East Asia	EC-12	NA	Other
						Trading Partner			
Japan	1980	5.30	14.10	3.10	...	22.40	5.80	21.50	50.30
	1985	7.70	13.10	5.10	...	25.90	6.90	25.50	41.70
	1990	11.20	10.50	5.20	...	26.90	15.00	27.10	31.10
	1990[b]	11.10	10.40	5.10	...	26.60	15.00	26.90	31.50
	1995[b]	12.30	11.40	10.70	...	34.40	13.20	26.30	26.20

a: Figures in parentheses are exports to Hong Kong.
b: Direction of Trade Statistics (IMF) have been used to calculate the shares in this row.

Source: United Nations Commodity Trade Statistics (unless otherwise indicated)

Second, the countries in East Asia have very different levels of protection and are at very different stages of development. This makes the distribution of gains from an FTA rather uneven. With discriminatory liberalization under an FTA, poorer countries which are also more highly protected are likely to lose or gain less than their relatively open and richer counterparts. This raises the specter of compensation that, as noted in the context of the ASEAN, is a barrier not easily overcome.

Third, the number of countries in the region is large which makes the task of far-reaching negotiations required for an FTA a daunting task. We saw earlier how difficult it has been for even six ASEAN countries to make progress towards the AFTA. It has taken the countries 25 years to reach the "framework agreement" and progress on serious preferential liberalization is still out of sight. In this background, it is not clear how disparate countries such as China, Japan, Korea and the members of ASEAN can be engaged in a dialogue, which will lead to a free trade area among them.

The external factors at work against an East Asian FTA are even more formidable. Because of perceptions that its markets are de facto closed to outsiders, Japan has been a persistent target of aggressive unilateralism by the United States during the last two decades. These actions have included voluntary export restraints, structural impediments initiative, and Super 301 threats. Smaller countries in the region such Korea and China have also been subject to Super 301 threats. Initiatives by these countries for a free trade area, which can potentially divert trade from the United States, are almost certain to be met with retaliation by the latter.

From the viewpoint of smaller nations, this external environment is quite different from that faced by Mexico in negotiating the NAFTA. Apart from the fact that, with the United States as the other negotiating party the threat of overt retaliation did not exist, Mexico was simply not very vulnerable to such actions. In 1990, Mexico exported 71% of its goods to North America and only 13% to Western Europe and 6% to East Asia. For the latter regions, imports from Mexico amounted to approximately a half percent of their total imports.

The situation is dramatically different for countries such as China and Korea. They not only face an environment which is hostile to an FTA in East Asia but are also *individually* very vulnerable to actions against them by the United States. In 1990, Korea sold a quarter of its exports to the United States. China's direct exports were not as large but once reexports through Hong Kong are taken into account, it too sent a quarter of its goods to the United States. With such large concentration of exports in the United States, risks for Korea and China of an FTA which the United States opposes are immense. This, in turn, suggests that an East Asian FTA is not a feasible proposition in the near future.

3.3.3 Region-wide Nondiscriminatory Liberalization? Maybe.

Having argued that sub-regional grouping and trading blocs which promote discriminatory liberalization are not worth the effort required to create and sustain them, I now turn to the discussion of the so-called "open" regional approach centered around a GATT-style, MFN-based nondiscriminatory liberalization.[112] I argue that though this regionalism has certain advantages over discriminatory approaches, it, too, has serious limitations.

The key element distinguishing this approach from a regional bloc will be nondiscriminatory nature of liberalization. The countries in the region will come together at a common forum and, very much in the spirit of the

---

[112.] To my knowledge, a proposal to this effect has been made for the first time in a recent World Bank (1993) report. Petri (1992) offers a similar proposal but makes the United States, Australia and New Zealand a part of the overall scheme. Because intra-regional trade among these countries and East Asia is so intense, the economic case for this proposal can be hardly disputed. But the same factors, which make an open trading bloc a la Bhagwati and Cooper politically infeasible, also cast a serious doubt on the workability of this proposal.

various GATT rounds, negotiate reductions in trade barriers. Any concessions made by a country to another will be extended automatically to all WTO members. In the following, I offer a detailed discussion of the positive as well as negative side of this approach.

3.3.3.1 The Positive Case

(i) No Trade Diversion. Because tariff reductions are nondiscriminatory under this approach, by definition, there can be no trade diversion. In terms of our VCR example, if Indonesia lowers its tariffs on Japanese VCRs in return for a tariff concession from Japan, the same reduction is extended to Korea and all other suppliers of VCRs. The reduction in tariff then benefits Indonesia's consumers rather than Japanese VCR producers.

A lack of trade diversion takes away one major obstacle in the way of a discriminatory bloc: Countries with high initial tariffs need not feel that they will lose as a result of liberalization. Any gains from liberalization will accrue to consumers inside the country rather than the partner country. Problems mentioned earlier regarding compensation will simply not arise.

(ii) External Constraints. This regionalism will certainly face a much less serious challenge from the United States. Because the liberalization is nondiscriminatory, it will improve the U.S. access to East Asia's markets as well. Indeed, the negotiations could go a long way towards answering the U.S. complaints about a lack of openness of markets in East Asia in general, and Japan and China, in particular.

More importantly, liberalization at the regional level may help alleviate two major problems that provide fuel for aggressive unilateralism in the United States against Japan and other trading partners. First, to the extent that such liberalization is likely to shift the region's exports away from the United States and towards East Asia, some of the current competitive pressure on the U.S. industry may be relieved. At the least, a decline in Japan's share in the U.S. market and possibly a rise in the share of domestic producers there will weaken the lobbies' case for trade-policy actions against the former. Second, the possible shift in exports towards East Asia may alleviate trade deficits of the United States with Japan and China. Because the overall trade deficit is a macroeconomic phenomenon governed by investment-savings gap, this redirection may not help the total U.S. trade deficit. But it may help lower *bilateral* trade deficit. If so, nondiscriminatory liberalization will weaken considerably the case for unilateral actions by the United States.

(iii) Low Adjustment Costs. Because liberalization will take place simultaneously in all the major countries of the region, this approach will help minimize the costs of adjustment. In the GATT style, liberalization will be in areas of mutual interest. Therefore, countries will improve export prospects at the same time that they subject their import competing industries to competition from abroad. In contrast, if liberalization is unilateral or, worse still, in response to Super 301 type of threats from the United States, adjustment costs will be higher. In the spirit of the GATT rounds, it may also be possible to allow the liberalization process to be spread over a period of, say, 10 years. This will further smoothen the path of adjustment.

(iv) East Asia's Role in World Economic Affairs. In recent decades the United States has become what Jagdish Bhagwati calls a Diminished Giant. Simultaneously, East Asia, particularly Japan, has emerged as the major economic power in the world. Gradually, commensurate with their current economic weight and future potential, Japan and the Greater China region (including China, Hong Kong and Taiwan) must assume the leadership role in the world economic affairs. Japan has already emerged as a major donor country in the world. Within East Asia, it now enjoys the same central role as the United States in the Americas and Germany in the EC. It provided more than half of the official development assistance commitments to East Asia in 1992 against only 6% from the United States. More than 30% of the region's net direct foreign investment in 1990 came from Japan compared with 10% from the United States. Parallel with these developments in Japan, China is rapidly becoming a major engine of growth in Asia. According to a recent World Bank report, Greater China has become the world's `fourth growth pole' after Europe, North America and Japan. The report notes that imports into Greater China region are already two-thirds as much as Japan and will surpass the latter by the year 2002 if growth continues at the present rate.[113] Import liberalization by China in the years to come will further enhance that country's role in global economic affairs. Region wide liberalization could then serve as a stepping stone to the eventual leadership role for East Asia in general and Japan and China in particular.

[113.] See the article by Laurence Zuckerman in the *Wall Street Journal*, May 17, 1993.

3.3.3.2 The Negative Case

The discussion up to this point makes nondiscriminatory liberalization almost too good to be true. And it is. Though, as just described, there is much to be gained from this type of liberalization in the long run, the short to medium run economic effects are not favorable. This means that it will be difficult to mobilize support for implementation of the scheme. Let me elaborate.

The existing levels of tariffs, at least in Japan, are relatively low. This means that potential gains from lowering this most transparent barrier to trade in Japan are limited. Indeed matters are worse than the official tariff rates may reveal. Japan gives very extensive trade preferences under the GSP to its East Asian trading partners. For example, in the case of Korea, 88% of the Japanese tariff lines facing it are either zero or below the MFN level. For approximately two thirds of the tariff lines, the GSP gives Korea a duty free access. A similar pattern applies to other countries.[114] This means that if Japan lowers its tariffs in a nondiscriminatory fashion, developing East Asian countries will lose the tariff preferences they currently enjoy. This is most likely to be a losing proposition for them.

There does not appear to be a substantial scope for gains from a reduction in tariffs in other countries either. Because tariff levels across countries are highly variable, the scope for quid pro quo is limited. Thailand, Indonesia and arguably China have the highest levels of tariffs. At the other extreme, Singapore and Hong Kong have virtually no tariffs while Japan imposes very low tariffs on its East Asian partners. In-between we have Korea and the Philippines with tariffs generally below 20%. Given this cross-country structure of tariffs, it will be rather difficult to engineer a MFN style liberalization.

The picture with respect to nontariff barriers is similar. Identifiable nontariff barriers are limited. We do not have information on all countries but in the cases where it is available, these barriers are not extensive. Japan employs few formal nontariff barriers. Among the major developing East Asian countries, the coverage of such barriers is currently less than 10%. In terms of formal barriers, perhaps China is most protective. But in reality, China's imports have risen sharply in recent years suggesting that its import regime is freer than may be suggested by formal restrictions.

[114.] Singapore pays a positive MFN tariff in only 8% of the cases. At 15%, among the ASEAN countries, Indonesia has the largest share of tariff lines with positive MFN rates.

This discussion leads to the conclusion that the only significant trade liberalization in the region may come from lowering the so-called "informal" barriers to trade that Japan is often alleged to have. In order to bring to the negotiating table the countries with high formal trade barriers, only Japan can make attractive concessions. But the problem with "informal" barriers is that either they may not exist or they are invisible. It is simply not clear how countries can negotiates on these barriers.

It is possible that purely on the basis of inter-temporal balance of trade, Japan's imports in the coming years will rise faster than its exports.[115] Then it may be argued that Japan can use this opportunity to aggressively lead other East Asian countries towards liberalization. But once again, it is difficult to imagine other countries participating in a negotiation when import expansion in Japan is expected to happen through market forces in any case and there are no formal offers on the table for a reduction in trade barriers.

A final and perhaps the most important point is that even if we can somehow identify substantial trade barriers in Japan and other countries which can be negotiated away on a nondiscriminatory basis, the likely decline in the terms of trade of the region could be substantial. This is because more than 50% of the region's imports come from outside countries. In the case of Japan, this number is as large as 70%. Unilateral liberalization by the region as a whole must worsen the terms of trade. Moreover, the current level of protection being low, it likely that such a reduction in the terms of trade will be welfare worsening.

This same problem—referred to as a free-rider problem—has been faced by the major negotiating parties at the GATT rounds. The United States, EC and Japan feared that the benefits of liberalization by them on the MFN basis would spill over to nonparticipating—mostly developing—countries. But as Finger (1979) has shown, they were able to avoid this problem by limiting liberalization to those goods in which they themselves traded intensively. Goods in which developing countries had a comparative advantage—agricultural products, textiles, shoes and other labor intensive products—were not liberalized. Given that Japan imports 70% of its goods from countries outside East Asia, a major expansion of its imports cannot occur without liberalization of products coming from outside the region.

---

[115]. The argument here is that Japan will not keep accumulating dollars for ever. It must spend them some time.

3.4 APEC and Regionalism in Asia

By the end of 1993, APEC, which came into existence in 1989 as a low-key consultative body, began to emerge as the central institution for promoting liberalization of trade and investment at the regional level.[116] Because APEC consists of not only East Asian countries as members but also the United States, its evolution into a regional trading bloc is not ruled out by the arguments made in this chapter.

I have discussed the role of APEC in promoting regional integration in detail elsewhere (Panagariya 1996b) recently. Here it suffices to note a fundamental conflict between Asian members of APEC and the United States. The former are keen to undertake trade liberalization only on the Most Favored nation (MFN) basis while the latter insists on reciprocity. In particular, the United States is unwilling to extend its liberalization commitments within the APEC context to the rest of the world, especially the European Union, without reciprocal liberalization by the latter. Thus, while the Asian members advocate liberalization along the lines of Section 3.3.3, the United States prefers to follow the discriminatory route.

A key development in APEC's history took place at its 1994 annual meeting in Bogor, Indonesia. At that meeting, APEC members signed a (non-binding) agreement to achieve free trade in developed member countries by the year 2010 and in developing member countries by 2020. Because of the conflict between Asian and American approaches to liberalization, the future of this agreement remains in doubt, however. At the 1995 Osaka meeting, the United States stood firm and offered no import liberalization to make progress towards the 2010 goal. Some developing-country members from Asia, particularly China and Indonesia, offered limited tariff reductions but even these did not go beyond what was planned by the countries as a part of their own trade reform policies or promised under the Uruguay Round agreement. At the 1996 meeting to be held in the Philippines, in view of the elections in November, even APEC enthusiasts are not expecting any liberalization offers from the United States. It is also unlikely that Japan and Canada will make any significant offers. Therefore,

---

116. It was not until its 1992 meeting in Singapore, that APEC decided to establish a permanent secretariat. In 1993, in order to pressure the European Union into bringing the Uruguay Round to its logical conclusion, the United States upgraded the November 1993 meeting of APEC into a high-profile Leaders' Meeting. The subsequent APEC annual meetings have been accompanied by summits of heads of states of member nations.

once again, the momentum for liberalization will have to come from developing-country Asian members, Australia and New Zealand. For signs of more substantive progress, which inevitably requires active participation from the United States, we must await 1997.

3.5 Conclusions

On the whole, this chapter takes a pessimistic view of regionalism in East Asia. The pessimism follows, inter alia, from low or negative gains in the case of sub-regional groupings such as the AFTA, insurmountable external and internal barriers to effective integration in the case of an Asia wide discriminatory bloc, and adverse terms of trade effects in the case of concerted nondiscriminatory liberalization by the region.

This leaves the possibility of pursuing a regional approach to liberalization on an APEC-wide basis. In 1993, in order to pressure the European Union into bringing the Uruguay Round to a speedy conclusion, the United States upgraded the November 1993 meeting of APEC into a high-profile Leaders' Meeting. That and the subsequent APEC summit in Bogor, Indonesia have led to a great deal of optimism towards the regional approach in some quarters. Indeed, at the end of the Bogor summit in 1994, an agreement was signed by APEC members to establish free trade by the year 2010 in developed-country members and 2020 in developing-country members.

Will this approach succeed? My answer is in the negative. The Bogor agreement is non-binding and some members have already gone on to declare that free trade does not mean zero tariffs. More importantly, there is a fundamental conflict between the interpretations of the Bogor agreement by the Asian members and the United States. While the former expect liberalization to be on the MFN basis, the latter insists on reciprocity. Given that countries outside APEC, especially those in Europe, will not liberalize in response to liberalization by APEC members, reciprocity necessarily amount to taking a discriminatory approach and turning APEC into an FTA.

Given this conflict, the future of the 2010/2020 goal is in some doubt. Therefore, as suggested by Bhagwati (1995), the best strategy for East Asian members of APEC will be to use this forum to push for further multilateral liberalization. On the one hand, they should develop a consensus among themselves that APEC will not be turned into another preferential trading arrangement and, on the other, they should persuade the American members that multilateral free trade, not a spaghetti bowl of preferential free trade areas should be the centerpiece of the emerging world trading system. Recently, many economists have noted that a weakness in the WTO system is the absence of a deadline for achieving worldwide free trade. APEC could remedy this weakness by persuading WTO to adopt the 2010/2020 deadline for free trade on a worldwide basis.

References

Ariff, Mohamed, and Tan, Eu Chye. 1992. "ASEAN-Pacific Trade Relation Relations," in *ASEAN Economic Bulletin*, Vol. 8, No. 3, pp. 258-283.
Bhagwati, Jagdish, 1995, "U.S. Trade Policy: The Infatuation with Free Trade Areas," in Bhagwati, J. and Krueger Anne O., eds. in *The Dangerous Drift to Preferential Trade Agreements*, Washington, D.C.: American Enterprise Institute for Public Policy Research, 1995.
Bhagwati, Jagdish and Panagariya, Arvind. 1996a. "The Theory of Preferential trade Agreements: Historical Evolution and Current Trends," *American Economic Review. Papers and Proceedings*, May
Bhagwati, Jagdish and Panagariya, Arvind. 1996b. "Preferential Trading Areas and Multilateralism: Strangers, Friends and Foes," in Bhagwati, J. and Arvind Panagariya, eds., *The Economics of Preferential Trade Agreements*, 1996, AEI Press, Washington, D.C., forthcoming. (Chapter 2, this volume)
Finger, J.M. 1979. "Trade Liberalization: A Public Choice Perspective," in Amachen, R.C., Haberler, G., and Willett, T., eds., *Challenges to a Liberal International Economic Order*, Washington, D.C.: American Enterprise Institute.
Foroutan, Faezeh. 1993. "Regional Integration in Sub-Saharan Africa: Past Experience and Future Prospects," in Melo and Panagariya, eds.
Krugman, Paul. 1993. "Regionalism versus Multilateralism: Analytical Notes," in Melo and Panagariya.
Lee, Hiro and Woodall, Brian. 1998. "Political Feasibility and Empirical Assessments of a Pacific Free Trade Area," in *Economic Development and Cooperation in the Pacific Basin*, ed. Hiro Lee and David W. Roland-Holst (Cambridge, U.K.: Cambridge University Press, 1998).
Melo, Jaime de, and Panagariya, Arvind. 1992. *The New Regionalism in Trade Policy*. The World Bank, Washington, DC.
Melo, Jaime de, and Panagariya, Arvind, eds. 1993. *New Dimensions in Regional Integration*. Cambridge University Press.
Melo, Jaime de, Rodrik, Dani, and Panagariya, Arvind. 1993. "The New Regionalism: A Country Perspective" in Melo and Panagariya, eds.
Panagariya, Arvind. 1996a. "Free Trade Area of the Americas: Good for Latin America?" Center for International Economics, *World Economy*, forthcoming. (Chapter 5, this volume)
Panagariya, Arvind. 1996b. "APEC and the United States," paper presented at the Conference on *International Trade Policy and the Pacific Rim*, University of Sydney, Australia. (Chapter 4, this volume)

Pangestu, Mari, Soesastro, Hadi, and Ahmed, Mubariq. 1992. "A New Look at Intra-ASEAN Economic Cooperation," in *ASEAN Economic Bulletin*, Vol. 8, No. 3, pp. 333-352.

Petri, Peter, "One Bloc, Two Blocs or None? Political-Economic Factors in Pacific Trade policy," in K. Okuizumi, K.E. Calder, and G.W. Gong, eds., *The U.S.-Japan Economic Relationship in East and Southeast Asia: A Policy Framework for Asia-Pacific Economic Cooperation, Significant Issues Series* 14(1), Washington, D.C.: Center for Strategic and International Studies.

Sopiee, Noordin. See Chew Lay and Jin, Lim Siang, eds., 1987, *ASEAN at the Crossroads: Obstacles, Options, and Opportunities*, ISIS, Kuala Lumpur.

Summers, Lawrence. 1991. "Regionalism and the World Trading System," in *Policy Implications of Trade and Currency Zones*. Federal Reserve Board of Kansas City.

Viner, Jacob. 1950. *The Customs Union Issue*. New York, Carnegie Endowment for International Peace.

Winters, Alan. 1993. "The European Community: A Case of Successful Integration?" in Melo and Panagariya, eds.

World Bank, 1993. *East Asia and the Pacific Regional Development Review: Sustaining Rapid Development*, Washington, DC.

4.   APEC and the United States

4.1 Evolution of the U.S. Trade Policy

In this panel, I have been assigned the task of articulating the North American view on the Asia Pacific Economic cooperation (APEC) forum. Of course, just as there is no single Asian view on APEC, there is no single North American view on it; but to minimize the confusion that can result from this multiplicity of views, I will organize my discussion around the U.S. strategy towards APEC. In examining this strategy critically, I hope to cover the alternative views on the subject.

The major objective, which has guided the U.S. trade policy in recent years, particularly under President Clinton, is export expansion. Though all instruments, including aggressive unilateralism a la Super 301 and Special 301 have been used to achieve this objective, the instrument which has assumed the central role recently is preferential trading arrangements (PTAs).[117] In the Western Hemisphere, with the North American Free Trade

Originally published, as chapter 14, in *International Trade Policy and the Pacific Rim*, ed. John Piggott and Alan Woodland (London: McMillan Press Ltd., 1999). The paper was presented at the APEC Symposium of the IEA Conference on International Trade Policy and the Pacific Rim, University of Sydney, Australia, July 15-17, 1996. I am grateful to Sethaput Suthiwart-Narueput, a referee and the editors for extremely helpful comments on earlier drafts of the paper.

[117]Section 301 of the U.S. Trade Act of 1974 introduced a provision for retaliation against foreign practices that "unreasonably" restrict U.S. exports. The Omnibus Trade Practices Act of 1988 strengthened Section 301 of the 1974 Act by introducing what are called Super 301 and Special 301 provisions. Accordingly, the United States Trade Representative is required to identify priority foreign practices, which, if eliminated, will have the greatest benefit for U.S. commerce, and seek a removal of those practices under the threat of retaliation. Investigation of policies of foreign countries which restrict U.S. exports of goods and services is done under the Super 301 provision and of policies which deny American residents the protection of intellectual property rights (e.g., patents, trademark and copyright) is taken under Special 301 provision. It is expected that with the strengthened dispute settlement machinery

Agreement (NAFTA) already established, the United States is promoting the Free Trade Area of the Americas. This arrangement is expected to give U.S. firms preferential access to the entire Western Hemisphere. In Europe, the United States has encouraged a Trans-Atlantic Free Trade Area (TAFTA), proposed originally by Klaus Kinkel of Germany. In Asia, at the APEC ministerial meetings and through the American-led Eminent Persons Group (EPG), she has resisted liberalization based on the Most Favored Nation (MFN) principle and insisted on reciprocity for large countries such as the United States.[118]

It must be acknowledged that the United States is not unique in promoting PTAs. The European Union has done the same on a larger scale and for much longer. What is different about the United States, however, is her history. Until recently, unlike Europe, the United States had been a staunch opponent of regional arrangements and the prime force behind multilateralism. Having witnessed the pernicious effects of discriminatory trade and payments regimes during the Great Depression, the United States emerged at the end of the Second World War as the champion of a nondiscriminatory trade regime firmly grounded in the Most Favored Nation principle. Speaking for the U.S. policy makers, Howard Ellis (1945) denounced bilateral arrangements in the strongest terms:

> There are good reasons for believing that no device portends more restrictions of international trade in the postwar setting than bilateral arrangements. (Saxonhouse 1996)

The U.S. commitment to multilateralism manifested itself in her efforts to create the International Trade Organization (ITO), an institution intended to establish a rules-based trade regime throughout the world. But because the U.S. Congress failed to ratify it, the ITO was stillborn. Undeterred, the United States took advantage of the General Agreement on Tariffs and Trade (GATT), signed in 1947, and led the world into a series of highly successful rounds of multilateral trade negotiations. By 1979, when the Tokyo Round was completed, GATT members had negotiated seven such rounds. Along the way, the United States had stood firmly behind the multilateral approach

---

at the World Trade Organization and expected implementation of the Trade-Related Intellectual Property Rights Agreement of the Uruguay Round Agreement, the scope for unilateral actions under Super 301 and Special 301 is considerably reduced.

[118]The EPG were appointed to advise APEC in 1992 for a term of three years which expired in 1995. The United States, being the incoming chair of APEC at the time, got to appoint the EPG chairman and chose C. Fred Bergsten of the Institute for International Economics for the job.

and squarely rejected all calls for participation in regional arrangements including a North *Atlantic* Free Trade Area proposed by the United Kingdom. The only regional arrangement the United States did support was the European Economic Community, which she saw as a necessary counter-weight to the emerging Soviet power.

The turning point in the history of U.S. trade policy came in 1982 when, at the GATT ministerial meeting in Geneva that year, she tried to get the eighth GATT round started. But the European Community, which was then suffering from economic difficulties, described as "Euro-sclerosis", frustrated her efforts. At that point, a disappointed William Brock, the United States Trade Representative (USTR), saw the regional approach as the only alternative left to keep the process of trade liberalization moving ahead. In the absence of multilateral process, he saw open-ended, ever-expanding free trade areas (FTAs) as an alternative instrument of achieving worldwide free trade.[119] Negotiations were opened with Israel and Canada and FTA agreements concluded with them in 1985 and 1988, respectively.

In the meantime, the Uruguay Round was launched successfully in 1986. But the European Community, preoccupied now by its Single Market initiative, remained a reluctant player in the ensuing negotiations. This gave the United States a reason as well as an excuse to continue pursuing PTAs.[120] In 1989, negotiations were opened with Mexico which, in 1992, culminated in the signing of the North American Free Trade Agreement (NAFTA).

Happily, despite Lester Thurow's famous pronouncement that 'GATT is dead,' GATT did not die and the Uruguay Round was concluded successfully in December 1993. The United States' threat to pursue regional arrangements of its own had the desirable impact of bringing a reluctant European Community to the negotiating table. The GATT has been revived, revitalized and, at last, transformed from a treaty into a proper international institution known as the World trade Organization (WTO).

Today, with the original objective behind the switch in the U.S. policy towards preferential trading having been achieved, it would seem that there

---

[119] As Bhagwati (1993) notes, Brock's approach was not geographically circumscribed and he had offered FTAs to even Egypt and the Association of South-East Asian Nations (ASEAN).

[120] Reason because the EC needed the extra push to start negotiating seriously; excuse because the United States had by now developed a taste for negotiations in a regional context and would have wanted to pursue NAFTA irrespective of EC's willingness to negotiate seriously under GATT.

is no further need to promote PTAs. But the taste of bilateral negotiations and the preferential access they bring have changed the dynamics of trade-liberalization process. The United States has decided to "walk on both legs." From a staunch opponent of bilateralism, she has turned into an aggressive proponent of it. The original U.S. vision of promoting liberalization on the Most Favored Nation principle has been replaced by demands for reciprocity and the simple-minded view that *any* reduction in trade barriers is a good thing. This switch in the U.S. thinking is best summarized in the following assertion by Lawrence Summers (1991), the Deputy Secretary of Treasury in the Clinton Administration:

> (E)conomists should maintain a strong, but rebuttable, presumption in favor of all lateral reductions in trade barriers, whether they be multi, uni, bi, tri, plurilateral. Global liberalization may be best, but regional liberalization is very likely to be good.

Jagdish Bhagwati and I have argued elsewhere (Bhagwati 1995, Panagariya 1996a, and Bhagwati and Panagariya 1996a) that this is a flawed vision, if it can be called vision. Writing in 1950, Jacob Viner, who pioneered the theory of preferential trading, was himself puzzled by the general support of PTAs by pro-free-trade economists of his time. "The major explanation", he wrote, "seems to lie in an unreflecting association on their part of any removal or reduction of trade barriers with movement in the direction of free trade." Viner then went on to explain that clever politicians had always known that a reduction in trade barriers can, in fact, be used to *increase* protection and, in so doing, he provided the essential idea behind the later development of the concept of effective protection.

In addition to the possibility that PTAs can slowdown progress on the multilateral front, there are at least four reasons for skepticism towards PTAs as an instrument of trade liberalization.[121] First, being discriminatory in nature, they can and do lead to trade diversion.[122] Because weaker,

---

[121]Whether PTAs are a building or stumbling block to multilateral free trade is a contro-versial issue. The rapidly growing theoretical literature on this subject is reviewed in Bhag-wati and Panagariya (1996a). For contributions favorable to PTAs, see Krugman (1991), Summers (1991), Frankel and Wei (1997) and Goto and Hamada (1996). The last of these contributions favors unequivocally an APEC FTA.

[122]Trade diversion is said to have occurred when, as a result of the tariff preference, a member country expands its exports to another member by displacing more efficient suppliers located outside the union. Trade creation occurs when such expansion is at the expense of the less efficient suppliers in the importing member country. Trade diversion is likely to reduce welfare and trade creation likely to increase it.

uncompetitive industries are often the ones that succeed in lobbying against foreign competition, PTAs are often voted in when trade diversion is the dominant force. This is a point made forcefully in the recent theoretical work by Grossman and Helpman (1995) and Krishna (1995). Similarly, the careful empirical work of Kowalczyk and Davis (1996) shows that in NAFTA, the sectors which were allowed the longest phase out periods for implementing the accord in the United States were the one where the U.S. lobbies were most powerful. Most importantly, the recent World Bank study by Yeats (1996) provides systematic evidence of wholesale trade diversion in the Southern Cone Common Market popularly known by its Spanish acronym MERCOSUR. The view that a PTA does not lead to serious trade diversion if member countries trade a lot with each other and are neighbors—the so-called "Natural Trading Partners" hypothesis, promoted by Krugman (1991) and Summers (1991)—has been shown to have no foundation in theory by Bhagwati and Panagariya (1996). It has also been shown to be inconsistent with reality by the World Bank study just mentioned.

The second problem with PTAs is that they can lead to increased protection against outside countries. In bad times, pressures for protection grow and when a PTA member is unable to raise trade barriers against a partner, the burden of increased trade barriers falls disproportionately on the outside countries. Such increases in trade barriers can turn even an initial trade creation into trade diversion.[123] This is not idle speculation. Outside tariffs in Israel went up after she concluded FTAs with both EU and the United States.[124] Similarly, in the aftermath of the Peso crisis, Mexico raised tariffs on outside countries on 503 items from less than 20% to 35%.[125]

---

[123]This point was made forcefully by Bhagwati (1993).

[124]For details, see Halevi and Kleiman (1994).

[125]In my various presentations and discussions, I have frequently encountered the argument that in comparison with the increases in trade barriers in the wake of the macroeconomic crisis in Mexico in early 1980s, the recent tariff increases were minuscule. There are two problems with this argument. First, since early 1980s, there has been a complete reversal in the conventional wisdom on how countries should respond to balance-of-payments crisis. In the past, the uniform advice, including that given by the International Monetary Fund, to countries facing balance-of-payments crises was to raise trade barriers. Today, the advice is take the opportunity to carry out trade reforms that are difficult in times of stability. As a result, even India, the last major bastion of protectionism, ended up liberalizing its trade regime after a balance-of-payments crisis even though she had no PTA with the United States or EU. Second, Mexico was given a massive $40 billion debt-relief package to deal with the recent peso crisis which was not available at the time of the previous crisis.

Another way the burden can be transferred to outside countries is through increased anti-dumping and safeguard actions against outside countries.

Third, in FTAs, which seem to be the dominant form of PTAs today, the rules of origin have been creating a spaghetti bowl. This problem is bound to be compounded as overlapping FTAs proliferate. As it is, the rules of origin in NAFTA are complicated. Now suppose Chile, who already has an FTA with MERCOSUR, joins NAFTA. Because MERCOSUR does not have an FTA with NAFTA, the rules of origin for Chile's entry into NAFTA are likely to be more complicated than those for NAFTA. The rules of origin will open a further avenue for trade diversion. Thus, a manufacturer in Chile will have to make a decision on whether to buy his components in the Southern Cone or North America depending on whether he wants to sell the final product in MERCOSUR or NAFTA. If he relies on a single source of supply, he will be able to satisfy the rules of origin for only one of the two destinations. Moreover, if the most efficient supplier happens to be in Asia, trade diversion will be inevitable.

Finally, measures, which are otherwise WTO inconsistent, have begun to sneak back into PTAs. One such example is the trade-balancing requirement within MERCOSUR. The WTO has just outlawed this Trade-Related Investment Measure or TRIM. Yet the members of MERCOSUR have introduced this requirement for firms operating within the union. Thus, an Argentine company operating in Brazil must export as much Brazilian goods to Argentina as it imports from the latter. Similarly, voluntary export restraints (VERs) have been outlawed by the Uruguay Round Agreement. Yet, such VERs were resurrected on tomato imports into the United States from Mexico within the context of NAFTA. At the moment, we do not have evidence of such WTO-inconsistent measures being widespread but they certainly have the potential to subvert the multilateral process down the road.

4.2 APEC and the United States

To ensure open access for U.S. firms in Asian markets, her own pursuit of NAFTA notwithstanding, the United States has actively opposed the formation of an exclusively Asian trading bloc. Thus, when in December 1990, Prime Minister Mahathir Mohamed of Malaysia proposed the East Asian Economic Group (EAEG), the U.S. Secretary of State James Baker vehemently opposed it. Baker's efforts at the ASEAN post-ministerial conference held in July 1991 led to the downgrading of the group to an East Asian Economic Caucus (EEAC) and prevented Japan and Korea from joining it.

The Australian Prime Minister R.J.L. Hawke had proposed APEC in January 1989 without consulting the United States. Seeing its importance, the Bush Administration quickly moved to ensure a seat for the United States and her FTA partner, Canada, at the first formal meeting of the organization held in Canberra in November 1989.[126] Because of its diverse membership, APEC proceeded cautiously, aiming to develop closer ties through consultation, cooperation and consensus rather than formal negotiations. Indeed, during its first four years, it operated without a formal secretariat.

As Barfield (1996) points out correctly, 'it was the Clinton administration that moved to change the focus of APEC from an informal consultative mechanism to a more formal organization promoting trade liberalization—and ultimately preferential trade arrangements—within the Pacific region.' The impetus provided by Clinton at the Seattle meeting in November 1993 culminated the following year in the Bogor declaration. Led by President Suharto of Indonesia, APEC members agreed to establish free trade by the year 2010 in the developed member countries and by 2020 in the developing member countries. Though the meaning of 'free trade' in this context has remained unclear and no strategy for achieving the goal has been articulated, the agreement was a departure from APEC's past practice of limiting itself to a low key, consultative approach.

Since the Bogor meeting, the United States' approach has been to encourage unilateral liberalization by developing Asian members but to resist any reductions in its own trade barriers on an MFN basis. The ground work for this approach had been laid down by the American-led EPG in its second report (APEC 1994). The EPG noted

... considerations suggest that, while APEC members should implement unilateral liberalization to the maximum extent possible, it will be expedient to pursue a strategy of negotiated liberalization as well. The largest members, including the United States, are unlikely to liberalize unilaterally when they can use the high value of access to their markets to obtain reciprocal liberalization from others. The same view applies to other economies in the region.

---

[126]In a recent paper, Bergsten (1996), whose views mirror those of the Clinton Administration on the U.S. trade policy in Asia, puts the following positive spin on the U.S. success in blocking an exclusively Asian trade bloc: "By joining East Asia and North America, APEC has eliminated any possibility of the three-bloc world that was widely feared a few years ago."

The closely related consideration is that APEC as a whole is the world's largest trading region, considerably larger than even the EU. ... the region would give away an enormous amount of leverage if its members ... especially its large members—were to liberalize unilaterally to any significant degree. (APEC 1994)

Thus, the EPG essentially ruled out liberalization by the United States within the APEC framework unless it is discriminatory, though the same was welcome if undertaken by smaller economies of the region, mainly developing Asian countries.

It may be argued that, because the EPG did not represent the United States but served the APEC, its views cannot be taken as representing the U.S. position. But the 1995 Economic Report of the President echoes the EPG when it focuses on liberalization by Asian members of APEC but states little about the corresponding liberalization by the United States. To quote the report:

Although the opportunities for U.S. businesses are tremendous, the obstacles are often very large. Between 1989 and 1992, automobile sales in Malaysia, the Philippines, and Thailand doubled, but tariffs on automobile imports into those countries remain high at between 17 and 57 percent. ... Market-opening initiatives through APEC will help reduce these barriers, creating tremendous opportunities for U.S. companies and workers.

There is little mention in the report of the high tariff on textiles and apparel and footwear in the United States and the gains from removing them. Nor is there any mention of a speedier phase out of the Multi-fibre Arrangement (MFA) in products of interest to Asian exporters.

Finally, it may be noted that at the Osaka ministerial in 1995, whatever liberalization was announced came from developing Asian countries such as China and Indonesia. The only liberalization announced by the United States was that of *exports* of certain goods with possible military use.[127] Mickey Kantor, the United States Trade Representative at the time and now the Commerce Secretary, insisted that future trade liberalization would allow 'no free riders.' (Barfield 1996).

It is unlikely that the U.S. objective of improved market access in Asia without a corresponding liberalization of her own markets within the APEC framework will actually be attained. At the time of writing (middle of

---

[127]See the *Economist,* November 25, 1995, pp. 75-76.

November, 1996), preparation for the 1996 APEC summit, to be held in the Philippines, were under way. At this summit, the United States planned to use APEC as one of the fora for developing consensus for liberalization in the area information technology, a subject that was expected to be discussed more fully at the WTO ministerial in Singapore. Developing Asian countries, for their part, planned to announce modest liberalization on an MFN basis. Prospects for more substantial liberalization by Asian countries within the APEC framework without the United States undertaking similar liberalization appeared dim.

4.3 Liberalization within the APEC Framework

Let me now address more directly the possible ways of liberalizing trade within the APEC framework in the future. There is consensus among APEC members that whatever liberalization takes place should be GATT consistent. Indeed, given the recent tightening of multilateral rules under the Uruguay Round, it is difficult to imagine that any significant liberalization can be pursued in a manner inconsistent with GATT. Short of initiating another round of multilateral negotiations, this fact narrows down APEC's options to four modes of liberalization. These are: one-way trade preferences by developed to developing member countries under the Generalized System of Preferences (GSP), reciprocal trade preferences between developing member countries under the Enabling Clause of GATT, FTAs and customs unions under GATT Article XXIV, and unilateral liberalization on the MFN basis.

Of these four modes, the first two are unlikely to play any significant role in the APEC framework. Developed-country members are in no mood to offer trade preferences on a non-reciprocal basis. Nor are developing member countries in East Asia keen to trade preferences with each other on a discriminatory basis. The ASEAN Preferential Trading Arrangement (APTA), negotiated in 1977 and superseded by the ASEAN Free Trade Area (AFTA) in 1992, falls under this category but the exchange of trade preferences on account of it has been minimal (Panagariya 1993, 1994). Instead, the member countries have chosen to lower trade barriers on a nondiscriminatory basis. In any case, even if this mode was to be employed, since it cannot include developed countries, it will be done outside of APEC.

The main mode of trade liberalization in Asia has been either unilateral liberalization by developing countries as a part of their trade reforms or negotiated liberalization on an MFN basis under the auspices of the GATT. Though APEC and AFTA may have helped speed up the commitments for liberalization under these modes—Mr. Bergsten certainly likes to claim that to be the case—, they have not been the primary force.

For its part, the United States government is not in the least interested in offering reductions in trade barriers without reciprocity. In other words, she does not plan to lower trade barriers on a nondiscriminatory basis since such a move gives EU additional access to the U.S. market without her having to offer any reciprocal liberalization. Therefore, if trade liberalization within the APEC framework is to incorporate all members without violating GATT, the logical outcome is an APEC FTA or customs union. Though neither the U.S. Administration nor EPG has explicitly advocated such a bloc, it is the only possible implication of the demand for reciprocity with GATT consistency. And an FTA does sit well with Clinton Administration's newfound wisdom on trade policy which has elevated PTAs to more or less the same status as multilateral liberalization. Thus, echoing Lawrence Summers, quoted earlier, the 1995 President's Report (pp. 214-15) notes,[128]

Possibly the most distinctive legacy of this Administration in international trade is the foundation it has laid for the development of open, overlapping plurilateral trade agreements as stepping stones to global free trade. The Administration's plurilateral initiatives in North America, the rest of the Western Hemisphere, and Asia embody principles of openness and inclusion consistent with GATT. They will serve as vehicles for improving access to foreign markets...

Of course, the Asian member countries do not share the U.S. enthusiasm for either reciprocity or 'negotiated liberalization.' Instead, they have shown a clear preference for adherence to the MFN principle. At Osaka, the Asian view of 'concerted unilateralism' prevailed with each member being offered the opportunity to adopt voluntarily its separate path to liberalization. In pursuit of the Bogor goal of free trade by 2010 or 2020, the member countries were asked to provide first 'downpayment' for free trade at the next annual meeting in the Philippines in December 1996.

Thus, on the face of it, Asian members of APEC may have successfully countered the U.S. insistence on reciprocity. (As an aside, it may be noted that the EPG, which had advocated the U.S. position forcefully, their term having expired, were allowed to disband rather than be given another term.)

---

[128] In passing, I may note that, in early 1994, the Administration had also discussed the possibility of extending NAFTA to Korea. See Saxonhouse (1996) for details.

Saxonhouse (1996) certainly takes this view. But I am afraid I must agree with Barfield (1996), that in any future liberalization, the 'United States...is likely to demand reciprocity.' At Osaka, the Clinton Administration chose to adopt a low profile perhaps as a part of its overall strategy to avoid any new trade policy initiatives until the end of the forthcoming election. This stance was consistent with the Administration's decision to put all other trade policy issues—accession of Chile to NAFTA, China's entry into WTO, and acquisition of the 'fast track' negotiating authority—on to the back burner. But once the election is over, regardless of who wins it, we are likely to witness a return of the U.S. demands for reciprocity at APEC ministerial meetings.

4.4 An APEC FTA?

I have made the point that unless negotiations take place on a multilateral basis, reciprocity necessarily amounts to an FTA or customs union under GATT Article XXIV. Because a customs union requires the surrender of the authority to choose the external tariff, the bigger members of APEC—in particular, the United States—are not interested in it. This limits the choice to an APEC-wide FTA.

In Panagariya (1993, 1994), I have discussed at length why a discriminatory arrangement such as NAFTA is neither feasible nor desirable among countries in East Asia. In a modified form, most of those arguments extend to the larger set of countries included in APEC. Rather than repeat the arguments put forth there, let me venture to discuss a different argument made originally in Panagariya (1996a, 1996b) and developed fully in Bhagwati and Panagariya (1996a). According to this argument, because negotiable barriers to trade such as tariffs are high in some APEC members and low in others (see Appendix Table 1), an FTA among them will result in large redistributive effects, with some countries actually losing. In particular, the countries, which have high tariffs, are likely to lose from an FTA with countries with low tariffs.

To make the point most simply, suppose Indonesia and Singapore were to form an FTA. Because Singapore already has free trade, the FTA will amount to Indonesia offering Singapore a tariff-free access to its market without reducing the tariff on outside countries. As long as the FTA does not eliminate imports of different products from outside countries, there will be little change in Indonesia's internal price structure and hence no improvement in her internal efficiency.[129] Yet, she will lose the tariff revenue collected on imports from Singapore. The revenue will be transferred to exporters from Singapore who now have access to the internal price of Indonesia. Indonesia's preferential liberalization will hurt herself and benefit Singapore.

If Indonesia was to liberalize on an MFN basis, however, her internal price structure will come to correspond to the border price structure. Therefore, the usual efficiency gains will accrue. With the internal price of imports declining, the tariff revenue lost on imports from all sources will be passed on to Indonesian consumers. There is a fundamental difference between preferential and nondiscriminatory liberalization in that the former benefits largely the union partner while the latter benefits the country which liberalizes.[130]

As argued originally in Panagariya (1996a), this analysis undermines the popular view that NAFTA benefited Mexico. Having extended a large margin of preference to the United States without receiving the same in return, on balance, I will argue that Mexico lost from NAFTA. The analysis also explains why the exchange of trade preferences within the ASEAN framework has been minimal. The distributional conflict I have highlighted is reflected well in the following statement by a former foreign minister of Indonesia at the 25th anniversary celebration of the ASEAN:

Singapore and Malaysia are always telling us to lower tariffs and duties and let their goods into the country. But, in return, how about the free movement of labor? We will take your goods if you take our surplus labor supply. When they hear this and think about all those Indonesians coming to work in their countries, then they say, 'wait a minute, may be it's not such a good idea'.

As Table 4.1 shows, except in textiles, apparel and leather, tariffs on industrial products in the United States and Japan are low. Tariffs on all industrial products in Singapore are virtually nonexistent. In other countries, particularly China, Indonesia and Thailand, are high. Clearly, the scope for redistributional effects in the event of preferential liberalization is large.

---

[129] Strictly speaking, this assumes that Indonesia and Singapore are small relative to the rest of the world.

[130] As shown in Panagariya (1996c), this analysis remains valid in a modified form when the FTA is formed in the presence of import quotas.

4.5 Back to Multilateralism

At the present time, a discriminatory APEC bloc is neither desirable nor feasible. This naturally raises the question what role can APEC play in pushing for further trade liberalization?

On the Asian side, particularly among smaller members, there appears to be some enthusiasm for concerted unilateral liberalization. I must admit, however, that there is only limited scope for additional liberalization over and above what countries have committed themselves to under the Uruguay Round, or plan to undertake as a part of their own country reforms as, for example, in the case of Indonesia, Thailand and China. APEC may be able to speed up the implementation of the Uruguay Round or country reforms, but any progress beyond that is difficult to envisage. As regards bigger member countries, they are aware that while unilateral liberalization may bring triangular efficiency gains, they will also bring rectangular terms-of-trade losses. Therefore, they are unlikely to undertake any significant unilateral liberalization. This conclusion leaves in doubt the fate of the Bogor declaration for free trade by 2010 and 2020.

But maybe not. Representing as they do more than half of the world income and trade, APEC members could not only achieve that goal for themselves but also for the rest of the world. But that would require abandoning the pursuit of the illusory 'open regionalism,' which is nothing but *Maya* [or as T.N. Srinivasan (1995) calls it, an oxymoron] and using APEC's clout to nudge the world towards the sure, one-fold path to nirvana: multilateralism. In particular, APEC could push for the adoption by the WTO of the free trade goal by 2010 for developed countries and 2020 for developing countries.[131] Wolf (1996) has recently noted that an important ingredient missing from the WTO agenda is a deadline by which it aims to achieve global free trade. APEC's deadlines for free trade can, thus, become the missing deadlines of the WTO.

In addition, since investment liberalization has been an integral part of the APEC agenda, it could take lead in this area. Recently, the development of an investment code has become a priority item for the WTO. The agenda

---

[131]This suggestion essentially follows Bhagwati (1995). He suggests that APEC should transform its goal of open and free trade and investment in the region, from an APEC-alone liberalization, into an APEC initiative in conjunction with the G-7 to launch the next round of *multilateral* trade negotiations to reduce trade barriers on a nondiscriminatory, most-favored nation, basis.

for this item is being driven currently by the Multilateral Agreement on Investment (MAI) of the Organization of Economic Cooperation and Development (OECD). APEC could consider developing an alternative agreement on investment, which will serve better its membership. The developing Asian countries are not members of OECD and an OECD-driven investment code may not best serve their interests.

Table 4.1: Unweighted average percentage tariff rates pre- and post-Uruguay Round

Country	Australia		Canada		Indonesia		Japan		Korea		Mexico		Malaysia	
Product	Pre-UR	Post-UR	Pre-UR	Post-UR	Pre-UR	Post-UR	Pre-UR	Post-UR	Pre-UR	Post-UR	Pre-UR	Post-UR	Pre-UR	Post-UR
Paddy rice	11.0	1.0	70.0	0.0	9.0	9.0	500.0	444.0	49.0	49.0	8.0	8.0	49.0	49.0
Wheat	1.0	0.0	26.0	26.0	0.0	0.0	308.0	193.0	272.0	13.0	0.0	0.0	272.0	13.0
Grains	0.0	0.0	24.0	24.0	6.0	6.0	336.0	180.0	327.0	95.0	0.0	0.0	327.0	95.0
Non-grain crops	3.3	3.3	3.0	3.0	54.7	38.3	42.0	38.7	51.7	47.7	3.0	3.0	51.7	47.7
Wool	0.0	0.0	0.0	0.0	0.0	0.0	0.0	0.0	0.0	0.0	0.0	0.0	0.0	0.0
Livestock	0.0	0.0	0.0	0.0	0.0	0.0	0.0	0.0	118.0	83.0	0.0	0.0	118.0	83.0
Forestry	0.0	0.0	0.7	0.0	4.7	4.7	0.4	0.2	4.2	2.4	1.3	1.3	6.4	6.3
Fishing	0.0	0.0	0.1	0.5	13.4	13.4	4.1	2.7	14.8	10.3	5.5	5.5	7.5	4.8
Coal	0.0	0.0	0.0	0.0	2.6	2.6	0.4	0.3	2.2	0.6	0.6	0.6	1.8	1.8
Oil	0.0	0.0	0.0	0.0	0.7	0.7	0.0	0.0	2.4	2.4	0.0	0.0	0.9	0.9
Gas	1.7	0.7	1.6	1.6	0.7	0.7	1.7	0.0	1.8	1.6	0.9	0.9	1.5	1.5
Other minerals	0.7	0.5	0.0	0.0	2.4	2.4	0.6	0.0	4.4	2.7	4.8	4.8	3.5	3.5
Processed rice	1.0	0.0	7.0	7.0	0.0	0.0	36.5	36.5	78.0	41.0	0.0	0.0	78.0	41.0
Meat	4.5	0.5	26.0	26.0	12.7	10.7	308.0	193.0	114.0	32.5	19.5	19.5	272.0	13.0

Milk	19.0	7.0	157.0	157.0	0.0	0.0	207.0	207.0	111.0	111.0	4.0	4.0	111.0	111.0
Other food	0.0	0.0	0.0	0.0	0.0	0.0	0.0	0.0	0.0	0.0	0.0	0.0	0.0	111.0
Beverages and tobacco	0.0	0.0	0.0	0.0	0.0	0.0	0.0	0.0	29.5	20.8	0.0	0.0	29.5	20.8
Textiles	23.6	14.1	15.9	10.4	31.6	24.2	6.1	4.0	16.1	10.7	12.6	12.6	23.3	16.1
Wearing apparel	58.9	37.2	22.6	16.4	38.8	29.8	13.5	9.1	20.5	13.8	14.6	14.6	24.3	17.6
Leather	22.8	14.9	15.4	10.2	14.5	12.9	15.1	12.9	18.4	9.4	9.7	9.7	22.3	18.2
Lumber	15.7	7.4	9.2	4.0	27.5	24.6	4.4	1.6	16.8	12.0	12.6	12.6	24.5	17.9
Pulp paper	11.3	6.3	7.3	0.0	10.6	10.6	2.5	0.0	7.5	0.0	4.5	4.5	5.9	5.3
Oil and coal	1.6	0.9	0.8	0.5	3.7	3.7	1.6	1.4	7.7	4.2	2.5	2.5	8.2	7.1
Chemicals	11.2	7.3	10.9	6.0	5.6	5.6	5.4	2.5	15.3	6.7	8.9	8.9	7.7	6.7
Non-metallic mineral products	12.5	8.4	10.3	4.8	17.1	15.1	3.2	1.4	18.0	12.3	12.0	12.0	22.7	19.3
Primary ferrous metals	8.8	1.6	7.7	1.4	5.5	5.5	4.3	0.9	8.4	1.9	6.0	6.0	4.9	4.9
Non-ferrous metals	10.3	4.8	4.0	1.9	10.8	10.4	1.8	0.6	14.4	6.5	4.7	4.7	6.0	5.2
Fabricated metals	15.8	10.9	8.3	4.9	20.4	20.2	4.6	0.9	18.3	11.8	12.6	12.6	16.7	13.6
Transport	13.2	9.8	6.5	4.3	15.8	15.0	2.4	0.0	13.8	11.4	8.8	8.8	14.5	14.2
Machinery	12.6	7.8	5.1	2.3	14.6	14.2	3.8	0.1	18.1	7.1	11.7	11.7	8.4	5.4
Other manufacturing	15.5	11.6	10.4	4.2	32.2	28.6	4.1	2.3	18.6	8.8	15.4	15.4	14.4	12.6
Electricity, water and gas	0.0	0.0	0.0	0.0	0.0	0.0	0.0	0.0	0.0	0.0	0.4	0.4	0.0	0.0

Table 4.1 (Continued): Additional Countries

Country	New Zealand		Philippines		Singapore		Thailand		U.S.A.		China	
Product	Pre-UR	Post-UR	Pre-UR	Post-UR	Pre-UR	Post-UR	Pre-UR	Post-UR	Pre-UR	Post-UR	Pre-UR	Post-UR
Paddy rice	11.0	1.0	49.0	49.0	5.9	2.2	49.0	49.0	0.0	0.0	0.0	0.0
Wheat	1.0	0.0	272.0	13.0	7.0	2.7	272.0	13.0	13.0	4.0	0.0	0.0
Grains	0.0	0.0	327.0	95.0	14.1	5.3	327.0	95.0	0.0	0.0	3.0	3.0
Non-grain crops	3.3	3.3	51.7	47.7	22.2	7.5	51.7	47.7	42.0	42.0	13.9	11.8
Wool	0.0	0.0	0.0	0.0	2.3	0.9	0.0	0.0	8.0	5.0	15.0	15.0
Livestock	0.0	0.0	118.0	83.0	25.8	9.6	118.0	83.0	0.0	0.0	71.7	39.6
Forestry	0.0	0.0	3.0	3.0	0.0	0.0	6.2	4.9	0.0	0.0	7.3	7.1
Fishing	1.6	0.7	11.0	7.1	1.9	0.7	36.8	12.7	0.3	0.2	23.0	17.1
Coal	0.0	0.0	7.8	7.8	0.0	0.0	8.7	8.7	0.0	0.0	15.0	13.5
Oil	0.0	0.0	3.0	3.0	0.0	0.0	4.3	4.4	0.4	0.4	2.0	2.0
Gas	0.0	0.0	5.2	5.2	0.0	0.0	0.0	0.1	0.0	0.0	3.5	27.5
Other minerals	2.7	1.3	10.2	9.9	0.0	0.0	10.9	7.3	0.7	0.2	18.7	18.5
Processed rice	1.0	0.0	78.0	41.0	10.6	3.9	78.0	41.1	2.0	2.0	0.0	0.0
Meat	4.5	0.5	272.0	13.0	15.2	3.1	272.0	13.1	13.0	4.0	47.4	37.6
Milk	19.0	7.0	111.0	111.0	22.3	4.2	111.0	111.1	92.0	92.0	28.0	25.3
Other food	0.0	0.0	0.0	0.0	16.5	6.1	0.0	0.1	0.0	0.0	28.7	26.0
Beverage and tobacco	0.0	0.0	29.5	20.8	25.0	9.3	29.5	20.9	0.0	0.0	65.0	62.5
Textiles	10.9	8.2	33.6	23.3	1.2	0.4	56.6	26.6	9.6	7.4	55.0	38.9
Wearing apparel	40.5	31.3	39.7	26.3	3.9	3.9	56.7	22.9	17.9	15.9	83.3	39.9
Leather	34.3	25.6	25.4	25.4	0.5	0.5	43.2	28.5	7.4	6.6	64.8	43.4

Lumber	23.3	11.8	24.9	24.9	1.3	0.2	34.3	16.1	3.5	1.1	51.0	32.1
Pulp paper	20.3	0.0	25.1	24.1	0.0	0.0	24.3	20.3	1.7	0.0	31.3	27.2
Oil and coal	3.8	3.0	12.7	12.7	10.7	10.7	21.4	21.1	1.7	0.8	15.5	15.5
Chemicals	13.7	7.7	19.5	17.4	1.1	0.4	34.0	30.1	4.7	3.1	31.8	28.3
Non-metalic mineral products	13.3	9.5	26.6	26.4	0.0	0.0	31.9	25.8	7.6	5.2	45.9	35.2
Primary ferrous metals	10.8	8.5	12.8	12.8	0.0	0.0	14.2	13.8	3.7	1.0	22.3	18.9
Non-ferrous metals	15.3	9.5	20.8	19.0	0.0	0.0	16.2	11.7	1.7	1.0	11.9	10.9
Fabricated metals	16.6	13.2	30.7	30.6	0.0	0.0	33.6	31.8	4.1	2.2	44.4	34.5
Transport	14.4	12.3	22.4	22.2	0.9	0.9	50.6	41.1	2.9	2.5	69.3	69.3
Machinery	19.5	9.9	23.3	20.4	0.1	0.0	35.7	25.4	3.4	1.5	31.5	28.4
Other manufacturing	26.5	18.1	31.1	31.1	0.4	0.3	41.6	26.8	5.5	2.7	70.9	44.4
Electricity, water and gas	0.0	0.0	0.0	0.0	0.1	0.0	0.0	0.0	0.0	0.0	3.0	3.0

Source: The Pacific Economic Cooperation Council for APEC, 1995, Survey of Impediments to Trade and Investment in the APEC Region.

References

APEC, 1993, *A Vision for APEC*, Report of the Eminent Persons Group to APEC Ministers, Singapore, Asia Pacific Cooperation.

APEC, 1994, *Achieving the APEC Vision*, Second Report of the Eminent Persons Group to APEC Ministers, Singapore, Asia Pacific Cooperation.

Barfield, Claude E., 1996, "Regionalism and U.S. Trade Policy," in Bhagwati, J. and Panagariya, A., ed., 1996b.

Bergsten, C. Fred, 1996, "Globalizing Free Trade," *Foreign Affairs*, May/June, 105-120.

Bhagwati, Jagdish, 1993, "Regionalism and Multilateralism: An Overview," in Melo and Panagariya, (ed.).

Bhagwati, Jagdish, 1995, "U.S. Trade Policy: The Infatuation with Free Trade Areas," in Bhagwati, J. and Krueger Anne O., eds. in *The Dangerous Drift to Preferential Trade Agreements*, Washington, D.C.: American Enterprise Institute for Public Policy Research, 1995.

Bhagwati, Jagdish and Panagariya, Arvind, 1996a, "Preferential Trading Areas and Multilateralism: Strangers, Friends or Foes?" in Jagdish Bhagwati and Arvind Panagariya, 1996b, eds. (Chapter 2, this volume)

Bhagwati, Jagdish and Panagariya, Arvind, eds., 1996b, *The Economics of Preferential Trade Agreements*, 1996b, AEI Press, Washington, D.C., forthcoming.

Corbet, Hugh, 1995, "Progress of the APEC Process up to the Bogor Declaration," paper presented at the Conference *Economic cooperation in the Asia-Pacific Region* organized by the Sigur Center for east Asian Studies, Washington, D.C., June 22-23, 1995.

Council of Economic Advisors, 1995, *Economic Report of the President. 1995*, Washington, D.C., Council of Economic Advisors.

Ellis, Howard, 1945, "Bilateralism and the Future of International Trade," *Essays in International Finance* No. 5, Summer.

Frankel, J. and Shang-Jin Wei, 1997, "The New Regionalism and Asia: Impact and Options," in A. Panagariya, M.G. Quibria and N. Rao, eds., *The Global trading*

System and Developing Asia, Hong Kong: Oxford University Press, forthcoming.

Goto, J. and K. Hamada, 1996, "Regional Economic Integration and Article XXIV of the GATT," Discussion paper, Economic Growth Center (New Haven, Conn.: Yale Univbersity).

Grossman, Gene and Helpman, Elhanan, 1995, "The Politics of Free Trade Agreements," *American Economic Review*, September, 667-690.

Halevi, N. and E. Kleiman, 1994, "Israel's Trade and Payments Regime," paper prepared for the Regional Trade Group, Institute for Social and Economic Policy in the Middle East, Kennedy School of Government, Cambridge, MA.

Kowalczyk, Carsten and Donald Davis, 1996, "Tariff Phase Outs: Theory and Evidence from GATT and NAFTA," in Jeffrey Frankel, *Regionalization of the World Economy*, Chicago: University of Chicago Press, forthcoming.

Krishna, Pravin, 1995, "Regionalism and Multilateralism: A Political Economy Approach," mimeo., Economics Department, Columbia University, December.

Krugman, P., 1991, "The Move to Free Trade Zones," Symposium Sponsored by the Federal Reserve Bank of Kansas City, *Policy Implications of Trade and Currency Zones*.

Melo, Jaime de and Panagariya, Arvind, ed., 1993, *New Dimensions in Regional Integration*, Cambridge, Great Britain: Cambridge University Press.

Panagariya, Arvind, 1993, "Should East Asia Go Regional? No, No and Maybe." WPS 1209, World Bank, Washington, D.C. (Chapter 3, this volume)

Panagariya, Arvind, 1994, "East Asia and the New Regionalism," *World Economy* 17, No. 6, November, 817-39.

Panagariya, Arvind, 1996a, "The Free Trade Area of the Americas: Good for Latin America?" *World Economy*, forthcoming. (Chapter 5, this volume)

Panagariya, Arvind, 1996b, "Preferential Trading and the Myth of Natural Trading Partners," Center for Japan-U.S. Business and Economic Studies, Stern School of Business, New York University, Working Paper No. 200.

Saxonhouse, Gary R., 1996, "Regionalism and U. S. trade Policy in Asia," in Bhagwati, J. and Panagariya, A., ed., 1996b.

Srinivasan, T.N., 1995, "APEC and Open Regionalism," mimeo.

Summers, L., 1991, "Regionalism and the World Trading System," Symposium Sponsored by the Federal Reserve Bank of Kansas City, *Policy Implications of Trade and Currency Zones*.

Viner, Jacob, 1950, *The Customs Union Issue*, New York: Carnegie Endowment for International Peace.

Wolf, Martin, 1996, "A Vision for World Trade," *Financial Times*, February 27, p. 12.

Yeats, ALexander J., 1996, "Does Mercosur's Trade Performance Justify Concerns About the Effects of Regional Trade Arrangements? Yes!," World Bank, mimeo.

PART III   LATIN AMERICA

5. Free Trade Area of the Americas: Good for Latin America?

5.1 Introduction

Excluding Mexico, Latin America accounts for less than 2.5% of the world trade. Is the creation of a trading bloc between this economically small region and the members of the North American Free Trade Agreement (NAFTA) a good idea? Yes, answer many analysts, arguing that even though the effect of the bloc on the United States and Canada is likely to be small, it will bring large gains to Latin America. Afterall, for Latin America, trading freely with the United States is like trading freely with the world. And if free trade is supposed to bring gains, the Free Trade Area of the Americas (FTAA) must surely do so.

Unfortunately, this argument is based on flawed reasoning. In the policy debate, there is a strong tendency to equate free trade areas (FTAs) with free trade. But as Viner (1950) taught us many decades ago, this equation is erroneous: FTAs liberalize trade on a discriminatory basis by removing trade barriers exclusively against union members while free trade requires a removal of the barriers against all trading partners. Indeed, discriminatory liberalization under FTAs may *increase rather than decrease* protection and may, indeed, make the countries undertaking the liberalization as well as the world as a whole worse off. The conventional wisdom which emerged from Viner's seminal contribution was that, on balance, FTAs were likely to be harmful; the United States resisted all calls for the formation of trading blocs in the post-Second-World-War period.[132] In the mid-1980s, for a variety of

Originally published in the *World Economy* 19(5), 1996, 485-515. I am indebted to two referees, Jagdish Bhagwati and Dani Rodrik for comments on this paper and to John Nash, Maurice Schiff, Sethaput Suthiwart-Narueput and Wendy Takacs for discussions on related

reasons discussed in Bhagwati (1993, 1995), the United States turned to regionalism.[133] Canada-U.S.A. Free Trade Agreement (CUFTA) was concluded in 1988 and NAFTA in 1992. Most recently, in 1994, an agreement has been signed to create by 2005 a Free Trade Area of the Americas (FTAA) consisting of the entire Western Hemisphere except Cuba. Alongside these developments, the conventional wisdom on FTAs has been shifting. Such distinguished economists as Dornbusch (1993), Krugman (1991, 1993) and Summers (1991) have enthusiastically embraced regionalism as a principal instrument of free trade.[134] Summers (1991), a staunch supporter of trading blocs, has taken the following position

> (E)conomists should maintain a strong, but rebuttable, presumption in favor of all lateral reductions in trade barriers, whether they be multi, uni, bi, tri, plurilateral. Global liberalization may be best, but regional liberalization is very likely to be good.

In this chapter, I take issue with the advocates of NAFTA and FTAA and argue that the key issue is not which lateral is chosen but whether the given lateral is implemented on a discriminatory or nondiscriminatory basis. My central thesis is that when trade liberalization is discriminatory as in an FTA, within the Vinerian framework, the effects of freer trade have a strong mercantilist bias: a country benefits from *receiving* a preferential (or discriminatory) access to the partner's market and is hurt by *giving* the partner a similar access to its own market. When the country gives access to the partner on a preferential basis, it loses the tariff revenue collected on imports from the partner. The revenue goes to boost the terms of trade of the latter. The reverse happens when the country receives a preferential access from the partner. On balance, then, the country, which liberalizes most, is

---

work which helped improve this one. Thanks are also due to Gabriel Castillo for valuable research assistance.

[132]The United States supported the formation of the European Economic Community (EEC) purely for political reasons. At that time, the United States saw a united Western Europe essential to meet the growing Soviet threat. See Bhagwati (1993) in this context.

[133]The principal reason why the United States, an ardent supporter of the nondiscriminatory process, turned to preferential trading arrangements was the failure to secure an agreement from Europe and developing countries to start a new round of multilateral trade negotiations.

[134]A referee of this journal has pointed out that "from recent statements by Messrs. Krugman and other regional enthusiasts at least the emphasis is gone and newly found enthusiasm for the WTO can be detected." In the case of Krugman, this observation is supported by a recent presentation by him at the 1996 American Economic Association meetings in San Francisco.

likely to lose. In the context of NAFTA and FTAA, the United States and Canada already have virtual free trade on a nondiscriminatory basis while Latin America has high tariffs. Therefore, within NAFTA and FTAA, Mexico and Latin America will give a much greater discriminatory access to the United States and Canada than they will receive from the latter. The inevitable conclusion is that the static welfare effects of NAFTA and FTAA on Mexico and Latin America will be negative.

Of course, the traditional Vinerian analysis is insufficient to establish the case against NAFTA and FTAA from the viewpoint of Mexico and Latin America. Recently, it has been argued that the gains to a developing country from an FTA with a large, rich trading partner go far beyond the traditional static effects. These new, *non-traditional* gains arise from a guaranteed access to the large market of the rich partner, protection from predatory actions such as anti-dumping by the latter, a "lock" on the country's own reforms, and a steady flow of foreign capital. If these gains are sufficiently large, FTAA may be desirable despite adverse welfare effects in static terms.

In the following, I will examine these non-traditional gains critically and argue that, in the absence of any means of verification, their significance was greatly exaggerated by the proponents of NAFTA. The latter often claimed gains from NAFTA that simply did not exist and disregarded benefits of the General Agreement of Tariffs and Trade (GATT)—now the World trade Organization (WTO)—that did exist. In this context, it is critical to distinguish between the rules of the game in the European Union and those in NAFTA.[135] The European Union (EU) and NAFTA are fundamentally different institutions: the former is a customs union with high degree of capital mobility and a commitment to eventual labor mobility. The latter is an FTA with complex rules of origin and essentially hostile to labor mobility.

The chapter is organized as follows. In Section 5.2, I outline the basic Vinerian economics using a simple partial equilibrium model. In addition to pointing out the relevance of the mercantilist approach for the economics of FTAs, I also question the analytic basis of some key justifications for FTAs in recent writings. My analysis is not new; it derives from the basic Vinerian model and can be found in different forms in the literature. The chapter's

---

[135]By core members in the EU, I mean full members of whom there are 15 currently. Core members are to be distinguished from associate members, mainly countries in Central and Eastern Europe, for whom the rules of the game are different.

contribution lies in reminding readers of the forgotten lessons in the context of NAFTA and FTAA.

In Section 5.3, I discuss some aspects of regional arrangements between developed and developing countries—the so-called North-South arrangements—not covered by the Vinerian analysis. In Section 5.4, I subject NAFTA to a critical scrutiny and, in Section 5.5, I compare it to the EU. In Section 5.6, I take a close look at other Latin American countries and argue that, on balance, they will lose from FTAA. In Section 5.7, I address issues related to policy harmonization. My conclusion here is that policy harmonization within North-South regional schemes is a costly affair for southern countries. For one thing, as has been systematically shown in various contributions in Bhagwati and Hudec (1996), there is no compelling case for policy harmonization, specially when countries are disparate in terms of size, income levels and preferences. Moreover, even if a plausible case could be made for harmonization, it requires a global context.[136] Harmonization by southern partners in North-South schemes towards northern countries' standards will leave the former at a disadvantage vis-a-vis their other southern competitors in regions such as East Asia. A summary of main conclusions is provided in Section 5.8.

5.2 Mercantilist Bias in the Effects of Discriminatory Liberalization[137]

In a small open economy, and up to a point, even in a large open economy, the primary source of gains from trade liberalization is the reduction in home tariffs. Reduced protection at home leads to a more efficient allocation of resources and of consumer expenditures. Yet, in trade negotiations, the reduction in home tariffs is viewed by negotiators as a cost and a reduction in the partner country's tariffs as benefit. Because of this mercantilist bias, it is commonly suggested that the negotiations under the General Agreement on Tariffs and Trade (GATT) lead to the right outcome for the wrong reason.

---

[136]Bhagwati (1995) has argued persuasively that as far as labor and environmental standards are concerned, a case for harmonization can simply not be made.

[137]This section and Section 5.6 draw on Panagariya (1995).

Surprisingly, when it comes to regional integration, at least within the Vinerian framework, the mercantilist approach is right: gains from regional integration come primarily from a reduction in the partner country's tariffs. Though this point is implicit in the standard Vinerian analysis, to my knowledge, it has not been recognized explicitly. I will first explain the point within a simple model and then deal with complications that may undermine it.

5.2.1 Preferential Tariff Liberalization: The Basic Case

Consider a world consisting of three countries: A, B and C. Think of A as Mexico which has high tariffs initially. In Figure 5.1, $M_A M_A$ represents the import demand for a product by A. The height of this curve represents the marginal benefit from imports and, hence, the area under it the total (gross) gains from trade.

Before we introduce export supplies of B and C, recall that Viner introduced the concepts of trade creation and trade diversion using a case in which supply prices of both B and C are constant. An important drawback of this case is that, in equilibrium, imports come from only one country. That is, whichever country has a lower tariff-inclusive price supplies *all* imports. A more realistic case is the one in which imports come from both countries. This case is captured most simply under the assumption that the supply price rises with exports for one country, say B, and remains constant for the other, C. As I will discuss later, this case, too, has certain limitations but it captures the essence of our argument without requiring us to deal with the complications of the small-country case.

In Figure 5.1, I represent the export supply of B by the upward sloped curve $E_B E_B$ and that of C by the horizontal line $P_C P_C$. Under a nondiscriminatory tariff at rate t per unit, supplies from B and C, as perceived by buyers in A, are given by $E_B{}^t E_B{}^t$ and $P_C{}^t P_C{}^t$, respectively. Total imports into A equal OQ_3 of which OQ_1 come from B and $Q_1 Q_3$ from C. A collects tariff revenue in the amount represented by rectangle GHNS. The gains from trade amount to the area under the import-demand curve and above the domestic price plus the tariff revenue, i.e., triangle KSG plus rectangle GHNS. For country B, the gains from trade equal the area above $E_B E_B$ and below the net price received, P_C, and equals HUD. Country C neither gains nor loses from trade. Table 5.1 summarizes this information in column 1.

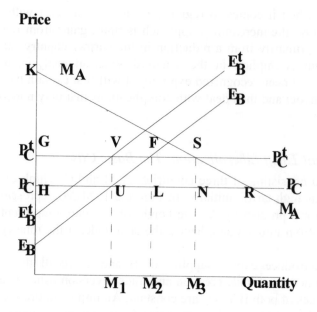

Figure 5.1: Welfare Effects of a Tariff Preference

Suppose now that A decides unilaterally to adopt a policy of nondiscriminatory free trade. The price in A declines to P_C, imports from B do not change, and imports from C rise by NR. Tariff revenue disappears but the gains from trade rise to KGS+GHNS+RSN. There is a net welfare gain of RSN. The extra gain comes from increased benefits to consumers. The gains to country B remain unchanged at HDU. Because of the perfectly elastic supply, country C neither gains nor loses from trade before or after trade liberalization by A. Therefore, the world as a whole benefits by area RSN. These changes are summarized in column 2 of Table 5.1.

Next, assume that A has the option to form an FTA with B or C. It should be obvious that the outcome of the FTA will depend critically on whether the partner country is B or C. For the moment, I assume that the partner country is B and return to the other case later. Because the rest of world is likely to be much larger than a single trading partner, *prima facie*, it is not unreasonable to assume that the rest of the world's supply is more elastic than that of the partner. Figure 5.1 represents this assumption in the extreme form by making C's supply perfectly elastic.

Under the FTA arrangement, A eliminates entirely the tariff on B but retains it on C. Imports from B rise to OQ_2 and those from C decline to Q_2Q_3. Though there is trade diversion, B gains from the FTA due to an improvement in its terms of trade. The net price received by the exporters of B increases from P_C to P_C^t and the gains from trade to B rise to HDU+HUFG. *Country B gains from A's liberalization precisely as mercantilists would predict.*

Because imports continue to come from C before as well as after the FTA and C's supply is perfectly elastic, the price in A is unchanged. But now that there is no tariff revenue on goods coming from B, A's gains from trade decline by GFLH. *Once again, as mercantilists would have argued, A loses from its own liberalization.* Because the FTA diverts imports Q_1Q_2 from the more efficient C to less efficient B, A's loss exceeds B's gain by area UFL. The world as a whole loses by area UFL. The last column in Table 5.1 shows these changes.

In his influential paper mentioned earlier, Summers (1991) chastises economists for paying too much attention to second best considerations while evaluating regional arrangements. Referring to trade diversion, he writes

> I find it surprising that this issue is taken so seriously—in most other situations, economists laugh off second best considerations and focus on direct impacts.

Taking issue with Summers' position in this and the earlier quotation, Bhagwati (1995) has recently retorted thus,

> My gut reaction is to wonder what Summers would say if, on hearing that he wanted our spending to be cut, I told him, 'Cut anything you want, wherever you wish, it does not matter what, as it all leads to reduced spending.' Or, on hearing that he wanted revenues to be raised, I advised him, a wonderful public finance specialist of the neoclassical variety, to raise any and every tax in any way that he could since all taxes raised revenue.

| Policy | Nondiscriminatory | Complete | FTA with B |
| | Tariff at Rate t | Free Trade | |
Country	(1)	(2)	(3)
A	KGS+GHNS	KGS+GHNS	KGS+GHNS-
		+RSN	GFLH
B	HDU		HDU+GFLH-
		HDU	UFL
C	0	0	0
World		KGS+GHNS	KGS+GHNS
	KGS+GHNS+	+HDU+RSN	+HDU-UFL
	HDU		

Table 5.1: Gains from Trade under Unilateral Liberalization and FTA.
(The table relates to Figure 5.1)

The analysis in this section complements Bhagwati's argument. The loss to A from its own liberalization arises primarily from the "impact effect" of the FTA rather than second- best considerations. If we assume that the initial imports from the trading partner are large, the loss due to trade diversion—triangle UFL in Figure 5.1—accounts only for a small fraction of A's loss. The large part of the loss—rectangle GVUH—is accounted for by the lost tariff revenue on the original imports from the partner. In denouncing trade diversion as a major concern, Summers has clearly overlooked the fact that FTAs can also give rise to *large redistributive effects* between countries and that, unlike efficiency effects which are triangles, redistributive effects are rectangles!

My analysis also raises doubts about the argument injected into the debate recently that countries which trade with each other a lot are "natural" trading partners and regional arrangements among them are beneficial. It is not clear what it means to be "natural" trading partners but a quotation from Summers (1991) may help.[138]

---

[138] As far as I am able to trace, the idea originated in Wonnacott and Lutz (1989). Krugman (1991) also makes this argument stating, "To reemphasize why this matters: if a disproportionate share of world trade would take place within trading blocs even in the absence of any preferential trading arrangement, then the gains from trade creation within blocs are likely to outweigh any possible losses from external trade diversion." Recently, Primo Braga, Safadi and Yeats (1994) have pushed the "natural trading partners" argument one step further by suggesting that, having become more interdependent in recent years, Latin American economies are more ripe for regional integration among themselves today than in the 1960s and 1970s. As discussed in the text, economic theory offers no basis for this conclusion.

Are trading blocs likely to divert large amounts of trade? In answering this question, the issue of natural trading blocs is crucial because to the extent that blocs are created between countries that already trade disproportionately, the risk of large amounts of trade diversion is reduced.

Drawing upon the analytic results from the past literature, particularly Lipsey (1958), Bhagwati (1993) has questioned the presumption that trade diversion is minimal if potential members trade with each other disproportionately more with each other. My analysis adds to Bhagwati's critique of the "natural trading partners" argument. It is evident from Figure 5.1 that the larger the initial quantity of imports from a trading partner, the greater the loss to the country liberalizing preferentially from a given trade diversion. That is to say, the more natural the trading partner according to Summers' definition, the larger the loss from a discriminatory trade liberalization with it!

Finally, it is being suggested lately that given low levels of trade restrictions than in 1960s and 1970s, chances that trade diversion will dominate trade creation are low. This is exactly opposite of the conclusion coming out of the Vinerian analysis. Thus, in Figure 5.1, if the initial nondiscriminatory tariff is sufficiently high, an FTA between A and B eliminates C as a supplier of the product. In this case, the FTA lowers the internal price in A and gives rise to trade creation. Under some conditions, this trade creation can outweigh the tariff-revenue loss and may improve welfare. By contrast, if the initial tariff is low, the chances that the formation of the FTA will eliminate imports from C and lower the internal price are poor.

5.2.2 Beyond the Basic Case

The conclusion that A's preferential liberalization hurts itself and benefits its union partner has been derived under the assumption that the supply of B is less than perfectly elastic and that of C perfectly elastic. In this setting, the union partner is a less efficient supplier of the product than the outside world. What will happen if the situation was reversed and A formed a union with C rather than B?

In Figure 5.1, a union between A and C lowers the price in A to P_C. Though there is no gain to the union partner, A's gain from the FTA exceeds that under nondiscriminatory liberalization. Relative to the initial, nondiscriminatory tariff, A gains area SNR plus the tariff revenue (not shown) on imports from the outside country B. We are back to the neoclassical world where A's liberalization benefits itself and not B.

This case clearly undercuts the arguments made in Section 5.2.1. Therefore, it is important to ask how relevant it is empirically. It is perhaps reasonable to assert that a union partner is likely to resemble B for some products and C in other products and, therefore, the effect of the FTA will be ambiguous in general. In the specific case of NAFTA, a common claim has been that, on net, Mexico is likely to gain because the United States is very large and, *therefore*, the most efficient supplier of a majority of Mexico's products.

There are at least two reasons why this conclusion is unwarranted. First, given that the outside world includes the EU, Japan, China, Korea, Hong Kong and numerous other highly competitive countries, the conclusion that the United States and Canada are the most efficient suppliers of a large majority of Mexico's products is highly suspect. Indeed, if it were true, we will be hard-pressed to explain the persistent demands for anti-dumping and other forms of protection in the United States. Second, recall that if the union partner is a large supplier of imports, the losses to A in the case of trade diversion are large and the gains to it in the case of trade creation are small. Therefore, even if the union partner is the most efficient supplier of the majority of A's imports, losses may outweigh the gains. In the case of NAFTA, the United States does account for a sufficiently large proportion of Mexico's imports that the losses to the latter in trade-diversion cases will outweigh the gains to her in trade-creation cases.

Before I conclude the discussion of static welfare effects of an FTA, two additional possibilities deserve to be considered: (i) export-supply curves are upward sloped for both B and C and (ii) exports of B and C are imperfect substitutes. In either of these cases, the small-country assumption is violated and a complete elimination of the tariff by A, whether on a discriminatory or nondiscriminatory basis, is not the optimal policy.

Bearing this fact in mind, let me note that the analysis of Section 5.2.1 remains valid under the following circumstances. In case (i), if the elasticity of supply of the outside country is high in relation to that of the union partner, a discriminatory tariff reduction is likely to hurt even when a nondiscriminatory reduction will not. The discriminatory tariff reduction will benefit B. In case (ii), if the imports coming from the union partner and the outside country are sufficiently close substitutes, discriminatory liberalization by A will hurt that country and benefit the union partner.

Because neither of these cases are implausible in reality, I conclude that the presumption is in favor of the conclusion, derived in Section 5.2.1, that within a discriminatory liberalization scheme, a country is hurt by its own liberalization and benefits from the partner's liberalization.[139]

5.2.3 FTAs under Quotas

Let us now briefly turn to the case of a quota. The first point to note is that under a quota, the wedge between the domestic and the border price—the so-called quota rent—is captured by the recipient of the license. For example, if import licenses are issued free of charge to domestic importers, license holders get the quota rent. If the government auctions the licenses freely, it captures the quota rent in the same way as it gets the tariff revenue in the case considered in Section 5.2.1. Either way, the quota rent, represented by GHNS in Figure 5.1 (assuming the quota to be set at GS on a nondiscriminatory basis), remains a part of A's gains from trade.

Consider now the formation of an FTA which frees B of the quota restriction but not C. It should be obvious that the results depend critically on how the quota on C is fixed. If the quota on C is fixed such that total imports from all sources do not change after the union is formed, our previous analysis remains unchanged. In terms of Figure 5.1, the import quota on C is fixed at FS. Country B, though freed of the quota restriction, continues to export GF. No quota rent is generated on imports from B, which now receives the full price, P_C^t. The results in column 3 of Table 5.1 are entirely unchanged.

A more plausible assumption is that the quota on C is fixed at the pre-FTA level of imports from that country. In this case, total imports into A will rise after the formation of the union, the price in A will fall and trade creation will take place. The net effect is still likely to be negative, however. For the partner's terms of trade will still improve (though by less than the full amount of the quota rent in the pre-FTA equilibrium) and a part of the rectangle GVUH will be lost. The basic conclusion of Section 5.2.1 remains valid.

---

[139]For further details, see Bhagwati and Panagariya (1996a) where the argument of this and previous subsection has been developed more fully. The imperfect-substitutes model is discussed in detail in Panagariya (1996a, 1996b). Finally, for a summary of the theoretical literature, see Bhagwati and Panagariya (1996b).

5.3 Non-traditional Gains from North-South Integration

The first regional movement, which flourished in the 1950s and 1960s, consisted of regional arrangements that were either North-North or South-South type. The original members of the European Economic Community and of the European Free Trade Area (EFTA) were all developed countries. Members of other regional schemes such as the Central American Common Market, Andean Pact, Association of South-East Asian Nations, and Economic Community of West African States were all developing countries.

The second regional movement, also referred to as the New Regionalism, can be traced to the beginning of negotiations for Canada-U.S.A. Free Trade Agreement (CUFTA) in mid 1980s. This movement began with the conversion of the United States to regionalism and has been characterized by several regional agreements between developed and developing countries. The most prominent of these is, of course, NAFTA, which supersedes the CUFTA and is designed to create a Free Trade Area among Canada, Mexico and U.S.A. The second enlargement of the European Community in 1986, which gave Greece, Portugal and Spain entry into the Community also had elements of North-South integration. Finally, a large number of Association Agreements between the European Community (EC) on the one hand and Central and East European countries on the other represent examples of North-South agreements.

In principle, developing county participants of North-South arrangements can expect three advantages that are not available in South-South arrangements. First, such arrangements guarantee access to a large market. If the rich partner's markets are subject to trade barriers initially, the FTA helps remove those barriers and, thus, *improves* the country's access to the former's market. If the rich partner's markets are already open, the FTA helps *maintain* the access in the event the former becomes more protectionist in the future.

Second, the FTA can shield the developing country member from administered protection in the rich country. For instance, the country may escape anti-dumping and safeguards actions by the rich partner to which other trading partners can be subject.

Finally, a regional arrangement with a large, rich trading partner can be an effective instrument of imparting credibility to reforms. An international treaty with a large and rich country can "lock" the reforms, making it difficult for more protection-minded future governments to reverse the actions of their predecessors.

These benefits are not without qualification, however. First, to the extent that the southern country has higher initial tariffs, the FTA is likely to worsen its terms of trade. In the limit, if the northern country already has free trade, there is no change in the southern country's access to the former's market as a result of the FTA. On the contrary, it is the northern country, which succeeds in acquiring access to the southern country *on a preferential* basis. In this case, the discriminatory access given by the developing country may be a hefty premium to pay in return for the promise by the rich country not to close its markets in the future.

Second, as was amply demonstrated during NAFTA debate, integration with a southern country generates fears of adverse income distribution effects on unskilled labor in the North. These fears, in turn, lead to adoption of provisions (e.g., restrictive rules of origin) which partially undo the free-trade agreement in precisely those areas where it is likely to generate trade creation.

Finally, the benefits in terms of enhancing the credibility of reforms can be easily overstated. As far as tariffs are concerned, a country can attain the same objective *on a nondiscriminatory basis* through the GATT bindings. Regarding other instruments such as anti-dumping, an FTA does not offer any more restraint than the GATT. But that is likely to precisely enhance the possibility of such action against countries outside the union. This is the point made forcefully by Bhagwati (1993). To quote him,

> Imagine that the United States begins to eliminate (by outcompeting) an inefficient Mexican industry once the FTA goes into effect. Even though the most efficient producer is Taiwan, if the next efficient United States outcompetes the least efficient Mexico, that would be desirable trade creation...
>
> But what would the Mexicans be likely to do? They would probably start AD actions against Taiwan...

In the light of these benefits and costs of North-South regional arrangements, let us look closely at their evolution in the two major regions: North America and Europe.

5.4 NAFTA

In the Western Hemisphere, the North-South integration began with NAFTA. To assess the future desirability of similar FTAs, it is best to review briefly the main achievements of NAFTA. The following is the list of major changes to be implemented over a period of 15 years.

Liberalization of imports of **fresh fruits and vegetables** from Mexico into the United States and that of **corn** (and other grains) in the opposite direction.

- Liberalization of tariffs and quotas on North American trade in **textiles and apparel**.

- Removal of most tariffs and non-tariff barriers (NTBs) on **cars** by Mexico within five to ten years.

- Mexico agrees to a rapid access for the U.S. and Canadian firms to Mexico's **telecommunications** market. Mexico is to eliminate the majority of tariff and NTBs to its telecommunications equipment market upon implementation of NAFTA.

- In the **government procurement** area, over a period of 10 years, Mexico will open up to North American companies.

- NAFTA commits Mexico to a speedy implementation of the GATT **intellectual property** rights.

- Member countries agreed to provide national treatment to **investors** of another NAFTA member.

- The North American Agreement on **Environmental Cooperation** commits NAFTA members to improve environmental protection laws and enforce existing laws. Persistent failures are subject to a dispute settlement procedure, which can assess monetary fines up to $20 million.

- The North American Agreement on **Labor Cooperation** does the same in the area of labor laws and labor standards.

Let us evaluate the likely effects of these changes.

5.4.1 Static Welfare Gains

From the viewpoint of static welfare effects, it is difficult to argue that Mexico will be a net beneficiary. Tariffs in Mexico are close to 20% in many sectors affected by NAFTA while those in the U.S.A. and Canada 5%. Moreover, Mexico already enjoys preferential access to the United States market under the Generalized System of Preferences (GSP). According to Erzan and Yeats (1992), for the year 1986, Mexican exports to the United States which faced a tariff of 5% or more and also had one or more significant nontariff barriers accounted for only 8.5% of total exports. Hence, NAFTA is virtually certain to improve the U.S. access to Mexico without a major change in Mexico's access to the U.S. market. Put differently, NAFTA will worsen Mexico's terms of trade.

The only sectors where Mexico appears to have won important new concessions *over other exporters* are fruits and vegetables and textiles and clothing. In fruits and vegetables category, items in which Mexico had major interests such as orange juice and sugar are subject to special agreements that effectively limit import surges. And in textiles and clothing, Mexico's gains are likely to be limited for four reasons.

First, during 1980s, Mexico consistently underutilized its Multifiber Arrangement (MFA) quotas with the United states. Erzan and Yeats (1992) place Mexico's average quota utilization rate over 1985-89 in the United States at 51.5%. Though, as discussed in Whalley (1995), quota underutilization may mean many different things, this evidence suggests that the gain from the MFA-quota liberalization may turn out to be rather limited. Second, under NAFTA, imports are subject to strict rules of origin based on "triple transformation." These rules are likely to limit Mexico's preferential access to the U.S. market in textiles and clothing. Third, the gains from tariff liberalization are limited due to a tiny share of textiles and clothing in total Mexican exports to the United States. The average tariff on Mexico's clothing and textiles exports in the United States in 1987 was 17.3%.[140] The eventual removal of this tariff would seem to be a significant gain. But given that clothing and textiles account for less than 2% of its total exports to the United states, the associated gain, even if such exports double, cannot be very large. Finally, to some degree, the dismantling of the MFA under the Uruguay Round will erode Mexico's preferential access to the United States' market.

---

[140]See Erzan and Yeats (1992), footnote 14.

By comparison, concessions granted by Mexico—virtually all of them on a preferential basis—are many and more substantial. Given the relatively high restrictions on outside countries—recall the highest tariff rate is 20%— NAFTA is bound to lead to a substantial transfer of tariff revenue to the U.S. exporters. The liberalization in the automobile sector and government procurement is also likely to benefit mostly the United States. There may be some efficiency gains in the telecommunications sector where the U.S. industry is said to be highly efficient but not enough to offset the losses in other areas. Whalley (1993) was right on the mark when, discussing the willingness of larger countries to go along with the demands of smaller countries for regional arrangements albeit at a price, he predicted

> The current danger for Mexico in NAFTA is that the price will be paid in the form of adverse exclusionary arrangements which are against Mexican national interest, particularly autos, with potential impediments to third-country inward capital flows and arrangements which effectively reserve the Mexican import market for US suppliers.

5.4.2 Non-traditional Gains

In the long debate preceding the approval of NAFTA in the United States, economists were virtually unanimous that the arrangement was beneficial to Mexico. Not only the advocates of regionalism such as Dornbusch and Summers pushed for NAFTA, traditional skeptics such as Cooper (1993) and Corden (1993) also supported it. A key factor behind this consensus was the belief that NAFTA offered Mexico certain non-traditional gains not available through any other means.[141]

Surprisingly, the existence of these gains was accepted as a matter of faith. In all the writings prior to the approval of NAFTA by the United States—by believers and skeptics of regionalism alike—I have not found any critical assessment of these gains. Recently, Bhagwati (1995) has confronted the issue head on. Following him, let me attempt a full-scale critical examination of the non-traditional gains from NAFTA.

---

[141]Especially after Ross Perot declared his opposition to NAFTA, even economists critical of the regional approach found it difficult to oppose NAFTA lest they be viewed as supporting Perot's position and hence against free trade. The author is proud to say, however, that during December 1993 when the Congress was about to vote, he wrote and submitted to the Wall Street Journal an article entitled "Death to NAFTA: Long Live Free Trade." Of course, the Journal promptly rejected the article.

5.4.2.1 Market Access

According to this argument, NAFTA *improves* and *maintains* Mexico's access to the large North American market. I have already argued that with the exception of fruits and vegetables, *improvement* in Mexico's access to North American market on account of NAFTA is minimal. This is not only because the U.S. and Canadian markets are already quite open but also because NAFTA has 200 pages of rules of origin. Though the stated purpose of these rules is to ensure that goods do not get imported from low-tariff country for transshipment to a high-tariff union member, given their complexity, they are bound to be misused for protectionist purposes.

An extension of the argument under consideration is that NAFTA guarantees Mexico *future* market access in case the U.S. and Canadian markets close. In my view, this argument simply plays on the fears of weaker nations and has no basis in reality. I can imagine the United States threatening Japan, EU, China, South Korea and even India and Brazil with new trade restrictions unless these latter opened their own markets further. But it is hard to imagine the use of such threats against a relatively open country such as Mexico with or without NAFTA. Given its own obligations under various GATT agreements, the United States is also unlikely to raise its own MFN tariffs. And in the unlikely event of an all-out trade war, irrespective of NAFTA, the United States is likely to move closer to, not away from, its trade partners to the south.

5.4.2.2 Shelter from New Protectionism in the United States

It is sometimes suggested that NAFTA shelters Mexico from administered protection in the United States.[142] The reality, however, is that NAFTA provides Mexico no more reprieve from anti-dumping actions than available to other countries. Nor does it banish the use of safeguard actions. Indeed, the special agreements on sugar and orange juice explicitly allow for the play of administered protection in the event of import surges in these sectors. Furthermore, side agreements on labor standards and environment give the United States *new* powers to subject Mexico to dispute settlement procedures which can lead to fines of up to $20 million.

---

[142]For instance, in a letter to the author, Jeffrey Schott of the Institute for International Economics writes, "...NAFTA is a GATT-plus accord that goes beyond the GATT commitment regarding contingent protection and import safeguard actions."

5.4.2.3 Credibility to and Lock on the Reforms

This is perhaps the most loudly expressed and least articulated argument made by proponents of NAFTA. As commonly expressed, the argument says that an international treaty with the world's richest country guarantees that reforms undertaken by the current government cannot be reversed by less re-form-minded future governments. This, in turn, promotes a healthy envi-ronment for investment—both domestic and foreign—and growth. In its ex-treme form, the argument turns FTAs into a simple formula for growth: sign a regional pact with a rich country and you will prosper. The costs in terms of redistribution of tariff revenue to partner-country exporters, trade diver-sion and side agreements are then minuscule in relation to benefits. The ar-gument definitely deserves a close examination.

The first point to note is that the causal relationship between NAFTA and credibility to reforms may be reverse. Rather than NAFTA giving credibility to reforms, very likely, it was the (perceived) credibility of Mexico's reforms, which led the United States to sign NAFTA in the first place. By the time the United States got serious about NAFTA, Mexico's reforms were perceived as irreversible even by markets. Without that perception, massive capital inflows including direct foreign investment into Mexico could not have taken place. Though the recent crisis has proved both the United States and markets wrong, it does not detract from the fact that the perception of credibility played an important role in facilitating the negotiation, signing and passage of NAFTA. Put differently, if the United States Congress was voting on NAFTA today, without a shred of doubt, the vote will be negative.

We must also acknowledge that, ironically, NAFTA may have contributed to the recent macroeconomic crisis Mexico. It is now becoming clear that the foundation of the crisis had been laid at least as early as 1993. Determined not to let NAFTA slip away at any cost, Salinas government used the massive capital inflows from the United States, caused to a large degree by recession and low interest rates there, to maintain an overvalued peso. This, in turn, allowed Mexicans to maintain a high level of imports including consumer goods. A large proportion of these goods came from the United States. The imports promoted the image of a healthy Mexican economy on the one hand and increased the stakes of U.S. exporters in Mexico on the other. Both factors helped prop up support for NAFTA in the United States. But, in the meantime, much needed adjustment in the monetary policy and the exchange rate was delayed.

The crisis aside, can we still claim that NAFTA offers a lock on Mexico's reforms. To answer, we must be clear about what we mean by "reform" in this context. If by reform, we mean *macroeconomic stability*, the recent crisis has already proved the argument to be false.[143] As a general point, macroeconomic stability comes largely from a country's own actions rather than the signing of an external pact. Chile does not have NAFTA but has managed its affairs well in recent years; it has had no crisis. Mexico had NAFTA but managed its affairs poorly; it suffered a crisis.

Next, let us look at microeconomic reforms. The most obvious first candidate in this area is trade policy. In evaluating NAFTA's contribution to *trade reform* and its credibility, we must compare it to tariff bindings offered by the WTO. Each member of the WTO has the option to bind its tariffs on different commodities at specified levels within the WTO framework. Once this is done, countries whose exports are adversely affected can challenge tariff increases beyond the bindings in the WTO. This is the mechanism, which has sustained the tariff reductions of industrial countries under the various GATT rounds during the last four decades. Neither the United States nor Japan nor a host of European countries signed any regional pacts to lend credibility to their "trade reform."

There is no doubt that the WTO bindings offer a superior lock on tariffs than NAFTA. First, the WTO bindings are nondiscriminatory and apply to more than 120 countries while NAFTA locks tariffs on just two countries. In terms of economic efficiency, this makes the WTO mechanism superior. Second, on the face of it, violation of an agreement is less likely when there are dozens of potential challengers than just two. The old argument that compliance within the GATT/WTO framework is weak is no longer valid, now that a new, much tighter, dispute settlement mechanism is in place at the WTO. Finally, GATT bindings are not accompanied by rules of origin. Under NAFTA, the rules of origin have the potential to subvert the liberalization even within the union.

But, for the sake of argument, suppose for a moment that the proponents of NAFTA are right in that the NAFTA discipline works while GATT discipline does not. Now if protectionist pressures in Mexico rise in the

---

[143]It may seem that proponents of NAFTA claim "lock in" effects only on the policies actually covered in the agreement. But in policy discussions, I have found these claims to go well beyond the agreement. As an example, consider the following assertion by Jeffrey Schott in the letter to the author mentioned earlier, "Furthermore, the 'lock-in' effect applies to domestic policy reforms undertaken by the developing countries, and reduces the risk of policy reversals..."

future, how will the government respond? True, that the purpose of the lock is not to have to respond. But as we know from experience in virtually all countries, there are times every government has to respond to protectionist demands. With NAFTA effectively locking the protection against the United States and Canada at zero and GATT discipline subject to abuse, the government may be left with no option but to raise tariffs against outside countries. With 70% of Mexico's imports coming from the United States, this increase in the outside tariff will have to be very substantial, indeed, to grant the desired level of protection.[144] By contrast, in the absence of NAFTA, the necessary increase in the tariff will be small and, being nondiscriminatory in nature, less damaging to Mexico's welfare.

Does NAFTA help contain the use of nontariff barriers more effectively than GATT? As already noted, the agreement does not limit the use of instruments such as anti-dumping and safeguard actions, which are governed by the WTO discipline. Nor does it provide any discipline against the use of direct import quotas against nonmembers beyond that provided by GATT. Some proponents of regionalism argue, however, that in times of macroeconomic crises, countries will not be able to resort to *exchange controls* if they are locked in a regional arrangement with a developed country.[145] As far as I know, this claim is incorrect. NAFTA creates an FTA among member countries but beyond that says nothing about the use of exchange or import controls in times of macroeconomic crises with respect to outside countries. Whatever discipline exists comes from International Monetary Fund (IMF). Under Article IV, countries are required to consult with the IMF before they can introduce any new exchange controls. In the 1960s and 1970s, the Fund gave permission to use these restrictions with relative ease. But lately, the Fund has been more conservative. It should be remembered, however, that the Fund discipline, which is weak in any case, applies to current account restrictions only. Countries, both developed and developing, employ exchange controls relating to capital account transactions.

---

[144]Since the writing of the original draft of this paper, after the recent peso crisis, Mexican tariffs on outside countries on 502 products have been raised to 35%. Because pre-NAFTA tariffs in Mexico were 20% or lower, this tariff increase implies a 75% or larger tariff preference to NAFTA members.

[145]Paul Collier of Oxford University made this point at a World Bank conference during a paper presentation by the author.

Some proponents of NAFTA also argue that it will discourage the adoption of arbitrary domestic policies designed to favor one firm over others. This adherence to nondiscriminatory policies will, in turn, discourage rent-seeking activities. Once again, apart from the national treatment provision for investors of union members, there is nothing in the NAFTA document, which supports this contention. But if national treatment itself is ill defined—note that the argument begins by asserting that the government discriminates between domestic firms—this provision cannot help very much. Perhaps the argument rests on a belief that the U.S. firms likely to be hurt by the discriminatory policies will be looking over Mexican government's shoulder and bring moral pressure on the latter to be even handed. Quite apart from issues of national sovereignty that this line of reasoning raises, its validity is highly suspect. If the U.S. firms do acquire the ability to exert pressure on the Mexican government as a result of NAFTA, they will themselves seek preferential treatment. Domestic firms will, in turn, form alliances with U.S. firms to continue their quest for rents. The net result will very likely be an increase rather than decrease in rent-seeking activities and, worse yet, redistribution of rents from domestic to foreign firms.

Finally, proponents of NAFTA also argue that the provision on intellectual property rights will result in better copyright and patent laws and the side agreements on labor and environmental standards will lead to improved enforcement of the existing Mexican laws. Though I deal with this subject separately later, it may be noted here that these agreements were not sought by Mexico and, as such, not viewed by the country as being in its own interest. The view that higher standards are in Mexico's interest even if it did not seek them is not only paternalistic, it is also wrong. Higher labor and environmental standards in Mexico, without similar changes in competing developing countries, will surely lower Mexico's competitiveness in certain sectors. As for tighter intellectual property rights, at least in the short run, they will make technology imports more expensive. Reduced access to or increased prices of medicines are almost sure to hurt the poor.[146]

The contention of proponents of NAFTA that the arrangement will lead to a steady flow of foreign capital has been proved to be decisively wrong by

---

[146]See Panagariya (1996c) for a detailed analysis of the impact of tighter intellectual property rights on developing countries and Bhagwati (1996) and Bhagwati and Srinivasan (1996) for a discussion of the validity of the demands for higher labor and environmental standards by developed countries from developing countries.

the recent crisis. But for a Herculean international effort led by the United States—for which credit cannot go to NAFTA—Mexico was in danger of defaulting on its debt. As for direct foreign investment (DFI) rather than capital flows in general, the evidence provided by Whalley (1993) on the CUFTA should have a sobering effect on us. Whalley found that between 1987 and 1990, the DFI flow into Canada from the United States flattened while that from outside countries rose sharply.

5.5 A Digression to the European Union

Lest I should appear opposed to *all* forms of regional integration, let me hasten to express my support for the European Union (EU) as defined by its core membership of 15 countries. To begin with, the origins of the EU were political and, regardless of whether it created or diverted trade, it yielded major political benefits. In its various incarnations, for several decades, the EU served as an effective bulwark against the Soviet bloc. For this reason alone, it was well worth having the EU.

But this is not all. On economic grounds as well, it is much easier to defend the EU than NAFTA. Similarly to the United States, and unlike NAFTA, there is a strong commitment to deep integration within member states of EU. The EU is intended to be a *Common Market* with a common external tariff and free capital mobility which it already has and free mobility of labor which it seeks. The common external tariff eliminates the need for the rules of origin. It also provides a genuine lock on trade reform: a member state cannot raise its outside tariff without all members willing to do the same.[147] The EU also prohibits anti-dumping actions by member states against one another. Instead, members are subject to a common competition policy.

The strength of EU's commitment to integration is also reflected in the existence of compensation mechanisms designed to help the members who

---

[147]This point is developed formally in Panagariya and Findlay (1995). We should not forget that the lock works in both directions: the common external tariff can impede liberalization by weaker members if the dominant members in the union are more protectionist. This is clearly a risk for Uruguay who, as a member of MERCOSUR which is a customs union, must adhere to the latter's common external tariff. But the EU's record in this area has been excellent: it has not only lowered the common external tariff during successive GATT rounds but also led new members such as Greece, Portugal and Spain into faster liberalization than would have been the case otherwise.

either lose large amounts of tariff revenue or are poorer. Adjustment assistance and income convergence have been central goals of the EU. The Regional Development Fund was created in 1972 explicitly in response to UK's fears that some of its regions will suffer on account of its entry into the European Economic Community (EEC). Funds were also earmarked in the mid-1980s to smoothen the entry of Greece, Portugal and Spain.

Before turning to the Free Trade Area of the Americas, a word on the recent European Agreements (EAs) between EC and the Central and East European (CEE) countries is in order. These agreements effectively create an FTA between the EU and each of the CEE members in six to ten years' time. Many of the criticisms of NAFTA apply to these agreements. What is different, however, is the political context and eventual expectations. Politically, the CEE countries see these agreements as an instrument of distancing themselves further from Russia—a way to lock-in their newfound freedom. Equally important, they also see the agreements as a first step towards full membership in the EU, which can eventually turn the immediate economic losses into gains.

5.6 The Free Trade Area of the Americas

Let us now look at NAFTA from the viewpoint of Latin American countries other than Mexico. There are two main issues: how is NAFTA likely to impact them and should they make efforts to enter NAFTA. The first of these issues can be illustrated with the help of Costa Rica whose trade regime was studied carefully recently by the UNDP-World Bank sponsored Trade Expansion Program (1992). According to the study, fears have been expressed that NAFTA will lead to a displacement by Mexico of Costa Rica's exports to the U.S.A. and that it will also divert investments to Mexico. Because the United States alone accounts for more than 50% of Costa Rica's exports and an equally high proportion of its imports, *prima facie*, such fears may seem justified. But as the TEP report points out, a serious injury can happen only in the case of products which are currently subject to high barriers in the United States and are important to Costa Rica. There are few products, which satisfy both these conditions. For some exports into North America, common to Mexico and Costa Rica, the two countries both enjoy duty-free access. For example, this is true of the "maquilla" electronics industry as well as Costa Rica's major traditional exports. Sugar is the major exception but in that case, Mexico's access has itself been limited by special agreements. Main areas where NAFTA can have some adverse impact is non-traditional agricultural exports, which are not particularly large for Costa Rica and apparel. Not surprisingly, the TEP report concludes, "Overall then, a Mexico-U.S. agreement offers little reason for pessimism,..."

What applies to Costa Rica perhaps applies to a large number of other countries. As argued above, within NAFTA, there was limited room for discriminatory liberalization in the United States and Canada. Discriminatory liberalization by Mexico was more extensive but its market is relatively tiny. Not surprisingly, estimates of the effects of free trade within North America on third-country exports are generally small. Laird (1990) estimates that complete removal of tariffs within North America reduces the exports of other countries in the Western Hemisphere to the United States by less than .8%. Erzan and Yeats (1992) estimate that the total trade diversion from tariff elimination in North America will amount to 0.5% of U.S. imports from nonmembers. Of this, only 6% will fall on countries in the Western Hemisphere!

Turning to the issue of entry, I do not share the enthusiasm of many for a rush to sign an FTA with NAFTA and, eventually, create a Free Trade Area of the Americas. For reasons that must be clear by now, it is highly doubtful that Latin American countries stand to gain much from entering into an arrangement which gives their rich counterparts—U.S.A. and Canada—a much greater preferential market access than the latter are able to offer in return. Table 5.2, taken from Lustig and Primo Braga (1994), provides the information on trade barriers in Latin America. Unilateral trade reforms have virtually eliminated quantitative restrictions in the countries shown and lowered the average tariff rates considerably. Yet, the highest tariff rates at 20% or more remain high. Discriminatory liberalization with the United States under these circumstances is unlikely to confer major gains and will, very likely, lower welfare. Indeed, in the end, if FTAA does come into being, gains to developing countries in the region will come largely from improved access to each other's market than from any additional access to the U.S. and Canadian markets.

A different twist is added to the issue if we bring in the possibility of the EU forming FTAs with countries in Latin America. Given the frequent claim that EU markets are less accessible to outsiders than North American markets, an argument can be made that Latin American countries may be better off seeking FTAs with the former. Not surprisingly, possibilities have been raised of an FTA between the Southern Cone Common Market (MERCOSUR) and the EU. Whether the United States will favor such an arrangement or not and whether it can go ahead even if the latter is opposed remains to be seen.[148]

If one goes by the intensity of trade, for a large number of countries in Latin America, the EC is a larger trading partner than the United States.[149] Tables 5.3 and 5.4 show the direction of exports and imports, respectively, of Mexico and 10 other Latin American countries. Based on exports, for 6 of these countries—Argentina, Brazil, Chile, Paraguay, Peru and Uruguay— even the EC12 has been a larger trading partner in 1990 and 1993 than the United States.[150] Particularly striking is the relationship between MERCOSUR countries and the United States. The United States' exports to and imports from MERCOSUR have been 2.5% or less of her total exports and imports, respectively. Proportions of exports of Argentina, Brazil and Uruguay to the United States show a persistent decline over the three years shown. Only Paraguay shows a slight increase in 1993 over the corresponding proportion in 1990. Another interesting case is Chile. the United States and the EC accounted for roughly equal proportion of Chile's exports in 1985 (28%) but by 1993, their importance had declined. In 1993, the EC accounted for 25% and the United States 16% of Chile's exports. On the import side, the United States is more important for Chile than the EC. On balance, these data combined with more substantial restrictions in the EC lend some support to the view that many Latin American countries may be better off forming an FTA with the EC than NAFTA.

If countries do rush to join NAFTA or the EU as they certainly will, it is critical that they minimize the margin of preference to the potential partner. The inescapable implication of this prescription is that they must liberalize externally as they liberalize within an FTA framework. For instance, a country such as India will be eventually tempted to seek entry into the EU. But before doing so, it is important for her to carry its unilateral trade liberalization much farther. At the current tariffs which go up to 65% and average more than 35%, the potential transfers of tariff revenue to EU

---

[148]A referee has noted that one way to turn what is at present merely a declaration of intentions on the part of MERCOSUR and EU into serious negotiations for an FTA will be for the United States to voice opposition to such a move. Thus, the US influence has its limits.

[149] As the analysis in Section 5.2 shows, the import share of the partner country is far from a compelling criterion to consider FTAs.

[150]Recall that the EC, now European Union, has 15 members as of January 1, 1995.

Table 5.2: Tariffs and Liberalizing Reforms in Latin America and the Caribbean

Country	Year[a]		Average Unweigted Legal Tariff Rates(%)		Tariff Range(%)		Coverage of QRs as % of tariff lines, unless otherwise noted	
	Pre-reform	Post-reform	Pre-reform	Post-reform[2]	Pre-reform	Post-reform[2]	Pre-reform	Post-reform
Argentina	1987	1991	42(p)	10	15-115(p)	0-22	62 (of dom. Prod.)	8
Belize		1992	NA	NA		5-65%		NA
Bolivia	1985	1994	35	7.50	0-100	5-10	NA	Minimal
Brazil	1987	1993	51	14.20	0-105	0-35	39	Minimal
Chile	1984	1992	35	11	35	11	Minimal	
Colombia	1984	1993	61	12	0-220	5-20	99	1.40
Costa Rica	1985	1992	53(p)	15(p)	0-1400(p)	5-20	NA	
Dom. Republic	1990	1994	NA	NA	NA	3-35	NA	Significant

Ecuador	1989	1994	53	9,3	0-290	5-37	100	Minimal
El Salvador	1992			NA		7-30		0[1]
Guatemala	1985	1993	50(p)	'15(p)	'5-90	5-20	6 (of dom. Prod.)	
Honduras	1985	1992	41(p)	'15(w,p)	5-90	5-20	NA	
Jamaica	1981	1993	NA	20	NA	5-30	NA	0[1]
Mexico	1985	1994	22.60	'12.5(w)	0-100	0-20	28	1.60
Nicaragua	1992		NA	NA			NA	NA
Panama	1991		88.20	59.80		0-90		
Paraguay	1988	1991	NA	16	NA	0-20(y)	NA	Significant
Peru	1990	1994	66	16	0-120	15-25	100	0[1]
Uruguay	1987	1993	32	18(y)	10-55%	6-20%		
Venezuela	1989	1992	37	10(m)	0-135	0-20	40	10

Notes to Table 5.2:

1. Some QRs exist for health and safety reasons.
2. In practice, several countries have higher actual tariffs than those in the table. These are tariffs that have been applied to some specific goods and/or temporarily to control sudden import surges.

a: where applicable; p: Including tariff surcharges; w: production-weighted average tariff; m: import-weighted average tariff; y: relates to year 1992.

Sources: See Lustig and Primo Braga (1994).

Table 5.3: Direction of Exports by Country of Origin

Country	World	Share in World	DCs	USA	EEC	Other DCs	LDCs	LAC	Asia	Other LDCs	Merco	Arg.	Braz.	Par.	URU
1985															
Argentina	9,648	0.50	49.10	12.10	26.40	10.60	50.90	18.10	5.80	27.00	6.90		5.10	0.90	0.90
Brazil	28,182	1.50	70.00	28.90	28.20	12.80	30.00	8.60	7.80	13.60	3.20	2.20		0.60	0.4
Chile	4,139	0.20	70.80	20.70	32.20	17.90	29.20	14.50	10.50	4.10	7.90	2.10	5.50	0.10	0.2
Colombia	3,844	0.20	84.20	37.90	32.10	14.20	15.80	12.10	0.80	2.80	0.80	0.60	0.10	0.00	0.00
Costa Rica	1,220	0.10	79.10	46.70	17.30	15.10	20.90	16.90	0.30	3.60	0.20	0.20	0.00	0.00	0.00
Ecuador	3,493	0.20	66.70	56.50	6.10	4.10	33.30	8.70	23.00	1.70	0.50	0.30	0.00	0.00	0.00
Mexico	28,968	1.50	92.50	66.90	14.60	10.90	7.50	5.80	1.30	0.4	1.70	0.20	0.20	0.00	0.10
Paraguay	466	0.00	63.00	5.50	51.80	5.80	37.00	31.60	4.70	0.70	22.4	4.30	1.4		1.8
Peru	3,297	0.20	71.00	34.90	22.40	13.70	29.00	14.00	7.30	7.70	3.00	1.10	16.30	0.00	0.10
Uruguay	1,353	0.10	63.10	42.20	15.20	5.70	36.90	18.10	6.4	12.40	15.80	4.90	1.80	0.50	
Venezuela	13,914	0.70	84.10	49.10	20.90	14.10	15.90	14.30	1.30	0.30	2.00	0.00	10.50	0.00	0.00
U.S.A.	227,541	11.70	65.10		23.30	18.10	34.90	11.50	14.30	9.00	1.60	0.30	1.20	0.00	0.00
World	1,943,220	100.0	70.90	18.60	34.30	18.10	29.10	3.80	11.30	14.00	1.00	0.20	0.70	0.00	0.00
1990															
Argentina	13,844	0.40	52.60	12.00	31.90	8.70	47.40	25.00	7.70	14.70	13.70		10.90	1.20	1.60
Brazil	36,023	1.00	71.00	23.80	32.70	14.40	29.00	9.70	10.50	8.80	3.50	2.00		0.60	0.80
Chile	9,366	0.30	73.10	16.80	34.70	21.70	26.90	11.70	12.20	2.90	12	5.60	0.30	0.20	0.7
Colombia	6,995	0.20	85.4	48.70	26.00	10.60	14.60	11.10	1.40	2.20	1.60	0.4	0.50	0.00	0.00
Costa Rica	2,156	0.10	87.60	51.30	25.30	11.00	12.40	10.50	0.80	1.10	0.30	0.00	0.30	0.00	0.00
Ecuador	3,003	0.10	76.20	51.50	14.40	10.30	23.80	19.10	2.20	2.60	0.80	0.60	0.20	0.00	0.00
Mexico	41,032	1.20	93.50	75.10	9.20	9.20	6.50	3.80	2.10	0.60	0.90	0.30	0.50	0.00	0
Paraguay	1,156	0.00	53.30	4.80	46.60	1.90	46.70	38.80	6.00	1.90	33.80	3.60	29.00		1.30

Country	World	Share in World	DCs	USA	EEC	Other DCs	LDCs	LAC	Asia	Other LDC	Merco	Arg.	Braz.	Par	URU
Peru	3,764	0.10	70.30	22.60	27.40	20.20	29.70	13.60	8.60	7.50	4.10	0.30	3.80	0.00	0.00
Uruguay	2,169	0.10	44.00	15.50	22.40	6.10	56.00	38.60	5.30	12.10	33.20	5.40	27.4	0.4	0.00
Venezuela	17,895	0.50	77.20	55.50	11.50	10.10	22.80	20.30	2.00	0.60	2.30	0.00	2.20	0.00	0.00
U.S.A.	402,017	11.50	65.10		26.10		34.90	10.70	17.60	6.60	1.40	0.20	1.10	0.00	0.00
World	3,498,250	100.0	73.40	14.80	40.40	18.20	26.60	3.20	13.30	10.00	0.80	0.10	0.60	0.00	0.00
1993															
Argentina	14,059	0.40	42.90	9.20	27.20	6.40	57.10	37.40	6.70	13.10	23.90	10.30	18.70	1.80	3.40
Brazil	38,983	1.00	57.80	20.60	25.60	11.60	42.20	22.50	11.50	8.30	12.30	6.20	4.20	0.30	1.60
Chile	10,501	0.30	62.40	16.20	24.90	21.30	37.60	17.70	18.00	1.90	11.00	0.90	0.80	0.30	0.40
Colombia	7,824	0.20	73.10	41.80	22.30	9.00	26.90	24.20	0.80	1.90	1.70	0.20	0.00	0.00	0.00
Costa Rica	2,954	0.10	84.30	56.60	19.10	8.60	15.70	14.20	0.30	1.20	0.20	1.40	0.80	0.00	0.00
Ecuador	3,303	0.10	74.60	47.30	18.90	8.40	25.40	22.70	1.10	1.60	2.20	0.50	0.60	0.00	0.10
Mexico	51,274	1.30	93.50	79.50	5.80	8.20	6.50	4.80	1.50	0.10	1.10	7.10	32.30	0.00	0.80
Paraguay	843	0.00	45.90	6.40	34.60	4.90	54.10	52.20	1.70	0.20	40.20	0.70	3.70		0.10
Peru	3,372	0.10	63.50	23.70	26.10	13.70	36.50	18.70	14.80	2.90	4.60	17.90	22.20	0.10	
Uruguay	1,940	0.10	38.30	14.30	20.10	3.80	61.70	49.70	7.20	4.90	41.10	0.20	2.60	0.90	0.00
Venezuela	14,253	0.40	77.70	61.10	10.20	6.30	22.30	20.90	1.20	0.20	2.80	0.90	1.20	0.10	0.00
U.S.A.	487,491	12.80	56.40		21.40		43.60	16.40	19.30	7.90	2.20	0.90	0.70	0.00	0.10
World	3,804,550	100.0	66.50	15.80	34.20	16.50	33.50	5.00	18.00	10.50	1.30	0.50	0.70	0.00	0.10

Source: Direction of Trade Statistics (IMF)

Table 5.4: Direction of Imports by Country of Destination

Country	World	Share in World	DCs	USA	EEC	Other DCs	LDCs	LAC	Asia	Other LDCs	Merco	Arg.	Braz.	Par.	URU
1985															
Argentina	3,813	0.20	64.20	18.90	31.20	14.00	35.80	31.80	1.50	2.50	16.40		14.40	0.40	1.70
Brazil	14,035	0.80	48.80	22.40	14.60	11.90	51.20	11.20	4.60	35.40	5.00	3.50		0.40	1.00
Chile	2,641	0.10	62.00	25.80	22.80	13.40	38.00	29.30	5.60	3.10	13.90	4.20	9.00	0.50	0.20
Colombia	3,895	0.20	76.10	37.70	20.40	18.10	23.90	21.60	0.80	1.50	6.30	3.4	2.60	0.00	0.20
Costa Rica	1,059	0.10	66.10	39.80	15.10	11.20	33.90	30.30	2.90	0.70	2.00	0.30	1.70	0.00	0.00
Ecuador	1,765	0.10	71.70	33.50	21.50	16.60	28.30	20.40	4.80	3.10	7.70	0.80	6.80	0.00	0.10
Mexico	18,432	1.00	95.00	74.00	11.40	9.60	5.00	3.40	0.90	0.80	2.60	1.40	1.20	0.00	0.00
Paraguay	660	0.00	35.80	15.00	14.30	6.50	64.20	58.70	4.50	1.00	57.60	11.00	45.70		0.10
Peru	1,625	0.1	72.00	30.50	23.70	17.80	28.00	24.40	1.60	2.00	15.80	10.00	5.60	0.00	0.90
Uruguay	760	0.00	33.80	8.50	19.00	6.40	66.20	38.20	1.60	26.30	32.40	13.00	18.50	0.80	0.10
Venezuela	6,902	0.4	86.80	49.30	25.40	12.10	13.20	9.80	2.10	1.30	5.40	1.10	4.30	0.00	0.10
U.S.A.	327,540	17.70	65.00		20.00		35.00	12.30	16.50	6.20	2.50	0.30	2.10	0.00	0.00
World	1,854,620	100.0	68.40	11.50	35.00	21.90	31.60	5.40	11.20	15.10	1.90	0.50	1.40	0.00	0.00
1990															
Argentina	4,971	0.1	67.60	23.70	31.70	12.30	32.40	26.60	3.90	1.90	15.70		13.00	1.1	1.70
Brazil	28,945	0.80	43.00	17.50	16.20	9.30	57.00	12.50	1.90	42.60	7.70	4.90		1.10	1.70
Chile	6,670	0.20	63.00	25.10	22.40	15.60	37.00	24.40	7.70	4.80	14.90	6.90	7.30	0.40	0.20
Colombia	5,158	0.10	76.00	39.50	20.30	16.20	24.00	19.70	2.30	2.00	4.80	1.4	3.20	0.00	0.20
Costa Rica	2,019	0.10	68.20	49.10	10.00	9.00	31.80	25.60	5.70	0.60	3.20	0.60	2.60	0.00	0.00
Ecuador	1,923	0.10	69.80	35.40	21.50	12.90	30.20	25.00	2.70	2.50	8.80	2.20	6.60	0.00	0.00

Country	World	Share in World	DCs	USA	EEC	Other DCs	LDCs	LAC	Asia	Other LDCs	Merco	Arg.	Braz.	Par.	URU
Mexico	40,141	1.10	92.30	70.70	12.00	9.70	7.70	3.30	4.00	0.40	2.10	0.80	1.30	0.00	0.10
Paraguay	1,676	0.00	40.20	18.30	13.30	8.60	59.80	39.30	17.20	3.20	31.90	8.80	22.70		0.4
Peru	2,430	0.10	61.30	32.00	17.10	12.20	38.70	33.30	2.80	2.50	14.20	7.70	6.00	0.20	0.40
Uruguay	1,368	0.00	39.90	10.60	21.00	8.30	60.10	48.50	4.00	7.70	41.60	19.20	21.50	0.80	
Venezuela	7,435	0.20	82.20	41.80	29.10	11.30	17.80	13.50	2.50	1.80	5.60	1.90	3.60	0.10	0.00
U.S.A.	494,128	13.90	61.50		19.50		38.50	10.10	20.10	8.20	2.00	0.30	1.60	0.00	0.00
World	3,556,480	100.0	68.80	11.10	38.40	19.30	31.20	3.60	12.70	14.90	1.30	0.30	0.90	0.00	0.00
1993															
Argentina	16,191	0.40	56.30	23.30	24.40	8.60	43.70	31.50	10.40	1.80	24.90		22.60	0.30	2
Brazil	24,959	0.70	62.20	24.30	24.40	13.50	37.80	17.30	7.30	13.30	11.40	9.60		0.4	1.50
Chile	10,463	0.30	56.90	24.90	18.90	13.10	43.10	22.70	12.70	7.70	16.50	5.00	10.60	0.30	0.50
Colombia	8,680	0.20	71.00	37.20	17.60	16.20	29.00	24.60	2.4	2.00	6.70	2.20	4.30	0.00	0.20
Costa Rica	2,818	0.10	77.40	54.90	15.00	7.50	22.60	18.50	3.60	0.50	3.70	0.20	3.50	0.00	0
Ecuador	2,956	0.10	69.50	37.10	19.50	12.90	30.50	23.90	4.70	1.90	8.30	2.50	5.80	0.00	0.10
Mexico	59,868	1.60	91.50	69.50	11.60	10.40	8.50	3.40	4.80	0.20	2.10	0.40	1.70	0.00	0.10
Paraguay	2,605	0.10	36.4	20.00	7.90	8.50	63.60	50.90	11.60	1.20	48.20	10.80	36.90		0.6
Peru	3,649	0.10	54.10	29.30	13.40	11.30	45.90	39.7	4.90	1.40	15.40	6.70	7.50	0.20	1.0
Uruguay	2,683	0.10	43.30	9.40	27.50	6.30	56.70	49.40	5.00	2.30	45.50	16.4	28.90	0.30	
Venezuela	11,108	0.30	75.60	41.40	21.20	13.00	24.40	16.00	7.40	1.00	5.50	2.00	3.50	0.00	0
U.S.A.	581,848	15.50	58.40		16.90		41.60	11.70	24.00	5.90	1.60	0.20	1.40	0.00	0
World	3,745,780	100.0	67.60	12.4	34.80	20.40	32.4	4.30	17.20	10.90	1.4	0.30	1.00	0.00	0

Source: Direction of Trade Statistics (IMF)

exporters due to preferential access to India's markets can be very substantial.

One final point remains. If the analysis of this chapter is correct, why is there such a rush on the part of the countries in Latin America to get into regional arrangements with each other and with the United States? Bhagwati (1995) provides an answer to the question as follows[151]

> If the question is raised because it is inconceivable that the governments of those countries would not be rational in their policy choices, then that assumption itself must be clearly rejected. For one thing, as we well know from aid experience and the economic development literature, one can seek something that *sounds* good but actually does harm. Besides, the objectives of the leaders may be diversified. Thus, for instance, they may expect to gain political kudos by going along with NAFTA because, by granting preferential access to U.S. exporting interests, and through the implied underlining of Mexico's special relationship to the United States, they may gain the support of the United States in reaching out for prizes in a variety of unrelated political arenas. Thus, for example, in the absence of NAFTA and the willingness of then-President Carlos Salinas de Gortari to put almost everything on the line for its passage, can one seriously imagine that the United States would have gotten Mexico into the OECD or backed President Salinas for the important job of the director general of the WTO?

5.7 Regionalism and Harmonization

Let me now turn briefly to the possible role of regionalism in promoting harmonization of domestic policies in the member countries of a union. The interest in this area has been sparked primarily by the pursuit of harmonization in areas of environmental standards, labor legislation, tax policy, exchange rates, monetary policy, product standards, competition policy, and intellectual property rights among countries within the EU and between EU and countries with which it has Association Agreements. The side agreements concluded by NAFTA members on environmental and labor standards have also given rise to an interest in harmonization issues.

---

[151]Footnotes 12 and 13, associated with the following quotation, have been dropped.

Though space constraints do not permit a detailed analysis, it is worthwhile to make two points. First, as systematic analysis in various contributions in Bhagwati and Hudec (1996), particularly Bhagwati (1996) and Bhagwati and Srinivasan (1996) demonstrates, the case for harmonization of policies across countries is too weak to deserve a serious consideration in either a regional or global context. Differences in labor and environmental standards are perfectly compatible with—indeed, under most circumstances, required for—economic efficiency.

Second, even if, for the sake of argument, we agree on the desirability of harmonization of certain policies, the issue is tricky in the context of North-South regional arrangements. The pressure in such schemes is on the southern country to bring its standards up to those of the northern country. Because the optimal standard for the southern country is likely to be different than for the northern country, such harmonization ends up becoming an instrument of protection for the northern country. In addition, even when the southern country's standard is below the optimum, it is likely to conform to that in other southern countries. If it adopts the standards of the northern country, it will be placed at a disadvantage vis-a-vis its southern competitors. The inevitable conclusion is that if the actual standards in southern countries are below whatever is viewed as "optimal," the right institution for raising them is a multilateral, not bilateral, forum. Specifically, issues of intellectual property rights and higher labor and environmental standards should be dealt with multilaterally by appropriate international organizations.

The inevitable implication of this discussion is that in considering harmonization at a regional level, countries must satisfy themselves that the issue is primarily regional in nature. Once this is done, it is difficult to think of cases where developing countries can use the regional mechanism for harmonization. Most of the examples I can think of are those of cooperation in infrastructure building including roads, dams and sharing of river water and have little to do with harmonization of policies.

5.8 A Summary of Conclusions

This chapter takes a negative view of NAFTA and FTAA. The main conclusions may be summarized as follows.

1. When trade is liberalized on a discriminatory basis as in regional arrangements, the mercantilist conclusion is essentially valid: A country gains from liberalization by the partner and loses from its own liberalization.

2. Because the United States had little tariff preferences to grant to Mexico while the reverse was not true, the static welfare effect of NAFTA is likely to be positive on the former and negative on the latter.

3. Non-traditional gains to Mexico from NAFTA were greatly exaggerated in the debate preceding its approval. NAFTA does not shelter Mexico from the U.S. anti-dumping actions. The first systematic analysis of the "lock-on-the-reforms" argument in this chapter reveals that the role of NAFTA in landing credibility to Mexico's reforms is minimal, perhaps even negative. NAFTA locks at most Mexico's tariffs against the United States and Canada. But this is not necessarily a good thing; the welfare effect of this discriminatory lock is very likely negative and, moreover, if protectionist pressures rise in the future, it could lead to a substantial increase in discrimination against outside countries. As for the provision on intellectual property rights and side agreements on labor and environmental standards, they were not sought by Mexico but, rather, forced on it. Higher standards in Mexico in these areas, without a corresponding change in other developing countries, will make Mexico less competitive against the latter.

4. EU and NAFTA are fundamentally different arrangements. EU has had an important political dimension. For several decades, it served as a bulwark against the Soviet Union and may have even contributed to the latter's demise. On economic front, the member countries of EU have a much stronger commitment to deep integration. The arrangement involves a customs union, has a free mobility of capital and seeks free mobility of labor. By contrast, NAFTA is a free trade area requiring complex rules of origin and is hostile to the movement of labor. Recent Association Agreements between EU and Central and East European countries have many of the flaws of NAFTA. But these agreements have an important political dimension: they allow the Central and East European countries to further distance themselves from the Russia. Moreover, to the extent that the agreements may lead to an eventual entry to the EU with full membership, in the long run, they may be desirable on purely economic grounds as well.

5. Static welfare effects of the proposed Free Trade Area of the Americas (FTAA) will be very likely negative on Latin America and positive on the United States. FTAA will do little to give Latin America a preferential access to the U.S. market while the reverse is not true. Because the most

efficient producers of many products are in East Asia, not North America, trade diversion will dominate FTAA.

6. MERCOSUR has more to gain (or less to lose) by joining the EU than NAFTA in an FTA. The member countries already have free access to the North American market. An FTA with the EU can help improve access to that market.

7. Great caution should be exercised in using regional arrangements to promote harmonization of domestic policies. To begin with, harmonization is not a desirable goal under most circumstances. Moreover, where harmonization can be justified, its pursuit at a regional level can be counter productive. This is particularly true of North-South arrangements. Optimal standards in many areas (e.g., environment standards) are likely to be lower for a southern than northern country. In cases where optimal standards are uniformly below the "optimum" due to a race to the bottom, harmonization must be done on a global basis.

References

Bhagwati, Jagdish, 1993, "Regionalism and Multilateralism: An Overview," in Melo and Panagariya.

Bhagwati, Jagdish, 1995, "U.S. Trade Policy: The Infatuation with Free Trade Areas," in Bhagwati, Jagdish and Anne O. Krueger, eds., *The Dangerous Drift to Preferential Trade Agreements*, Washington, D.C.: American Enterprise Institute for Public Policy Research.

Bhagwati, Jagdish, 1996, "The demand to reduce Domestic Diversity among trading Nations," in Bhagwati J., and R. Hudec, eds.

Bhagwati, Jagdish and Robert Hudec, 1996, eds., *Fair Trade and harmonization: Prerequisites for Free Trade?*, MIT Press: Cambridge, Mass., forthcoming.

Bhagwati, Jagdish and Panagariya, Arvind, 1996a, "Preferential Trading Areas and Multilateralism: Strangers, Friends or Foes?" in Jagdish Bhagwati and Arvind Panagariya, eds., *The Economics of Preferential Trade Agreements*, 1996, AEI Press, Washington, D.C., forthcoming. (Chapter 2, this volume)

Bhagwati, Jagdish and Panagariya, Arvind, 1996b, "The Theoretical Analyses of Preferential trading Areas," paper presented at the American Economic Association Meetings, San Francisco, January 5-7, 1996; to appear in the *American Economic Review. Papers and Proceedings*, May.

Bhagwati, Jagdish and T.N. Srinivasan, 1996, "Trade and Environment: Does Environmental Diversity Detract from the Case for Free Trade?," in Bhagwati, J. and R. Hudec, eds.

Cooper, R., 1993, "Round Table Discussion," in Melo and Panagariya.

Corden, Max, 1993, "Round Table Discussion," in Melo and Panagariya.

Dornbusch, R., 1993, "Round Table Discussion," in Melo and Panagariya.

Erzan, Refik and Alexander Yeats, 1992, "Free Trade Agreements with the United States. What's In It for Latin America?" Working paper No. 827, Washington, D.C.: the World Bank, January.

Krugman, P., 1991, "The Move to Free Trade Zones," Symposium Sponsored by the Federal Reserve Bank of Kansas City, *Policy Implications of Trade and Currency Zones*.

Krugman, P. "Regionalism versus Multilateralism: Analytical Notes," in Melo and Panagariya.

Laird, Sam, 1990, "U.S. Trade Policy and Mexico: Simulations of Possible Trade Regime Changes," mimeograph, Washington, D.C.: The World Bank.

Lipsey, Richard, 1958, *The Theory of Customs Unions: A General Equilibrium Analysis*, University of London, Ph.D. thesis.

Lustig, Nora and Carlos Primo Braga, 1994, "The Future of Trade Policy in Latin America," in Weintraub, Sidney, ed., *Integrating the Americas: Shaping Future Trade Policy*, New Brunswick and London: Transaction Publishers.

Melo, Jaime de and Arvind Panagariya, 1993, *New Dimensions in Regional Integration*, Cambridge, Great Britain: Cambridge University Press.

Panagariya, Arvind, 1995, "Rethinking the New Regionalism," presented at the World Bank Conference on Trade Expansion Program, January 23-24, 1995.

Panagariya, Arvind, 1996a, "The Meade Model of Preferential trading: History, Analytics and Policy Implications," mimeo, University of Maryland, Department of Economics.

Panagariya, Arvind, 1996b, "Preferential Trading and the Myth of Natural Trading Partners," Center for Japan-U.S. Business and Economic Studies, Stern School of Business, New York University, Working Paper No. 200.

Panagariya, Arvind, 1996c, "Some Economic Aspects of the TRIPs Agreement," mimeo., University of Maryland, College Park.

Panagariya, Arvind and Ronald Findlay, 1995, "A Political Economy Analysis of Free Trade Areas and Customs Unions," Robert Feenstra, Douglas Irwin and Gene Grossman, eds., *The Political Economy of Trade Reform*, Essays in Honor of jagdish Bhagwati, MIT Press, forthcoming.

Primo Braga, Carlos A., Raed Safadi and Alexander Yeats, 1993, "Regional Integration in the Western Hemisphere: Deja-vu All Over Again?," paper presented at the conference "New Investment Opportunities in Eastern Europe and Latin America," Bethlehem, PA, Lehigh University.

Summers, L., 1991, "Regionalism and the World Trading System," Symposium Sponsored by the Federal Reserve Bank of Kansas City, *Policy Implications of Trade and Currency Zones*.

Trade Expansion Program, 1992, *Costa Rica. Strengthening Trade Links to the World Economy*, 101-105.

Viner, Jacob, 1950, *The Customs Union Issue*, New York: Carnegie Endowment for International Peace.

Whalley, John, 1993, Regional Trade Arrangements in North America: CUSTA and NAFTA," in Melo and Panagariya.

Whalley, John, 1995, "The Impact of the MFA Phase Out on the Asian Economies," presented at the Asian Development Bank Conference on Emerging Global Trading Environment and Developing Asia, May 29-30, 1995.

Wonnacott, Paul and Lutz, Mark, 1989, "Is There a Case for Free Trade Areas?" in Schott, Jeffrey, *Free Trade Areas and U.S. Trade Policy*, Washington, D.C.: Institute for International Economics, 59-84.

6. An Empirical Estimate of Static Welfare Losses to Mexico from NAFTA

6.1 Introduction

In a series of papers [Panagariya (1995, 1996, and 1997) and Bhagwati and Panagariya (1996)], I have recently argued that when a country extends a tariff preference, the presumption is that it loses from the change while the partner benefits from it. Because a member country gives as well as receives tariff preferences in a Free Trade Area (FTA), in general, it may benefit or lose from the union. *Ceteris paribus*, the larger the country's imports from the partner relative to its exports to it and the higher the margin of preference it gives relative to that it receives, the more likely that it will lose from the arrangement. In the context of NAFTA, though Mexico's imports from the United States are *approximately* equal to its exports to the latter, the extent of tariff preference granted by it is far greater than the tariff preference received by it. Therefore, the presumption is that purely in terms of static welfare effects, Mexico has been hurt by NAFTA.

In this note, I offer a rough estimate of the losses to Mexico from NAFTA. Section 6.2 outlines the basic framework within which the empirical calculation is done, Section 6.3 carries out the calculation, and Section 6.4 concludes.

6.2 The Theoretical Framework

Let us begin by first recalling Viner's (1950) analysis, which serves as the basis of our calculation. In panels a and b of Figure 6.1, curves $M_A M_A$ represent import demands of country A for two different commodities, while curves $P_B E_B$ and $P_C E_C$ are corresponding export supply curves of countries B

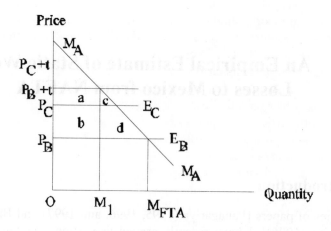

Figure 6.1-Panel a: The Trade Creation Case

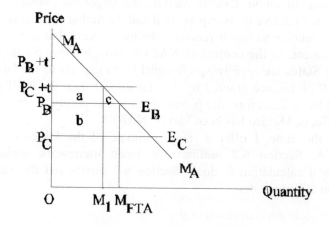

Figure 6.1-Panel b: The Trade Diversion case

and C, respectively. We can think of A as Mexico, B as the United States and C as the rest of the world. Initially, I make the standard Vinerian assumption that export supplies of B and C are perfectly elastic. Because this assumption gives rise to some unrealistic outcomes, I will later modify it.

For the commodity shown in panel a, B's supply price is lower than that of the outside country, C. As a result, under a nondiscriminatory tariff, all imports come from B. The internal price in A is P_B+t where t is per-unit tariff. Area a+b represents tariff revenue. If A now forms a union with B, the internal price in A falls to P_B and imports expand to OM_{FTA}. This is a trade-creating union in which the less efficient home producers of A are replaced by the more efficient suppliers in B. Tariff revenue disappears and consumers' plus producers' surplus expands by area a+b+c+d. The net gain to the country is area c+d.

For the product shown in panel b, B is a less efficient supplier than C. Therefore, under a nondiscriminatory tariff, all imports come from C. A union between A and B in this case "diverts" trade from the more efficient C to the less efficient B. All imports now come from B instead of C. The internal price in A falls to P_C and total imports rise to OM_{FTA}. The price decline helps replace some of the less efficient domestic suppliers by suppliers in B and generates a net increase in the consumers' plus producers' surplus of a+c. But, because tariff revenue disappears, the net gain to the economy is area c-b, which can be negative. *Ceteris paribus*, the more A imports of the product in panel b, the more it loses from the tariff preference.

The model in Figure 6.1 has two important limitations. First, in panel a, where the union is trade creating, the external tariff plays no role whatsoever. Even if Country A lowers the tariff on a nonpreferential basis, the outcome is the same. A model in which a trade-creating union makes no distinction between preferential and nondiscriminatory trade liberalization can hardly be considered compelling to defend preferential trading. Second, in both panels a and b, country A imports the product from a single source both before and after preferential liberalization. This is a highly unrealistic feature of the model. If we look at trade data, no matter how disaggregated, the sources of imports are highly diversified.

Complete specialization of the source of imports is the result of perfectly elastic supply of exports of both B and C. To permit diversification, we must allow for an upward-sloped supply of at least one of B or C. In Figure 6.2, I present the case when the supply curve of the partner, B, is upward-sloped and of C horizontal. This is not an entirely implausible case: the rest of the world is a much larger entity relative to two countries forming a union and, moreover, consists of a large number of highly competitive countries. Not surprisingly, this case has been at the heart of a large body of the literature on preferential trading [Lipsey (1958), Berglas (1979), McMillan and McCann (1981) and Lloyd (1982)].

As before, $M_A M_A$ represents the import-demand curve of country A and $P_C E_C$ the export supply of country C in the absence of a tariff. Partner country B's export supply is given by $E_B E_B$ and is upward sloped. Under a nondiscriminatory tariff, export supplies from the two sources, as viewed by agents in country A, are $P_C^t E_C^t$ and $E_B^t E_B^t$. Country A imports OM_3, of which OM_1 come from the potential partner B and $M_1 M_3$ from the outside country C. Country A collects rectangle GHNS in revenue.

Suppose next that as a part of an FTA agreement, country A removes the tariff on B but not C. This change shifts the export supply curve of B, as viewed by agents in A, down to $E_B E_B$. Imports from B expand to OM_2 with quantity $M_1 M_2$ diverted from country C to B. Because country A no longer collects tariff revenue on imports from B, it loses the rectangular area GHLF entirely. This loss is similar to the loss of area b in panel b of Figure 6.1. The difference is that whereas in Figure 6.1, area b is entirely a deadweight loss due to higher production costs in country B, in Figure 6.2, only UFL is the deadweight loss. The remaining area, GHUF becomes an extra producers surplus for exporting firms in country B. Moreover, as long as any imports continue to come from country C, the internal price in A cannot change and there are no gain corresponding to area c in panel b of Figure 6.1.

Thus, in the realistic case shown in Figure 6.2, the tariff preference by country A hurts itself and benefits the preference recipient country, B. In a complete reversal of "natural trading partners" hypothesis, the more A imports from the partner, the more it loses from the tariff preference it gives.[152] Of course, tariff preference *given* by country A is only half the story. As a part of the FTA, country A also *receives* a tariff preference from country B, which leads to a transfer of B's tariff revenue to its exporting firms. The net effect on A's welfare, thus, depends on the tariff revenue lost and extra profit made on exports to B. The larger the tariff preference country A gives and the smaller the tariff preference it receives, the more A loses from the FTA.

---

[152] A detailed critique of the natural trading partners hypothesis is provided in Bhagwati and Panagariya (1996).

6.3 The Case of NAFTA

In the NAFTA arrangement, because Mexico's tariffs were initially high and the U.S. tariffs low, and Mexico already enjoyed tariff preferences in the U.S. market under the Generalized System of Preferences (GSP), it gave a much larger tariff preference than it received. Indeed, to quota Fred Bergsten (1997), an ardent supporter of regional arrangements including NAFTA,

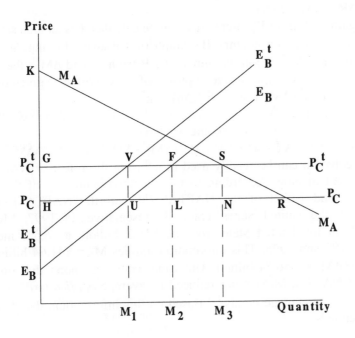

Figure 6.2: The loss to country A from a preferential removal of tariff is GFLH.

NAFTA amounted to a 4% expansion of the American economy, to include a country that accepted virtually every demand placed upon

it in the negotiations *and which made virtually all concessions.*
(Italics added, *Economist*, September 27, 1997)

Given this lopsided exchange of preferences, it stands to reason that Mexico lost on a net basis from NAFTA.

Because the NAFTA tariff preferences are to be phased over a period of fifteen years, to obtain an approximate measure of the effect of the preferences to-date, Figure 6.2 must be modified slightly. Letting tariff preference be Δt, The post-preference export supply curve of B is represented by the dotted line $E_B{}^{tp}E_B{}^{tp}$ in Figure 6.3. The loss to A from this partial preference is given by rectangle GH'L'F'. Denoting by M_1 the initial imports from the partner, the change in imports from the partner by ΔM_1 and the change in revenue by ΔR, we have

(1) $\Delta R = -(M_1+\Delta M_1)\Delta t$

The gain to A from B's preference can be calculated as an area similar to trapezium GH'U'F' on country B's graph (not drawn). Letting Δt^* be the tariff preference, $M_1{}^*$, the initial imports by B from A, and $\Delta M_1{}^*$, the change in B's imports from A, the change in profits of A's exporters is given by

(2) $\Delta \pi = (M_1{}^*+\Delta M_1{}^*).\Delta t^*-(1/2)\Delta M_1{}^*.\Delta t^*$

Adding (1) and (2), we can obtain a rough measure of the net effect of free trade area on country A's income. we have

(3) $\Delta y = \Delta R + \Delta \pi = -(M_1+\Delta M_1)\Delta t + (M_1{}^*+\Delta M_1{}^*).\Delta t^*-(1/2)\Delta M_1{}^*.\Delta t^*$

This equation can be readily used to measure the effect of NAFTA on Mexico's real income. According to the executive summary of the report "Operation and Effect of the NAFTA" (henceforth "NAFTA Report"), released by the United States Trade Representative, in 1997, Mexico's imports from the United States rose by $15.2 billion, a 36.5% increase, between 1993 and 1996. This information implies M_1 = $41.64 billion and hence $M_1+\Delta M_1$ = $56.84 billion. The same report also notes that since the signing of NAFTA, Mexico has reduced its average *applied* tariffs on U.S. goods by 7.1 percentage points.[153] Based on this information, the change in tariff-revenue is

$\Delta R = -\$(56.84 \quad .071)$ billion $= \$4.04$ billion

---

[153]Though the average *applied* tariff rate is not defined in the executive summary, as normally used, it refers to tariff revenue divided by the value of imports at world prices and gives us the right measure of t or Δt for our calculations.

Figure 6.3: The loss to Country A from tariff preference GH' is GH'L'F'.

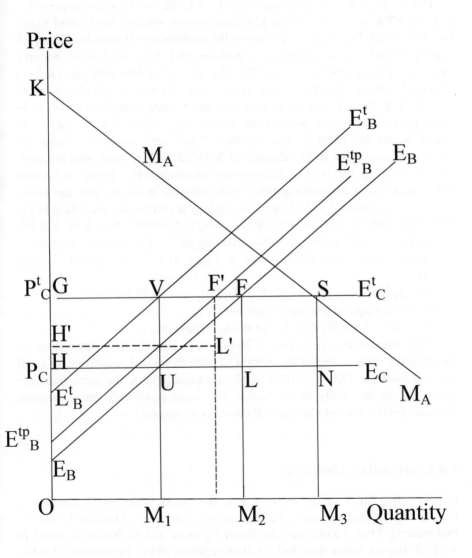

Note that the figure $56.84 billion of imports in 1996 is considerably smaller than $67.5 billion reported in a recent issue of the *Economist* (October 18, 1997, p. 22). Thus, the $4.04 billion loss errs on the side of underestimating the loss.

The NAFTA Report also states that U.S. tariffs on Mexican imports averaged 2.07%, and over half of Mexican imports entered the United States duty-free." This leaves unclear whether the average rate is calculated over *all* imports or only those subject to a positive duty (i.e., on half of imports, yielding a true applied rate of 1.035%.) To ensure that Mexico's gains are not mistakenly underestimated, I will assume that the rate is calculated on all imports. The Report goes on to state that the United States has lowered its tariffs by 1.4 percentage points since the signing of NAFTA. It adds, "The United States would have made some of these tariff reductions under the Uruguay Round even in the absence of NAFTA." This means that the margin of preference received by Mexico was less than 1.4%. To err on the side of overestimating Mexico's gains, I will assume, however, that the entire 1.4% tariff reduction by the United States was preferential. According to the *Economist* (July 5, 1997, chart 1, p. 22), Mexican exports rose from $40 billion in 1993 to $72 billion in 1996, yielding $M_1^* = $40 billion and $\Delta M_1^* = $32 billion. Therefore, the increase in Mexican exporters' profits can be written

$\Delta\pi = $[72 .014—(1/2) 32 (.014)] billion = $0.78 billion

The net change in Mexico's income is

$\Delta y = \Delta R + \Delta\pi = $(- 4.04 + .78) =—$3.26 billion.

Thus, Mexico may have lost $3.26 billion in 1996. Unless external tariffs are lowered, thus, reducing the margin of preference and redistributing tariff revenue from the U.S. exporters to Mexican consumers, the same or larger annual losses are likely in the future. The latter possibility arises because Mexican preferences are to rise in the forthcoming years.

6.4 Concluding Remarks

In concluding this note, let me now state the biases in the rough calculation done here. As already noted, the calculation understates Mexican losses for two reasons. First, I have used the lower figure of $56.84 billion reported in NAFTA Report rather than $67.5 billion reported in the *Economist* (October

18, 1997) for Mexican imports from the United States. And second, tariff preference to Mexico in the U.S. market is lower than 1.4%.

The estimate also overstates the losses if the world supply of exports is also upward sloped. In that case, the exchange of tariff preferences improves the terms of trade of NAFTA members vis-a-vis the rest of the world which is beneficial to them. This can be an important omission from my calculation and, for this reason, the losses are probably smaller than the above number. The calculation is unaffected, however, by the changes in trade flows caused by the peso devaluation following NAFTA. As long as the devaluation does not alter the terms of trade, the revenue transfer must take place irrespective of what caused trade flows to shift. And, in any case, the devaluation must worsen, rather than improve, Mexico's terms of trade, adding to the losses we have calculated.

References

Berglas, Eitan, 1979, "Preferential Trading: The n Commodity Case," *Journal of Political Economy* 87, No. 21, 315-331.

Bhagwati, Jagdish and Panagariya, Arvind, 1996, "Preferential Trading Areas and Multilateralism: Strangers, Friends or Foes?" in Jagdish Bhagwati and Arvind Panagariya, eds., *The Economics of Preferential Trade Agreements*, 1996 (AEI Press, Washington, D.C.) 1-78.(Chapter 2, this volume)

Lipsey, Richard, 1960, "The Theory of Customs Unions: A General Survey," *Economic Journal* 70, 498-513.

Lloyd, Peter J., 1982, "3x3 Theory of Customs Unions," *Journal of International Economics* 12, 41-63.

McMillan, John and McCann, Ewen, 1981, "Welfare Effects in Customs Union," *Economic Journal* 91, 697-703, September.

Panagariya, Arvind, 1995, "Rethinking the New Regionalism." Paper presented at the Trade Expansion Program Conference of the UNDP and World Bank, January 1995, forthcoming in Nash, John and Wendy Tackacs, eds., *Lessons in trade Policy Reform*, World Bank, Washington, D.C.

Panagariya, Arvind, 1996, "The Free Trade Area of the Americas: Good for Latin America?" *World Economy* 19, no. 5, September, 485-515. (Chapter 5, this volume)

Panagariya, Arvind, 1997, "Preferential Trading and the Myth of Natural Trading Partners," *Japan and the World Economy*, forthcoming.

Viner, Jacob, 1950, *The Customs Union Issue*, New York: Carnegie Endowment for International Peace.

Subject Index